www.wadsworth.com

wadsworth.com is the World Wide Web site for Wadsworth and is your direct source to dozens of online resources.

At *wadsworth.com* you can find out about supplements, demonstration software, and student resources. You can also send e-mail to many of our authors and preview new publications and exciting new technologies.

wadsworth.com
Changing the way the world learns®

Public Opinion

Measuring the American Mind

BARBARA A. BARDES

University of Cincinnati

ROBERT W. OLDENDICK

University of South Carolina

Wadsworth
Thomson Learning™

Australia • Canada • Denmark • Japan • Mexico • New Zealand • Philippines • Puerto Rico
Singapore • South Africa • Spain • United Kingdom • United States

Political Science Publisher: Clark Baxter
Senior Development Editor: Sharon Adams Poore
Assistant Editor: Cherie Hackelberg
Editorial Assistant: Melissa Gleason
Marketing Manager: Jay Hu
Marketing Assistant: Cara Durr
Print Buyer: Mary Noel

Permissions Editor: Robert Kauser
Production Service: Pre-Press Company, Inc.
Cover Designer: William Reuter
Cover Crowd Photo: Corbis/Bettmann
Compositor: Pre-Press Company, Inc.
Printer/Binder: Webcom Limited

Printed in Canada
1 2 3 4 5 6 03 02 01 00 99

For permission to use material from this
text, contact us:
Web: www.thomsonrights.com
Fax: 1-800-730-2215
Phone: 1-800-730-2214

**Library of Congress
Cataloging-in-Publication Data**
Bardes, Barbara A.
  Public opinion: measuring the American
mind/Barbara A. Bardes, Robert W. Oldendick.
    p. cm.
  Includes bibliographical references and index.
  ISBN 0-534-56043-1 (alk. paper)
  1. Public opinion—United States. 2. Public
opinion polls.
I. Oldendick, Robert W. II. Title.
HN90.P8B37   1999
303.3'8'—dc21   99-16353

**For more information, contact
Wadsworth/Thomson Learning
10 Davis Drive
Belmont, CA 94002-3098
USA
www.wadsworth.com**

International Headquarters
Thomson Learning
290 Harbor Drive, 2nd Floor
Stamford, CT 06902-7477
USA

UK/Europe/Middle East
Thomson Learning
Berkshire House
168-173 High Holborn
London WC1V 7AA
United Kingdom

Asia
Thomson Learning
60 Albert Street #15-01
Albert Complex
Singapore 189969

Canada
Nelson/Thomson Learning
1120 Birchmount Road
Scarborough, Ontario M1K 5G4
Canada

♻ This book is printed on acid-free recycled paper.

Contents

❧ ❋ ❧

List of Figures

List of Tables

Preface

It seems that every day the media reports polling data on some aspect of life in the United States. Whether it's a report on alcohol and drug use among high school students, the public's latest approval ratings of the President, or a "trial heat" on which candidate is leading in the upcoming election, the American public is presented with information on a wide range of subjects that may have some impact on their lives. Given the widespread use of polls in this country, our goal for this book is to characterize "the American mind," meaning contemporary public opinion in this country, but also to describe how public opinion data are collected, how they are used, and the role they play in the American political system.

One objective of this book is to provide information on how survey data are collected and the types of factors that a good consumer of polls should know in evaluating public opinion data. Characteristics of a survey, including the way the sample was chosen, the design of the questionnaire, and how the data were collected, are discussed fairly extensively in order to provide you with questions you should ask when presented with poll results.

A second objective is to demonstrate various ways in which public opinion data are used. Data from surveys have become increasingly important to federal agencies as well as to state and local governments. Candidates for public office depend on surveys for deciding how to develop their campaigns. The results of survey research are important to academic researchers in a variety of fields, including political science, sociology, mass communications, and public health. The media make use of surveys in their coverage of elections as well as in their reporting on public policy issues. Our discussion of the use of public opinion data provides an overview of the many ways in which survey data are a part of American political life.

Any text on public opinion must provide information on what the public believes, and this is the focus of much of this text. We discuss how Americans come to hold opinions on issues and politics, and then describe the American public's views on a number of social-welfare issues, racial questions, cultural issues, and foreign policy issues. We also look at how the public expresses its political views and attachments to the system.

Finally, we consider the role which public opinion plays in the American political system. Does public opinion matter in our democratic system, and how is public opinion translated into public policy? As part of this discussion, we also take a critical look at the way in which public opinion data are collected and used; we then identify several factors that may change the way in which poll results are used.

We present data on a number of different issues, but these represent only a minute fraction of the vast array of current and historical survey data available. Such data are becoming more available through the Internet, so we have included in each chapter a section on "Polls, Polling, and the Internet." This section identifies sites at which data are available or which contain information about polling and the survey industry. The range of topics for which data are available is virtually limitless, and we encourage you to visit these sites and explore your interests concerning the American mind.

An effort such as this is not completed without the assistance of a number of people. We would like to thank the staffs of Raymond Walters College of the University of Cincinnati and the University of South Carolina's Institute of Public Affairs for their support. In particular, we would like to thank Michael Link for his assistance in creating the data files and data processing, and to acknowledge the research assistance of Todd Anderson and Sherri Downing-Alfonso, as well as the clerical assistance of Freda Atkinson. This manuscript has benefited significantly from the suggestions of the reviewers Ted Jelen, University of Nevada, Las Vegas, William Jacoby, University of South Carolina, and Clyde Wilcox, Georgetown University. Finally, we would like to thank Clark Baxter, our publisher, Sharon Adams Poore and Melissa Gleason of ITP/Wadsworth Publishing Company for their support and skillful editing. Their work has resulted in a much improved product.

Barbara A. Bardes
Robert W. Oldendick

Public Opinion

Part I

Public Opinion and American Democracy

1

Public Opinion and American Democracy

Questions to Consider:

Was public opinion important to the Founding Fathers?

What do we mean by public opinion?

Does public opinion really matter to elected officials?

In historical perspective, the importance of public opinion in the United States is evident in the origin of the nation. The authors of *The Federalist* refer to "... the public voice proclaimed by the representatives of the people ..." and while the Founding Fathers were wary of the evils resulting from an overbearing majority, they recognized the need to acknowledge the public's voice in developing public policy (Federalist No. 10: 81). Although the general notion of "public opinion" was anticipated in the works of Plato and Aristotle, as well as the Romans (Palmer, 1936: 231–232), we can trace the modern concept of public opinion to Rousseau in 1744 (Hubert, 1992: 30). The idea that emerged from the Enlightenment of a mass public competent to exercise its sovereignty was instrumental in shaping the role of the public in the democratic society that developed in the United States.

In addition to a system in which the individual is the focus of the political process, traditional democratic theory assumes that each member of the electorate is interested in public issues, motivated by principle, aware of relevant facts, and capable of making decisions rationally. In a democratic system, the opinions of the public are to be translated into action (Hennessy, 1981: 13–15).

As stated succinctly by Achen, the starting point of democratic theory is that ". . . public opinion on policy matters" (1975: 1220). It is the views of adults on policy issues that we refer to as "the American mind."

Elisabeth Noelle-Neumann (1984: 76) has noted that David Hume's basic principle, that it is on opinion only that government is founded, became the doctrine of the Founding Fathers of the United States. The importance of public opinion has been evident throughout this country's history. Lincoln, for example, wrote that in politics ". . . public sentiment is everything. With public sentiment, nothing can fail. Without it nothing can succeed" (quoted in Minow, Martin, and Mitchell, 1973: 10). Lyndon Johnson's decision not to run for re-election in 1968 was in large part attributable to the erosion of public support for the Vietnam War and, consequently, his presidency (P. Converse, 1987). Similarly, public disapproval of his performance in office, along with a myriad of other factors, contributed to Richard Nixon's decision to resign the presidency in 1974. Modern political campaigns, not only for the presidency but at all levels, are replete with references to "what the public wants."

The role that public opinion should play in American democracy is a topic for debate in contemporary politics. During the U.S. House of Representatives' consideration of impeachment of President Clinton in late 1998, there were daily polls on the public's views of impeachment and the way that the president was handling his job. During this same period, numerous polls were conducted on how Americans felt this country should deal with Saddam Hussein and the situation in Iraq. Supporters of the president cited polls in his defense, while critics of the president focused on the need for legislators to fulfill their constitutional duty, even if it seemed to contradict "what the public wants."

In his description of the place of public opinion in American politics, Philip Converse (1987) described the exchange that took place during the Iran-Contra hearings in which Lieutenant Colonel Oliver North chastised the members of Congress for failing to support the Contra resistance in Nicaragua, and was in turned chastised by Senator Warren Rudman. Senator Rudman indicated that Congress had been appropriately reflecting public sentiment, pointing out that public opinion polls had been running 75-25 against support for the Contras. In Converse's view, what was significant about this event from the standpoint of public opinion was that (1) nobody challenged the accuracy of the public opinion figures and (2) nobody challenged Rudman's claim of basic authority for the voice of the public. Throughout the history of the United States, the important role played by public opinion has evidenced itself in many ways.

DEFINING PUBLIC OPINION

Despite—or perhaps because of—its long history in American political discourse, there is no generally agreed upon definition of "public opinion." For example, V.O. Key (1967: 14) defined public opinion as "those opinions held by private persons that governments find it prudent to heed." For Monroe (1975: 6), public opinion "is the distribution of individual preferences within a population. In other words, *public* opinion is simply the sum or aggregation of *private* opinions on any particular issue or set of issues." In Simon's (1974: 7) terms, public opinion ". . . is the aggregate of views people hold regarding matters that (the pollsters decide) affect or interest the community," while for Hennessy (1981: 4) it is "the complex of preferences expressed by a significant number of people on an issue of general importance." Erikson, Luttbeg, and Tedin (1980: 2–3) define this concept as "the combined personal opinions of adults toward issues of relevance to government." Cummings and Wise (1974: 168) view it as ". . . the expression of attitudes relevant to government and politics" while Noelle-Neumann (1984: 62–63) holds that it involves ". . . opinions on controversial issues that one *can* express in public without isolating oneself." For Weissberg (1976: 9), public opinion is simply ". . . a preference for a course of action."

While these definitions have a common element, they each differ slightly to reflect the varying points of view and areas of emphasis in the study of this phenomenon. We think it fruitless to attempt to establish *the* definition of public opinion, and rather than adding to this list, we will adopt that of Erikson, Luttbeg and Tedin, which not only best reflects our view of the important elements of this concept but also serves to structure the approach taken throughout this book:

> **Public opinion** is the combined personal opinions of adults toward issues of relevance to government.

The first element of this definition, "combined personal opinions," was a source of some controversy in the early development of modern public opinion research in the United States. As discussed below, critics of the use of polling techniques to measure public opinion, such as Blumer, argued that the summation of individual opinions in a "one person, one vote" style was exactly what public opinion was *not*. In the critics' view, public opinion was more accurately reflected in the views of the relatively small group of influentials in the community, who paid more attention to and were more knowledgeable about matters of public affairs (Blumer, 1948). Variations of this view held that public opinion in a community was represented by the integration of the views of all its major interest groups, or that it was articulated by certain community leaders, such as a newspaper editor or elected officials, who could claim some heightened sense of the "community interest."

As Philip Converse (1987) has noted, however, the development of the public opinion polling industry has served to homogenize and stabilize the definition of public opinion. In his words, "it is ironic that it is exactly this kind of 'one person, one vote' tally of opinions as reported by polls and surveys which has now become the consensual understanding the world around as to a baseline definition of public opinion." In Blumer's (1948) view, a design that selected unrelated individuals from the whole and assigned an equal weight to the opinion of each was a travesty in any realistic understanding of public opinion. As Converse (1987: S14) notes, however, ". . . it is now true that just such responses, elicited in just the same way and counted up with equal weights, are in fact brought forcefully to the attention of authorities at all levels of government."

As Converse goes on to recognize, public opinion as measured by sample surveys is not the same as "effective" public opinion. That is, the "public opinion" that is effective in the political arena is not identical to that reported in public opinion polls; while they are often reasonably convergent, they can at times diverge remarkably. This acknowledgement does not suggest, however, that the definition of public opinion offered here needs to be modified. Rather, examining the conditions under which these two types of public opinion converge or are at odds, and the factors underlying these conditions, is an important consideration to investigate as part of the present definition. The combined personal opinions of individuals in a jurisdiction, equally weighted, is central to our approach to the study of public opinion.

The second component of this definition, "of adults," stems from our focus on the role of public opinion in the political process. We focus on the opinions of those 18 and older—the voting age population—because it is the opinions of this group to which elected officials and policy makers are more likely to pay attention. While those under 18 certainly hold opinions—which, as we shall show in Chapter 3, can sometimes be important to policy makers—for the most part public officials pay more attention to the views of the potential electorate. Most of the widely known general public opinion polls conducted in the United States (for example, those done by the Gallup, Harris, and Roper organizations, CBS News/*New York Times,* NBC News/*Wall Street Journal,* ABC News/*Washington Post,* CNN/*USA Today,* and the *L.A. Times*) collect data from this voting age population. There is also a great wealth of data on the opinions of the adult population available for **secondary analysis** (that is, analysis by researchers other than those who originally collected the data). Given these considerations, we have centered much of our attention on the opinions "of adults." Examining the opinions of subgroups—the "informed" public, demographic groups, registered voters—is not excluded by this definition; rather, it is another important consideration to investigate.

In exploring the final component of this definition, "issues of relevance to government," we have adopted an extremely broad-based approach. Any issue of relevance to any level of government (federal, state, or local) and at any point in the political process—during the campaign, prior to the vote on an issue, after a policy has been adopted—falls under the scope of our definition of public opinion. For example, the public's views of a candidate's strengths and weaknesses, the image of his or her opponent, and the most important issues in the campaign are, from this perspective, "issues of relevance to government." Similarly, citizens' views on national concerns (for example, how to regulate the tobacco industry), state matters (increasing the state sales tax on gasoline), and local questions (where to locate a new correctional facility) are included under this definition. The public's evaluation of government programs or services—from the federal food stamp program, to state parks, to the local schools—its approval or disapproval of the way various individuals and institutions are performing their roles, the needs it feels should be addressed by government, as well as its general beliefs about the principles underlying the governmental process, are all topics that will be considered under this broad conceptualization of "relevance to government."

Private sector concerns about what the public thinks, while certainly a part of the larger "American mind," will not be addressed in this work. Although market researchers employ many of the same techniques for gathering information as those who study public opinion, their interests are largely outside the realm of "relevance to government." Our concern is not with what the public thinks is the best brand of peanut butter. Knowing how they feel about government regulations that require peanut butter manufacturers to specify the ingredients on the labels of their products, however, is a question that falls under our definition of "public opinion."

By adopting this relatively simple and straightforward definition, we leave unanswered a number of questions, including differences in **intensity of opinion** (the strength of an individual's views on an issue), the knowledge that underlies opinions, the division of opinion, the role of multiple publics, and the impact of public opinion on policy. On the question of intensity of opinion, for example, one of the points that critics such as Blumer make of the type of definition we have proposed here is that it treats all opinions equally. That is, the views of the individual who had never thought about an issue until asked about it by a survey interviewer are treated the same as those of a person who held a passionate view on the matter. In our "one person, one vote" framework, each individual's position on an issue is treated equally. The effect that differences in intensity of opinion might have on other actions a person might take (for example, contacting a legislator, writing a letter to a newspaper) or how such variations on issues such as gun control may lead to policies that appear to conflict with "majority rule" are fertile subjects for more extensive investigation.

A similar concern can be raised over treating equally the opinions of people who have potentially quite different levels of knowledge on an issue. The person whose first thoughts on an issue came in response to the interviewer's question are equivalent to those of the person who has spent a great deal of time reading about, thinking about, and refining their position, in our "democratic" conceptualization of public opinion. How the views of those with less knowledge may be more unstable and easily shifted by new information and events, and how the more knowledgeable person may be better able to use her knowledge to influence the opinions of others, also present interesting avenues for further inquiry.

The term "issues of relevance" implies some form of controversy or division of opinion. In defining the scope of "public opinion," we treat as a separate class those topics on which there is uniform agreement or disagreement, known as **valence issues** (Stokes, 1966). The number of valence issues in American politics is relatively small. While there is general consensus over the basic principles of democracy in abstract terms (for example, democracy is the best form of government; every citizen should have an equal chance to influence government policy), there is disagreement over even the specific applications of these principles (Prothro and Grigg, 1960). We can view "law and order" as a valence issue; virtually no one opposes law and order (Scammon and Wattenberg, 1970). This topic moves from a valence issue into our sphere of public opinion when the discussion turns to the means for achieving "law and order." Harsher punishment for criminals, more emphasis on rehabilitating offenders, gun control, and the death penalty are examples of issues over which there is considerable disagreement among the American public. Whether in the domain of social-welfare policy, foreign policy, or social issues, and at each level of government, public opinion in the United States is characterized more by conflict than consensus, and virtually all issues "of relevance to government" involve some degree of controversy. Describing these divisions of opinion and the differences that exist among various groups will be considered extensively in Chapters 6 through 10.

Another consideration in interpreting "public opinion" involves the existence of **multiple "publics"** for any particular issue. By our definition, all adults in a jurisdiction are members of the general public whose "combined personal opinions" are to be considered in determining public opinion. In addition to having their views included as part of the general public, citizens can make their views known to policy makers through other means, such as writing letters, contacting their representatives directly, or working through groups of which they are members. Take, for example, a case in which a local gun control ordinance is being considered by the city council. Mr. Jones is a gun enthusiast and a member of the National Rifle Association (NRA), and is active in his neighborhood civic association. If the city council was presented with results of an opinion poll of a representative sample of the public (see Chapter 4), then the views of Mr. Jones, and those who felt as he did, would be appropriately represented as part of the general public. In addition, the NRA might stage a rally, organize a letter writing campaign, or arrange to have its members contact council members individually. In this way, Mr. Jones's views might be made known as a member of an "interested public." Similarly, if the neighborhood association were to hold a special meeting or make a concerted effort to influence the council's vote on this issue, Mr. Jones's views might be made known as a member of this "concerned public." For any public policy question, there are a number of potential "publics" on both sides of the issue. Although the views of such special publics are an important component in the policy process, they are not what we consider "public opinion." They are important to our treatment of this topic, in that the views of "multiple publics" can affect how public opinion is translated into public policy.[1]

DOES PUBLIC OPINION MATTER?

In our approach to public opinion we begin with the premise that, in a democratic society, what the public wants is in some way translated into public policy. Given the large number of potential influences on policy, however, establishing a definite linkage between public opinion and public policy is extremely difficult. Even if we find that a legislator's or council member's vote on an issue corresponded with the sentiment of his or her constituency, we don't have proof that public opinion had an effect. Correspondence between public opinion and public policy may result from the fact that lawmakers and their constituents often have similar background characteristics and experiences, so that they share the same views on many issues. It is also possible for congruence between opinion and policy to arise as a result of leadership by policy makers (policy affecting opinion) or from manipulation of public opinion by government officials (Weissberg, 1976: 242). As Page and Shapiro (1983: 176) have noted, "it is hard to tell whether correspondence between opinion and policy arises from democratic responsiveness, from leadership or manipulation of opinion, or from some combination of these."

Much of the research on the "linkage" between public opinion and public policy has centered on the correspondence between the legislative votes and the views of their constituents. For example, Miller and Stokes (1963) examined the relationship between the views of members of Congress, their nonincumbent opponents, and their constituents, and found a modest degree of correspondence between the views of legislators and those of their constituents in the domains of social welfare, foreign involvement, and civil rights. Similarly, Adams and Ferber's (1980) analysis of the roll-call votes of members of the Texas House of Representatives and the votes of their constituents on the same issues demonstrated a fairly high level of consistency between them.

Other approaches have examined public opinion and policy outcomes. Monroe (1979) studied the correspondence between national survey data and federal policy outcomes and found that policy decisions were consistent with public preferences about two-thirds of the time, although his later work in this area (Monroe, 1998) indicated that such consistency had dropped to 55 percent during the period from 1980 to 1993. Similarly, Page and Shapiro's (1983) analysis of changes in preferences and changes in policy in the United States showed a substantial congruence between changes in opinion and policy.

Despite the difficulties in proving that public opinion has a direct impact on policy, various methods of examining this question have shown that opinion-policy congruence does occur. As summarized by Monroe (1979: 8), there is a "definite tendency for public policy to be in accordance with public opinion, though the relationship is decidedly imperfect." This linkage between opinion and policy is imperfect in the sense that there is not a strict correspondence between the public's desires and government actions. Rather, opinion is linked to policy in that the public's preferences provide broad guidelines within which policymakers can operate. Public opinion is more effective in preventing totally objectionable policies than in specifying a policy mandate. As Weissberg (1976: 242) has noted, "... linkage mechanisms probably narrow down both public demands and government responses to a point where almost any publicly considered policy will be at least tolerable (though not preferred) for most people."

Evidence from policymakers, while largely unsystematic, also provides an indication that the influence of public opinion is primarily indirect. For example, in a discussion of the impact of polls on the policy environment, the former Chairperson of the Consumer Product Safety Commission observed that the group used polls to alert it to issues that are bothering people and to problems that the Commission was not explaining well or that needed more attention. As the chairperson noted, "the polls suggest *how* we should pursue a given objective and, in a negative sense, how we should *not* attempt to pursue a given objective" (Cantril, 1980: 138). As part of this discussion, Paul Warnke, principal U.S. negotiator on the second Strategic Arms Limitation Treaty (SALT), described a somewhat different function of polls. In his view, the effect of polls on SALT had more to do with the tactics of presentation than with the substance of the treaty. Polls showed that Americans wanted to see a reduction in nuclear weapons and also that they didn't trust the Russians. In presenting the treaty to the American public, it was important to show both how the treaty reduced the threat of nuclear weapons and how this did not depend on trust of the Soviet Union (Cantril, 1980: 142-4). Data from polls provide the broad contours within which policy making takes place.

In a similar vein, Philip Converse (1987: S22) asserts that "few politicians consult poll data to find out what they should be thinking on the issues . . . but they have very little interest in flouting the will of their constituency in any tendentious, head-on way." He makes an indirect, but rather persuasive argument, for the impact of polls when he notes that the influence of polls must ". . . occur in very large doses among political practitioners, or it would be extremely hard to explain why such users pay many millions of dollars a year for this expensive class of information." This mounting acceptance of public opinion data is, in his view, best symbolized by the daily polls of the national electorate done for President Reagan by his pollster, Richard Wirthlin (Converse, 1987: S17–S22).

A number of methods have been used to evaluate the impact of public opinion on public policy. The general conclusion from these studies is that while the public's desires are not perfectly satisfied, the political system produces acceptable outcomes in a majority of the cases. It is not the case that the public makes its desires known through public opinion polls and these desires are then directly translated into policy, nor should we expect it to be. Rather, policy makers at all levels of government are influenced by public opinion as they take account of the public's views not only in their decision-making but also in identifying those issues that are important to the public and the broad outlines within which government can operate.

PUBLIC OPINION VS. PUBLIC JUDGMENT

In completing the description of the way in which we have chosen to present "public opinion," we should note the distinction between this term and "**public judgment.**" Yankelovich (1991) believes that the "public opinion" that is reported on the basis of polls is misleading because it reflects people's top-of-the-head views rather than their thoughtful, considered judgments. In his terms, public judgment is a "state of highly developed public opinion that exists once people have engaged an issue, considered it from all sides, understood the choices it leads to, and accepted the consequences of the choices they make" (Yankelovich, 1991: 6). He argues that enhancing the quality of public judgment is necessary to ensure effective self-governance in the United States.

Yankelovich cites capital punishment as an example of an issue on which the citizenry has reached "public judgment." In describing Americans' views on this topic, he notes that prior to the 1970s, a majority of the public was not in favor of the death penalty for murder and other serious crimes. Support for the death penalty built slowly over the next two decades, and reached an average of 73 percent during the 1980s. Moreover, interviews with people who took this position show "that most have struggled with the argument that imposing the death penalty means that some innocent people will die" (Yankelovich, 1991: 26). In contrast to the snap judgments reflected in polls where the views of the public may change significantly when presented with the consequences of a decision, supporters of capital punishment "realize and accept this implication, but they do not change their views even when contemplating these consequences" (Yankelovich, 1991: 26).

We do not disagree with Yankelovich over the distinction between "public opinion" and "public judgment"; the criticism that respondents to public opinion polls make "snap" judgments, as opposed to those individuals who have actually considered both sides of an issue, is one that has long been recognized (Gallup, 1947). We do not believe, however, that public opinion, as we have described the term, is a less important consideration than public judgment in the way in which government decisions are made in the United States. From our perspective, examining (1) the reasons some people are more informed about various topics, (2) the factors underlying an individual's position on an issue, and (3) the determinants of varying levels of intensity of opinion are all important components of an overall understanding of "public opinion." These various components of public opinion, from how opinions are formed to their ultimate impact on the political process, will be examined in the following chapters. Limiting the scope to "informed" opinion or judgment would unnecessarily preclude a more complete examination of the factors that underlie differences in public opinion in the United States and their consequences for public policy.

OPINIONS, ATTITUDES, AND BELIEFS

Before concluding this description of our definition of "public opinion," we need to distinguish among the terms **attitudes, opinions,** and **beliefs.** Psychologists often differentiate these terms, and while such distinctions are numerous (Allport, 1935), attitudes are generally defined as relatively enduring orientations toward objects that provide individuals with mental frameworks for making economical sense of the world; opinions are the verbal expression of attitudes; and beliefs are the inclination to accept something as true. In one sense, attitudes may be said to go deeper than opinions and beliefs. As Katz (1960:163) has described it, the attitudes of individuals are the raw material out of which public opinion develops.

While such distinctions are important in considerations of attitude formation and change, these terms are often indistinguishable in discussions of public opinion. More than twenty years ago, Greenstein (1969: 28) noted that social scientists ". . . sometimes tend to equate the concept 'attitude' with its most prevalent indicator—a discrete response to a question of opinion in a public opinion poll." Similarly, the title of an extensive survey-based study by Free and Cantril (1969)—*The Political Beliefs of Americans: A Study of Public Opinion*—illustrates the interchangeable use of these terms.

For our purposes, the attitudes, opinions, and beliefs of the American public are all important in that they can have an impact on public policy. As such, each of them will be considered in our discussion of "public opinion." Americans' attitudes toward war, their opinions about whether the United States should or should not have sent troops to defend Kuwait from Iraq in Operation Desert Storm, and their beliefs about the extent to which this country should be involved in the affairs of other nations all could have had an effect on government decisions during that conflict. In this framework, it makes little difference whether these expressions are referred to as attitudes, or opinions, or beliefs; these combined personal expressions of adults toward issues of government are what we shall consider "public opinion."

THE PLAN OF THE BOOK

In defining public opinion, we have made reference to a number of topics to be considered in this book. How opinions are formed, the different levels of knowledge that underlie opinion, variations in intensity of opinion, the factors that account for such differences, and the impact of opinion on the political process are all topics to be examined more thoroughly.

Chapter 2 examines the origins of public opinion polling in American history and discusses how the nature of public opinion polling has evolved in the United States. We describe critical events in its development in this chapter.

Part II contains a description how opinions are measured and put to use. Chapter 3 provides some examples of the ways in which public opinion data are used, including use by candidates, office-holders, policy makers, researchers, and the media. Chapter 4 details the methods used to collect public opinion data and delineates some of the steps involved in the data collection process, including sampling, designing questionnaires, and interviewing.

Part III focuses on what Americans believe. Chapter 5 explores the origins of Americans' opinions, including opinion formation, political socialization and political learning. Partisan and ideological identifications and the sources of these identifications are covered in Chapter 6. Americans' domestic goals, for example, in the areas of social welfare, the economy, and education are the subject of Chapter 7, while Chapter 8 explores their views on racial issues. Highly controversial topics, including the death penalty, are investigated in Chapter 9. Opinions on global political issues, such as the U.S. role in the world and foreign aid, are treated in Chapter 10.

In Part IV, Chapter 11 takes a critical look at the current state of public opinion, its measurement, and its use, while Chapter 12 addresses some of the more important political issues that should be considered by those interested in "the combined personal opinions of adults toward issues of relevance to government."

Polls, Polling and the Internet

Most newspapers and networks have poll stories weekly. Take a look, for example, at the poll results reported in *USA Today* at:

> http://www.usatoday.com

or the home page of the *Washington Post* at:

> http://washingtonpost.com

How do these newspaper reports of polls relate the results to the democratic expression of the people's views?

NOTES

1. The question of multiple publics is distinct from the question of **"issue publics"** as discussed by Converse (1964) and others (e.g., Hennessy, 1981; Weissberg, 1976). An "issue public" is a group of people who are knowledgeable and have meaningful beliefs about an issue and who are more likely to write letters to the editor, contact public officials, or change their vote on the basis of this issue. Concerns about the effects of differences in interest and awareness among such publics parallel those in our previous discussion of the effect of such differences on public opinion. As noted earlier, identifying the size, correlates, and consequences of such "issue publics" is an important consideration in the analysis of public opinion.

2

Measuring American Opinion: The Origins of Polling

Questions to Consider:

What was the first American public opinion poll?

How did polling become a "science?"

Why do newspapers and networks poll?

How did the federal government become a polling operation?

T he concept of democracy itself, resting as it does on the consent of the governed, implies some means for determining how the public feels about public policy issues. But while "public opinion" has always had a prominent role, the way in which the public's views have been measured has changed dramatically over time.

The Founding Fathers were themselves somewhat mixed in their views about the role of the public in this country's political process. Even though they wanted to create a system in which the ultimate political authority rested in the hands of the people, they were wary of the unbridled will of the citizenry. As Madison wrote in *Federalist No. 10*, ". . . the public good is disregarded in the conflicts of rival parties, and that measures are too often decided, not according to the rules of justice and the rights of the minor party, but by the superior force of an interested and overbearing majority" (*Federalist No. 10:* 54). Similarly, *Federalist No. 63* noted that, ". . . there are particular moments in public affairs when the people, stimulated by some irregular passion, or some illicit advantage, or misled by the artful misrepresentations of interested men, may call for measures which they themselves will afterwards be the most ready to lament and condemn" (*Federalist No. 63:* 410). The United States political system, with its representative government, separation of powers, and system of checks and balances, reflects these reservations concerning the power of "the public."

The way in which government officials have come to know what the public thinks has changed significantly over time. At the time of the Constitution's ratification, representatives relied upon personal contacts from citizens and leaders of various groups, letters to the editor, and marches and demonstrations as means for determining public opinion. While these sources are still used today and are important in learning how various segments of society feel about issues, more scientific means have been developed for assessing public opinion.

THE ORIGINS OF PUBLIC OPINION POLLING

We can trace the origins of public opinion research in the United States not to the desire of government officials to determine the public's views on issues, but rather to a fascination with information about the voting intentions of the electorate (Robinson, 1932: 51). Tallies of results from pre-election canvasses in 1824 have been cited by George Gallup as "the earliest counterpart of modern opinion surveys" (Gallup and Rae, 1940: 34–35). During this election, counts at regular public meetings, at militia musters, and at special meetings called to assess the public's presidential leanings, as well as tallies from "poll books" left at various public places such as taverns, were used to predict the outcome of the presidential election (Smith, 1990: 25–27). While there is some debate as to whether these methods were really the first "polls," there is little question that they were "a significant development in the assessment and quantification of public opinion and deserve a special place in the history of election polling" (Smith, 1990: 31).

Straw polls of this type served as an important means of assessing public sentiment for the next century. Newspapers such as the *New York Herald, Cincinnati Enquirer, St. Louis Republic* and *Boston Globe* conducted such polls not only for presidential elections but for some statewide and local contests as well. Other national periodicals, such as the *Farm Journal* and the *Pathfinder,* carried out straw polls during presidential election campaigns. Newspapers and magazines spent a great deal of resources on these polls not only because they thought the voting intentions of the American public had great news value, but also because the polls served to promote these publications (Robinson, 1932: 47–51).

The most prominent of these straw polls was conducted by the *Literary Digest.* The *Digest* poll—which Robinson (1932: 49) describes as "almost synonymous with straw polls"—began its predictions on presidential contests in 1916 and used straw polls during presidential elections through 1936. In addition to presidential races, the *Digest* used straw polls to assess public opinion on issues such as bonuses for war veterans, prohibition, and tax reduction.

The First Candidate Poll: Family Ties

In working on his doctoral dissertation in applied psychology at Iowa State University, George Gallup used survey methods to measure the readership of print media. This experience, together with his interest in public opinon and journalism, combined with the candidacy of his mother-in-law for Iowa's Secretary of State in 1932 to foster his interest in political polling. As a result, Gallup decided to test the utility of quota sampling for forecasting the election outcomes of 1934. This finding led, in part to his challenge to the *Literary Digest* in 1936. (J. Converse, 1987: 114; Moore, 1992: 46; Bradburn and Sudman, 1988: 14)

The method typically used by the *Literary Digest* was to mail ballot cards to a very large number of people, identifying them through telephone directories and automobile registration lists. As many as 20 million ballots were sent out during an election campaign. While there was often substantial deviation between the *Digest's* predicted percentage of the vote and the actual vote total, the *Digest* poll was fairly well-respected, having correctly predicted the presidential elections of 1920, 1924, 1928, and 1932 (Babbie, 1990: 67). Reports of the *Digest's* poll results were widely reported in newspapers across the country, with some even featuring them more prominently than their own polls (Squire, 1988 :126).

During the 1936 presidential campaign, the *Digest* mailed out more than 10 million straw vote ballots, using its usual procedure of drawing its sample from automobile registration lists and telephone books. Over 2.3 million ballots were returned. The prediction from these returns was that the Republican candidate, Alfred M. Landon, would receive 55% of the vote, Franklin D. Roosevelt, the Democratic candidate, 41%, and William Lemke, the candidate of the Union party, 4%. On election day, Roosevelt won 61% of the popular vote while Landon received 37%. The large discrepancy between the predicted and actual outcomes resulted from a bias in the sampling frame (that is, the list from which names were selected) and non-response, arising from a low response rate (Squire, 1988: 131). The bias in the **sampling frame** resulted from the fact that the names to whom ballots were mailed were taken largely from telephone directories or state automobile registrations. In 1936 such lists had a disproportionate number of upper-income respondents, and lower-income households were less likely to have telephones or cars and were more likely to vote for Roosevelt. **Non-response bias** resulted from the failure of everyone to whom ballots were mailed to return them. Even though more than 2.3 million ballots were received, this represented less than one-fourth of the number mailed out. Sample bias and non-response are both topics that will be discussed in more detail in Chapter 4. The "*Literary Digest* fiasco," as it has come to be known, is an important event in the history of public opinion research because it demonstrated dramatically the importance of proper survey design.

THE DEVELOPMENT OF SURVEY RESEARCH

During the period that straw polls were prominent in estimating the vote in-tentions and issue positions of the American public, developments were taking place that would ultimately lead to the scientific study of public opinion. While the straw polls of 1824 can be viewed as the earliest counterparts of modern opinion surveys, such surveys can also trace their roots to the social surveys that evolved in the late 1800s. In England, Charles Booth, among oth-ers, developed methods for collecting and analyzing data that became known as the "English social survey." Their procedures included fieldwork, compre-hensive coverage of some domain, an examination of detailed cases, quantifi-cation, and organization of the data by individual records. Examples of the ap-plication of these methods in the United States included the Pittsburgh Survey, which was an effort to provide an overview of the state of that city, and the Country Life Movement, which conducted surveys on agricultural condi-tions and practices (J. Converse, 1987: 21–26).

The first quarter of the twentieth century also marked the beginnings of the U.S. government's interest in surveys. As early as 1915, the Department of Agriculture was conducting surveys of the quality of life in rural America. The Department of Agriculture, along with other agencies such as the Works Progress Administration, continued to engage in a range of survey projects during the administration of Franklin D. Roosevelt.

It was during this period that **probability sampling** methods were devel-oped. The work of statisticians such as Bowley, Neyman, and Fisher was instru-mental in demonstrating the superiority of probability sampling over purpo-sive sampling procedures. During the 1930s, the Department of Agriculture and the Bureau of the Census applied probability theory to the design of na-tional samples of the American public (J. Converse, 1987: 202).

Advances in survey methods were also incorporated into research being conducted in the commercial sector. During the 1936 election campaign, three pollsters who had established themselves as market researchers— Archibald Crossley, George Gallup, and Elmo Roper—used these more scien-tific procedures in challenging the *Literary Digest*. Gallup was the most aggres-sive in this regard, selling his newspaper column with a money-back guarantee that his prediction would be better than the *Digest*'s and warning the *Digest* that it would regret its forecast of a Landon victory (J. Converse, 1987: 117). In response, W. J. Funk, editor of the *Digest,* commented, "Our fine statistical friend should be advised that the *Digest* would carry on with those old-fash-ioned methods that have produced correct forecasts exactly one hundred per-cent of the time" (*New York Times,* 1936: 21).

While their percentage estimates were far from perfect, the polls of Gallup, Crossley, and Roper each predicted a Roosevelt victory. Contrasted with the *Literary Digest*'s faulty estimate, these results were seen as vindication for the "scientific approach" for gauging public opinion (Jensen, 1980: 59).

In the aftermath of this election, government agencies, public opinion re-searchers, and market researchers carried out their surveys with confidence in their results. While some warnings were raised about the limitations of the **quota sampling** procedures commonly employed at the time, their use was generally seen as a necessity, since probability sampling did not seem a practical option for national surveys (J. Converse, 1987: 94).

During this period government agencies greatly expanded their use of surveys. The Department of Agriculture was one of the leading users. In 1935 a small interviewing unit was established to tap farmers' attitudes about the efforts of USDA farm programs. The utility of this information led to the creation of a Division of Program Surveys in the Bureau of Agricultural Economics, and the agency was instrumental in promoting the use of area probability samples and the development of standardized interviewing techniques (Bradburn and Sudman, 1988: 22–23; J. Converse, 1987: 138–139). While this program was founded to address farm issues, it fairly quickly expanded its scope to ". . . national and international problems that had meaning in their own right, such as national morale" (J. Converse, 187: 160). With the advent of World War II, the substance of these surveys further extended to the areas of American defense and involvement in the war and this unit conducted surveys for other federal agencies that needed survey data, such as the Office of Facts and Figures and the State Department.

Government use of survey research continued to expand during World War II. As part of the wartime effort, agencies such as the Research Branch of the Division of Morale of the U.S. Army, the Surveys Division of the Office of War Information, and Program Surveys of the Department of Agriculture conducted a wide range of surveys (J. Converse, 1987: 163). While the involvement of the federal government in surveys was scaled back after the war, the advancements in areas such as sampling, questionnaire design, and data collection made during this period solidified the base upon which modern public opinion research has been built.

THE ELECTION OF 1948:
A TEMPORARY SETBACK

If 1936 represented a breakthrough for advocates of the scientific approach to collecting survey information, the 1948 election provided a sharp reminder of its limitations. The preelection polls of Crossley, Gallup, and Roper each predicted a Dewey victory over Truman, by margins ranging from 5.0% to 15.1% (Mosteller, et al., 1949: 17). These polls led newspapers to run headlines such as "Poll Taker Finds Presidency Good As Settled" in the *Times-Picayune* and "Dewey Victory in November By Wide Margin Predicted" in the *Wilmington Morning News* (Mosteller, et al., 1949: 32) and, based partly on these poll findings, the *Chicago Daily Tribune* predicted a Dewey victory. On election day, Truman received 49.8% of the popular vote to Dewey's 45.4%, causing one commentator to note, "(E)veryone believes in public opinion polls. Everyone from the man in the street . . . up to President Thomas E.

Dewey" (Babbie, 1990: 67). The accompanying photograph of a victorious Truman is a stark reminder to survey researchers of the need to carry out all aspects of the survey process with great care.

A review of the events of 1948 by the Social Science Research Council (Mosteller, et al., 1949) identified a number of limitations of these election polls and led to some questions about the reliability of poll data. Two major limitations identified were (1) errors of sampling and interviewing, and (2) errors of forecasting. Quota sampling, which was used in the design of many of these surveys, is limited; the composition of the population may not be accurately known for the determination of quotas and the respondents who interviewers select may produce a **biased sample. Errors in forecasting** resulted from stopping data collection too soon, failing to identify likely voters adequately, and not allocating the undecided voters properly.

As a result of these incorrect predictions, major changes were made in the way in which surveys were conducted. One such change—which applied not only to pre-election polls but to surveys more generally—was to move from quota samples in which interviewers were responsible for respondent selection, and which were found to over-represent higher and middle-income respondents, to **modified area samples.** In addition, pre-election interviewing is now continued much closer to election day and polling organizations have developed some rather sophisticated methods for identifying potential voters and allocating the choices of the "undecideds" (Ladd, 1992: 27). As a result, the pre-election polls since this time have been more accurate. As shown in Table 2-1, since 1952 the average deviation between the final Gallup Poll and the actual election results has been 2.0%.[1]

AFTER 1948: CONTINUED GROWTH

The events of 1948 would prove to be only a temporary setback for survey research and the period from 1948 to the mid-1960s was one of steady growth. The improvements in survey methods following this election spurred a period of expansion not only in commercial polling and government surveys, but particularly in universities (DeMaio, Marsh, and Turner, 1984: 27). In the period after World War II, there was a dramatic increase in the amount of survey research conducted in university settings, led by the Bureau of Applied Social Research at Columbia University, the National Opinion Research Center (NORC) at the University of Chicago, and the Survey Research Center (SRC) at the University of Michigan (J. Converse, 1987: 239). Each of these organizations contributed uniquely to the development of survey research and programs originated by them, such as the American National Election Studies (NES) and the General Social Survey (GSS), continue to serve as important resources for survey researchers. These research programs will be discussed more fully in Chapter 3.

During the period between 1948 and the mid-1960s, there was also rapid expansion in commercial polling and audience research activities, led by organizations such as Gallup, Harris, Roper, Opinion Research Corporation, and

Table 2.1 The Accuracy of Gallup Pre-election Polls

Year	GALLUP Final Survey			ELECTION Results		Deviation*
1996	52.0%	CLINTON	49.0%	CLINTON		−3.0
1994	58.0	Republican	51.0	Republican		+7.0
1992†	49.0	CLINTON	43.2	CLINTON		+5.8
1990	54.0	Democratic	54.1	Democratic		−0.1
1988	56.0	BUSH	53.9	BUSH		−2.1
1984	59.0	REAGAN	59.1	REAGAN		−0.1
1982	55.0	Democratic	56.1	Democratic		−1.1
1980	47.0	REAGAN	50.8	REAGAN		−3.8
1978	55.0	Democratic	54.6	Democratic		+0.4
1976	48.0	CARTER	50.0	CARTER		−2.0
1974	60.0	Democratic	58.9	Democratic		+1.1
1972	62.0	NIXON	61.8	NIXON		+0.2
1970	53.0	Democratic	54.3	Democratic		−1.3
1968	43.0	NIXON	43.5	NIXON		−0.5
1966	52.5	Democratic	51.9	Democratic		+0.6
1964	64.0	JOHNSON	61.3	JOHNSON		+2.7
1962	55.5	Democratic	52.7	Democratic		+2.8
1960	51.0	KENNEDY	50.1	KENNEDY		+0.9
1958	57.0	Democratic	56.5	Democratic		+0.5
1956	59.5	EISENHOWER	57.8	EISENHOWER		+1.7
1954	51.5	Democratic	52.7	Democratic		−1.2
1952	51.0	EISENHOWER	55.4	EISENHOWER		−4.4
1950	51.0	Democratic	50.3	Democratic		+0.7
1948	44.5	TRUMAN	49.9	TRUMAN		−5.4
1946	58.0	Republican	54.3	Republican		+3.7
1944	51.5	ROOSEVELT	53.3	ROOSEVELT		−1.8
1942	52.0	Democratic	48.0	Democratic		+4.0
1940	52.0	ROOSEVELT	55.0	ROOSEVELT		−3.0
1938	54.0	Democratic	50.8	Democratic		+3.2
1936	55.7	ROOSEVELT	62.5	ROOSEVELT		−6.8

Note: No Congressional poll done in 1986.

*Average deviation for 30 national elections: 2.4 percent.

TREND IN DEVIATION:

Elections	Average Error
1936–1950	3.6
1952–1996	2.0

†The Ross Perot candidacy created an additional source of error in estimating the 1992 presidential vote. There was no historical precedent for Perot, an independent candidate who was accorded equal status to the major party nominees in the presidential debates and had a record advertising budget. Gallup's decision to allocate none of the undecided vote to Perot, based on past performance of third party and independent candidates, resulted in the overestimation of Clinton's vote.

Source: *The Gallup Poll Monthly,* November 1992; *Time,* November 21, 1994; *Wall Street Journal,* November 6, 1996.

Response Analysis. The latter part of this period also witnessed a growth in the use of surveys by government, as federal agencies such as the U.S. Information Agency, the Departments of Commerce, Labor, Agriculture, and Health, Education and Welfare, realized their need for survey information. A number of the data collection efforts started during this period provided the foundation for programs that continue today (Sudman and Bradburn, 1987: S73). As noted above, this was also a period of tremendous growth in academic survey work, as many researchers who were employed by the government during the war migrated to university settings with more technical expertise and greater scientific credibility gained through wartime experiences (J. Converse, 1987: 239-244). How academic researchers, commercial firms, and governments utilize survey data is discussed in the next chapter.

A SURGE IN TELEPHONE INTERVIEWING: THE DEVELOPMENT OF RANDOM-DIGIT DIALING

By necessity, much of the survey research done during this period involved face-to-face interviews. Interviewing by telephone was not considered a practical alternative for most probability samples due to noncoverage of the population. In 1936, it was estimated that 35 percent of the households in the United States had telephones. By 1960, this percentage had increased to 75 percent, and had risen to 93 percent by 1986 (Massey, 1988: 3). Today, approximately 95 percent of households in the United States have telephones (U.S. Census Bureau, 1996).

As telephone coverage increased, data collection by telephone became a more practical alternative for obtaining information from a representative sample of a population, and the increasing costs of face-to-face interviewing gave impetus to the search for a viable alternative. There was, however, a reluctance among survey practitioners to adopt telephone methods, since the procedures typically used for sampling from non-specified populations, such as residents of a city, a state, or the voting age population of the United States, generally involved selection from lists such as telephone or city directories. Such listings contain known biases in that they are incomplete, do not include households with unlisted or recently added numbers, and become less accurate as time passes from their date of publication. The problems of sampling for general telephone surveys were largely eliminated by the development of **random–digit dialing (RDD)**, which is a method that randomly selects telephone numbers from an exchange. More information about this technological advance that greatly facilitated an increase in surveying in the United States is given in Chapter 4.

GROWTH IN UNIVERSITY POLLS

As noted previously, in 1950 there were three academic survey research organizations: the Bureau of Applied Social Research at Columbia University, the National Opinion Research Center (NORC) at the University of Chicago,

---

Comparing Opinion by State

Most university-based survey organizations conduct statewide surveys. After the data have been analyzed, many of these studies are archived through the National Network of State Polls, which makes them available to other interested researchers. One use of such data is to compare public opinion in different states. For example, between March and June, 1994, Alabama, Kentucky, and New Jersey each asked survey respondents to rate their states as a place to live, with the following results:

Question: Overall, how would you rate (Name of State) as a place to live— excellent, good, only fair, or poor?

	AL	KY	NJ
DATE	3/94	5/94	6/94
Excellent	34%	44%	20%
Good	46	41	49
Fair	17	12	24
Poor	3	3	7

Similarly, polls taken in Florida, Illinois, and Rhode Island between September and November, 1996, found the following ratings of President Clinton:

Question: How would you rate the job that Bill Clinton is doing as president? Would you say excellent, good, fair, or poor?

	RI	FL	IL
DATE	9/96	11/96	11/96
Excellent	8%	10%	12%
Good	53	31	34
Fair	30	34	36
Poor	9	26	19

More information about the National Network of State Polls as well as access to data from state polls can be found at their website: http://www.irss.unc.edu/irss/nnsp/index.html.

---

and the Survey Research Center (SRC) at the University of Michigan. By the start of the 1960s, there were eight, and by 1970 there were 20. Currently, there are nearly 100 academic survey research organizations. Much of the growth in the number of academic survey research centers can be attributed to the increased demand for survey data that followed from increased governmental activities at the national, state, and local levels, as well as the need to evaluate these programs (O'Rourke, Sudman, and Ryan, 1996: 2-4).

If different levels of government are major consumers of survey data, then university survey units are among their principal suppliers. *Survey Research,* the newsletter of these academic organizations, regularly publishes brief reports of research done by these units. In 1996, it reported 147 projects; of these 31% were sponsored by the federal government, 19% by state governments, and 14% by local governments. The remainder were university supported or sponsored by non-for-profit groups, media organizations, or foundations.[2]

As the following examples demonstrate, surveys conducted by academic organizations address a broad range of issues and vary widely in scope. At the federal level, Temple University's Institute for Survey Research conducted a study for the National Institute for Drug Abuse that investigated the psychosocial antecedents and consequences of drug abuse and other deviant adaptations to stress across two generations. This study involved face-to-face interviews with 5,335 adults and 4,165 of their children. The Wisconsin Household Recycling Study conducted by the University of Wisconsin Survey Center provides an example of surveys done for state governments. This survey involved telephone interviews with 450 Wisconsin residents to evaluate the state's recycling program and assess citizen opinions and concerns. An example at the local level is City of Fort Worth Citizen Survey, done by the Survey Research Center at the University of North Texas, a telephone survey of 1,500 Fort Worth residents designed to determine citizen satisfaction with various city services and programs.

A common activity of many academic survey organizations is to conduct statewide surveys that may be sponsored by the university, done in conjunction with a newspaper or television station, or funded by client subscription. Of the 57 current members of the National Network of State Polls, 48 are university-based organizations.

More recent developments in survey research include innovations in the methods by which data are collected and recorded, such as CATI (computer-assisted telephone interviewing), audio-CASI (audio computer assisted self-interviewing), touch-tone data entry (TDE), voice recognition entry (VRE), and the use of the Internet to collect data. As will be evident in the description of these technologies in Chapter 4, like society in general, survey research has changed dramatically since the first straw poll of 1824.

Polls, Polling, and the Internet

The national organization of pollsters, people who study polls and media reporters of polls, is The American Association for Public Opinion Research. Visit the home page of this half-century-old organization at:

>   http://www.aapor.org

The original journal of public opinion scholarship is *Public Opinion Quarterly*, published by AAPOR. A complete and very usable index to all back issues is found at:

>   http://www.aapor.org/poq/

NOTES

1. This is not to imply, however, that such pre-election polls have been perfect or without their critics. For an example of some of the controversies that surrounded the 1980 election, see Ladd and Ferree (1981), while for those associated with the 1996 outcome, see Ladd (1996A) and Moore (1996B).

2. It should be noted that these reports do not represent all the research conducted by these organizations, since not all groups provide information on each of their studies and all reported studies are not printed in the newsletter.

Part II

How Are Opinions
Measured and Used?

3

How Public Opinion
Data Are Used

Questions to Consider:

How do candidates use polls to get elected?

Do polls shape government policy?

Why do the media sponsor polls?

What can researchers learn about Americans from polls?

In American politics, public opinion data are used for a variety of purposes. Candidates use polling information as part of their effort to win elective office. Once in office, elected officials frequently use surveys to determine how the public feels on a variety of issues. Such monitoring of public opinion is done not only by office-holders but also by the media, who make independent observations of the public's views on a range of issues, as well as take the public's pulse on the job performance of elected officials. Government agencies at all levels use surveys to assess their overall performance, as well as to evaluate specific programs and to determine the needs of those they serve. Academic researchers use survey information to test hypotheses and to attempt to uncover those factors that account for differences in attitudes and political behavior. This chapter describes each of these uses of public opinion data in more detail.

USE IN POLITICAL CAMPAIGNS

In describing the role of public opinion data in American politics, an obvious starting point is its use in election campaigns. Polling data are used throughout the campaign cycle and the polling that is done in a campaign varies considerably according to the resources available. Polling done for a presidential or senatorial campaign will generally be more extensive than that done for local candidates because far greater financial resources are available at the national level.

Benchmark Polls

A campaign that uses polling data effectively will typically conduct an extensive poll early in the process—that is, before a candidate has decided to run for office—that can be used as a benchmark for tracking the campaign's progress. Such a poll is designed not only to determine the candidate's standing (for example, name recognition and standing in trial heats), but also to identify issues and problems that the electorate views as important. It also identifies special groups within the electorate that may be receptive to special appeals (Roll and Cantril, 1980: 17–20).

The results of a **benchmark poll**—particularly for a non-incumbent—may be so negative in terms of lack of name recognition or the extent to which the individual is trailing in a trial heat that a potential candidate may decide against running. However, benchmark poll results are more commonly used to determine those issues the public feels are important, the stance on these issues that a majority of the public supports, the image that the electorate has of the candidate (and that of his or her potential opponents), and the subgroups that may be sources of voting strength or opposition. This information is used by the candidate's advisors or paid political consultants to aid candidates in (1) developing their issue positions and determining which issues should be stressed in the campaign, (2) identifying the characteristics (for example, competence or honesty) that are viewed positively and should be stressed, the areas in which the candidate's image needs improvement, and the characteristics on which opponents may be vulnerable, and (3) discovering groups whose views on a given issue may be distinct from other groups in a way that would make them responsive to a targeted appeal. If, for example, the benchmark poll for a re-election campaign reveals that the incumbent senator is perceived to be too much of a Washington insider, he or she may be advised to spend a great deal more time back in the state, visiting with the locals. Sometimes, the campaign consultant may advise the candidate to "dress down" and be more like an ordinary person when interacting with constituents.

Tracking Polls

Depending on resources, a benchmark survey is followed up at various points in the campaign by more polling to monitor a candidate's standing and to see whether the electorate's issue positions are changing or if new issues are emerging. This information is used to either support the strategy the candidate has been following or to suggest areas where changes are needed. Alternatively—or sometimes in addition to these follow-up surveys—a campaign may commission **tracking polls** over the final weeks of a campaign. Such tracking surveys generally consist of a relatively small number (100–200) of interviews that are conducted each day. The results of this daily interviewing[1] are then tracked and aggregated to determine if there are significant factors, such as a distinct trend in the preference of previously undecided voters, that would require some last-minute adjustment in campaign tactics, including the production of new television advertisements.[2]

As noted earlier, not all campaigns have the resources to mount repeated surveys or tracking efforts. While candidates for local offices may desire more extensive polling data, they are forced to use their more limited resources on other aspects of the campaign, and may only be able to conduct a single survey that reports their name recognition and identifies some of the issues that may be important in the campaign.

Pseudo-Polls

In the waning days of the campaign, the supporters of a single candidate or the local party organization may organize a telephone campaign that calls registered voters to ask if they have decided whom to vote for and whether they are planning to cast a ballot. Often, such telephone "get-out-the-vote" campaigns pretend to be a poll and then ask only two questions. The results of these telephone campaigns are used to organize the election day strategy of the candidate. Such telephone canvasses are a replacement for the old method of having a precinct captain visit each voter before the election.

In recent years, a technique that has been used more frequently is known as the **push poll**. As described by the American Association for Public Opinion Research (AAPOR), a push poll is

> a telemarketing technique in which telephone calls are used to canvass potential voters, feeding them false or misleading "information" about a candidate under the pretense of taking a poll to see how this information affects voter preferences. In fact, the intent is not to measure public opinion but to manipulate it—to "push" voters away from one candidate and toward the opposing candidate. Such polls defame selected candidates by spreading false or misleading information about them.

> (American Association of Public Opinion Research, 1996)

Such polls have been condemned by AAPOR, the National Council on Public Polls, and other professional survey organizations because they intentionally lie to or mislead respondents, and in so doing, they corrupt the political process. In most cases, there is no research component to a push poll and no data are actually collected. Instead, as many members of the electorate as possible are called without any sampling. The results of a such a poll, if released, "give a seriously flawed and biased picture of the political situation" (Gawiser, 1995: 1).[3]

Polling has become an industry in its own right with its own industry organizations. The American Association for Public Opinion Research is one
that combines major survey houses with media and academic practitioners.
However, there are at least three other major organizations of survey research
firms. CASRO (the Council of American Survey Research Organizations) has
more than 150 members. The "political pages" of *Campaigns and Elections*
monthly magazine listed 360 political polling and research organizations in
1996. Given such a sizable list, one might ask what all these firms do to stay in
existence. As we discussed above, polling for candidates takes place at all levels
of government, as does media polling about campaigns. The Cook Report for
the first six months of 1996 listed literally hundreds of polls reported in gu-
bernatorial races across the 50 states, more than four months before the actual
elections.

Given the amount of resources devoted to polling and the ever-increasing
attention given to survey results in developing campaign strategies, the political process in the United States is open to charges of paying more attention to
the "packaging" of a candidate rather than to the presentation of policy positions for the voters to evaluate in making their choices. Such a critique, however, ignores the fact that polling data are not the sole basis on which candidates develop campaigns. Their own views on issues, the position of their party,
the advice of other elected officials and advisors, as well as information from
focus groups, all play a role in the development of an election strategy. While
polling data does have an impact on how the candidate is "marketed," it is also
true that election polls attempt to determine the issue positions of the electorate and incorporate these into the campaign. This information can serve as
a base for the candidate, once elected, to use in formulating policies that conform to the wishes of his or her constituents.

USE BY OFFICE-HOLDERS

While public opinion data can be used effectively by any elected official, its
use is most visible—and probably most frequent—at the presidential level. The
first president to have a regular flow of polling information into his office was
Franklin D. Roosevelt (Roll and Cantril, 1980: 10). As described by Cantril
(1967), Roosevelt reviewed polls on a range of issues, from providing aid to
Britain prior to the United States' entry into World War II to providing farm
subsidies. In Cantril's view, "Roosevelt never altered his goals because public
opinion was against him or was uninformed. Rather he utilized such information to try to bring the public around more quickly or more effectively to the
course of action he felt was best for the country" (1967: 41).

The presidents immediately following Roosevelt, Truman and Eisenhower,
did not use polls extensively, although they were briefed on public attitudes
toward major issues (Bradburn and Sudman, 1988: 40). While John F. Kennedy
did not commission any polls directly, Louis Harris and others reported the

findings of many of their polls to him and "the published polls of Gallup and his colleagues were studied with great care" (Sorenson, 1965: 333).

Lyndon Johnson did, in contrast, commission polls, but his use of them was more effective in campaigning than in governing. On two of the more important issues of his presidency—the tax increase of 1966 and the Vietnam War—Johnson either went against the tide of public opinion or seemingly let it play little role in his decision (Bradburn and Sudman, 1988: 43). The use of polling information during the terms of Presidents Nixon and Ford was not as extensive as that of their successors, and has generally been characterized as ineffective. In contrasting the use of polls by Roosevelt and Nixon, Bradburn and Sudman (1988: 45–46) note that Roosevelt attempted to lead the public in the direction he thought was right, while Nixon's emphasis was "on retaining or recovering presidential popularity rather than making wise policy judgments."

The presidency of Jimmy Carter marked the institutionalization of public opinion as an important component of the governing process, together with an increasing role for the president's pollster as a policy advisor. Pat Caddell was Carter's pollster during the 1976 campaign and moved to Washington after the election. While he was not an official member of the White House staff, he continued to poll on issues for the president and gained influence in the policy process that was unprecedented for a pollster (Moore, 1992: 145).

One of the most visible—and perhaps most ineffective—uses of polling data by President Carter revolved around what has become known as the "malaise" speech. In early 1979, Carter's support among the American public was at a near-record low and was combined with a growing distrust of government, factors that together threatened the president's bid for reelection. While many of Carter's advisors saw these public attitudes as a normal reaction to the state of the economy and the administration's perceived ineffectiveness in dealing with it, Caddell argued that they reflected a more basic "crisis of confidence" (Moore, 1992: 149). At Caddell's urging, Carter cancelled a major energy speech just 48 hours before he was to give it on July 5, and retreated to Camp David to meet with his advisors (Bradburn and Sudman, 1988: 46). These actions heightened expectations for the speech that was aired on July 15. Rather than announcing a new energy policy, Carter—following the themes laid out by Caddell—proclaimed that there was a "malaise" affecting the American public and charged the people to restore faith and rebuild confidence in America. The views of the pollster were clearly evident in what has been termed "the most important speech" of the Carter presidency (Moore, 1992: 149). The reaction of the public and most commentators was surprise and disbelief rather than support for the president's view.

Polling data continued to play an important role during the presidency of Ronald Reagan. Reagan's pollster for the 1980 campaign was Richard Wirthlin, who continued his association with Reagan during his two terms, although he never worked directly in the White House. Instead, Wirthlin would meet with the president every three to four weeks and brief him on the public's view of the issues. The *Washington Post* reported that Wirthlin was doing nearly a million dollars a year in polling for the White House and the Republican National Committee and Moore reported that more polling was done for the Reagan administration than for any of Reagan's predecessors (Moore, 1992: 215). It is important to note that such polling by Wirthlin and his predecessor, Caddell, is usually under contract to the Republican or Democratic National Committee, paid for by contributions, not federal funds.

Although George Bush collected polling information during his presidency, his use of survey data was less extensive than that of his predecessor. Moreover, Bush was not above deriding the polls, referring late in the 1992 campaign to "those nutty pollsters" (*Charlotte Observer,* October 25, 1992) who showed him trailing Bill Clinton.

The Clinton administration raised the use of polls in governing to another level. During Clinton's first year in office, his pollster, Stanley Greenberg, was paid almost $2 million to conduct surveys and focus groups. More than any other president, Clinton "relies on polls and focus groups in helping to determine what he needs to be saying and how he should say it" (Perry, 1994: A-16). The influence wielded by the president's pollster has grown to the point that this position has been labeled "The Pollster General" (Schneider, 1997: 7).

After the mid-term elections of 1994, Clinton switched from Greenberg to the polling firm of Penn and Schoen, but this switch did not lessen the emphasis on polls. Under Penn and Schoen, the White House conducted a poll per night, using this information to shape policy positions in a way that gives governing the aspects of a "permanent campaign." Clinton's use of polls is alternately admired and criticized by his rivals who acknowledge that while these polls provide the president with an accurate reading of the public's pulse, they may enable Mr. Clinton to switch issue positions to take advantage of the public's current thinking on an issue.

Use of polls by other elected officials is done on a much smaller scale. While members of the House and Senate, governors, state legislators, and local elected officials could use public opinion data in the same way as the president, the resources are not available below the level of the chief executive. Members of Congress often must rely on national or statewide polls and use this information together with other sources (letters, contacts from contributors, feedback from staffers in their district) to determine the views of their constituents. Similarly, local elected officials are infrequently in a position to conduct a special-purpose poll and must rely more often on surveys conducted by departments or agencies within their jurisdiction to gain some idea of the public's feeling on specific aspects of the government's performance.

Polling can, however, become an important part of debates on new policy initiatives being considered by the president or Congress. When the Clinton administration embarked on its health policy reform in the early days of the first term, the potential transformation of the American health care system became the subject of multiple polls commissioned by interest groups in the health care industry, labor unions, the national parties, and, of course, the media, who were trying to cover the story. Private health institutes also engaged in polling on this issue. As the Clinton administration unveiled its proposal for public comment, the debate included data from all of these polls, inevitably showing conflicting desires on the part of the American public. Polling on any reform of the complex health care system faced certain obstacles as pollsters tried to evoke responses from the public on topics about which they had little information, such as managed care plans or coverage of mental disorders. In addition, polling on health care reform meant asking people about hypothetical reforms and trying to measure preferences in an unknown policy arena. Not surprisingly, many polls found considerable reluctance among publics to embrace major changes in the system, no matter how faulty it might be.

Controversy over the use of polls by officeholders will continue indefinitely. In one respect, the use of polls can be seen as consonant with democratic theory in that it provides a way for elected officials to find out what their constituents want. Conversely, officeholders who make extensive use of public opinion data are subject to the charge of governing by the polls, and of modifying their positions to satisfy public whims. Nonetheless, public opinion data seem to be playing an increasingly important role in the policy process.

USE BY GOVERNMENT AGENCIES

In Chapter 2, we described the use of survey research by the federal government before World War II and as part of the wartime effort. While the government's involvement in surveys was scaled back after the war, it increased greatly in the mid-1960s, and by 1980 government surveys accounted for five million of the 20 million interviews that were conducted (Sharp, 1984: 681). Brehm (1993: 9) has illustrated the scope of the federal government's involvement in surveys. He noted that in one year, the Department of Health and Human Services conducted interviews with 1,437,102 respondents that required over 1.2 million hours to complete.

Federal Government

While the government uses surveys for a great deal of data collection, the information collected is for the most part not attitudinal data, but rather demographic and behavioral indicators that provide the context in which to see how the American mind develops. A number of the major surveys carried out by the federal government are not of individuals but of institutions.[4] For example, among the many data collection efforts of the Census Bureau are an annual survey of state and local governments to obtain data on revenue, expenditures, debt, and employment, and a monthly sample survey of over 39,000 nonagricultural establishments to get data on employment, hours, and earnings by industry. The U.S. Department of Education conducts an annual survey of all institutions of higher education to collect data on total enrollment by sex, level of enrollment, type of program, racial/ethnic characteristics, and attendance status of students. The Department of Agriculture carries out annual

surveys of farm operators to collect data on planted acreage and livestock in-
ventories as well as total farm production, expenses, and specific commodity
costs of production. These surveys are a source of valuable information to decision makers interested in these specific policy areas. They also provide data
that may affect how individual citizens view issues related to these areas.

Major federal data collection efforts involving individuals focus largely on
demographic characteristics and behavioral indicators. One of the largest studies is the Census Bureau's Current Population Survey (CPS) which involves a
nationwide monthly sample survey of the civilian noninstitutionalized population, 15 years old or over, to obtain data on unemployment, the labor force,
and a number of other characteristics, and serves as a vehicle for studies on
other subjects, such as tobacco use and marital and birth history. This survey
uses a sample of about 60,000 households. The Survey of Income and Program
Participation (SIPP), also done by the Census Bureau, provides estimates of
money and in-kind income and participation in government programs. Re-
curring questions focus on employment, types of income, and noncash benefits. A listing of the significant programs or projects for which the Census Bureau provides information is provided in Appendix A.

In addition to the vast amount of demographic information collected by
the Census Bureau, information about various behavioral characteristics of the
American public comes from other federal agencies. For example, the National
Center for Health Statistics conducts the National Health Interview Survey
(NHIS), a sample of 42,000 households. This survey involves continuous data
collection covering the civilian noninstitutionalized population to get information on personal and demographic characteristics, illnesses, injuries, impair-
ments, and other health topics.

Other surveys conducted by the Department of Health and Human Services supply information on (1) topics such as health utilization, expenditures,
and insurance, in addition to related information on health status and disability
(National Medical Expenditure Survey); (2) the incidence, prevalence, consequences, and patterns of substance use and abuse (National Household Survey
on Drug Abuse); (3) how individuals view their health and what they do about
it in terms of seeking health care, the kind of care sought, and their ability to
perform normal functions (National Health and Nutrition Examination
Study); and (4) family planning, contraceptive use and efficacy, and other aspects of reproductive health, family formation, and dissolution (National Survey of Family Growth).

Other federal agencies gather information on topics such as crime victimization (U.S. Bureau of Justice Statistics, National Crime Victimization Survey);
family balance sheets, the terms of loans, and relationships with financial institutions (Board of Governors of the Federal Reserve System, Survey of Consumer
Finances); and energy-related household characteristics, housing unit characteristics, use of fuels, and energy consumption and expenditures by fuel type (U.S.
Energy Information Administration, Residential Energy Consumption Survey).

In addition to these ongoing data collection efforts, various federal agencies conduct surveys for a variety of different purposes, such as need assess-

ments, as part of an evaluation of a project or program, or in addressing a specific policy issue, for example an assessment of victims' ratings of police services (Newmark, Harrell, and Adams, 1995) or an evaluation of an elder abuse training program (Kohl, Brensilber, and Holmes, 1995). Beyond these surveys conducted directly by federal agencies, there are a number of programs in which the federal government sponsors surveys in the states. For example, in the Substance Abuse and Mental Health Services Administration's Center for Substance Abuse Treatment state demand and needs assessment project, approximately 250,000 interviews were conducted with members of the general population over a three-year period. In addition, a number of surveys of special populations—for example, students, arrestees, the homeless, and welfare recipients—were conducted as part of this effort. Similarly, the Centers for Disease Control sponsor the Behavioral Risk Factor Surveillance Survey, in which the states annually collect data on health risk factors and attitudes. Clearly, the federal government is a major user of the results of survey research.[5]

As these descriptions indicate, most of the information collected through government surveys involves factual or behavioral characteristics, with only a limited number of subjective items that are of primary interest in describing "the American mind."[6] Although the number of such items included in government surveys has increased in recent years, they still tend to be quasi-factual or to involve evaluations of specific programs.[7] In considering "the American mind," the data from government surveys are important because they serve as the analytic base for formulating policy and monitoring changes in the conditions of the American public that provides the milieu within which the American mind functions.

One agency that does collect considerable public opinion information is the United States Information Agency (USIA). USIA is responsible for advising the president, secretary of state, and other foreign affairs policymakers of foreign public opinion about the United States and its policies. It commissions public opinion surveys in nearly every country of the world. In 1996, the USIA spent $1.9 million on polling to determine how the minds of the rest of the world view America.

It is important to note that although the federal government conducts many surveys through its agencies, it also contracts with private commercial research firms and academic centers to collect data. In addition, many of the surveys that we will discuss below, as well as secondary data analyses, are funded through competitive government grants from agencies such as the National Science Foundation.

State Government

Although states, like the federal government, gather information on institutions, industries, and households as indicators of the state's economic well-being, they also sponsor surveys of public attitudes to guide and evaluate public policies. Individual states conduct a number of ongoing programs that utilize survey information (such as the Alcohol and Other Drug Abuse Treatment

Needs Assessment, the Behavioral Risk Factor Surveillance System, and Pregnancy Risk Assessment Monitoring System) with funds from the federal government. Many of these state surveys (as well as those commissioned by local governments) are conducted by the nearly one hundred survey research organizations affiliated with colleges or universities.

As at the federal level, individual state agencies use surveys for specific needs. In South Carolina, for example, the Department of Parks, Recreation, and Tourism (SCPRT) periodically conducts a survey of the state's residents age 12 and older to determine participation in and preferences for a variety of recreational activities (Oldendick, 1994). SCPRT also uses surveys of the general public to assess attitudes on specific policies, such as user fees for state parks (Link, 1997a). Other agencies also use surveys for assessing public opinion on issues such as a tax checkoff for the elderly (Oldendick, 1992b) or whether sex education should be taught in elementary schools (Link, 1997b), or for monitoring public perceptions of the agency's performance (Link, 1997c).

Many states use survey research to measure the public's views on education policy. The Michigan State Board of Education, for example, has surveyed the public annually about its perceptions of the system. In Massachusetts, the state Department of Education surveyed public high school students about use of drugs and alcohol and their experiences with violence and sex. Comparing the results of the 1994 poll to one taken four years earlier, officials noted that alcohol use was down but drug and tobacco use had remained at about the same levels as previously (the *Boston Globe,* May 20, 1994).

As these examples illustrate, states use public opinion in a variety of ways to determine how their citizens feel about policy issues, to identify needs that they have in areas such as aging, health, recreation, and transportation, to monitor their performance, and to evaluate specific policies or programs.

Local Government

Local governments use public opinion data in many of same ways as the federal government and the states. One of the primary uses at the local level is services evaluation. The City of Cincinnati, for example, has conducted a number of surveys designed to solicit citizen feedback on the services provided by various city departments, as well as to identify citizen budget priorities (Tuchfarber and Smith, 1995). Individual local government agencies also use surveys for needs assessments, to evaluate individual policies, or to monitor performance. For example, a survey conducted for the Georgetown County (S.C.) Recreation Department was designed to identify citizens' use of and perceived need for parks and recreational services in the county as well as to gauge support for different means of paying for improved services (Oldendick, 1996). The City of Cincinnati's public transit agency, Queen City Metro (QCM), has since 1978 conducted twice-yearly measurements of the public's use of the transit system. QCM has also employed survey data to assess the public's view of a tax increase for transit services (Tuchfarber and Weise, 1982), to evaluate a weekend fare experiment (Oldendick and Tuchfarber, 1984) and to develop a marketing plan (Tuchfarber and Oldendick, 1986).

USE BY INTEREST GROUPS

Not all of the public opinion data cited by public officials in policy debates is gathered by political parties or government pollsters. As noted in the discussion of the Clinton health care plan, policy debates inspire interest groups and, indeed, interested corporations and labor unions, to commission their own polls so that they will have appropriate data to cite during discussions with public officials or to release to the public in an attempt to influence public views. This type of interest group polling can have an impact on policy decisions on the national scene or at the state and local level. During the buildup to the Persian Gulf War, the Kuwaiti royal family and their supporters commissioned the Wirthlin Group to poll the American people about their support for a military invasion of Kuwait to repel the Iraqi army. The Wirthlin Group implemented weekly tracking polls to measure the opinions of American citizens. One of their findings (which was shared with the Bush White House) was that the American people did not support military intervention to preserve access to Kuwaiti oil reserves but did support military action for moral reasons (Wilcox, et al., 1991).

At the state and local level, interest groups also commission polls to have an impact on policy debates. Obviously, the sponsoring organizations are hopeful that they will be able to release poll results that back their own position or goals. For example, the Coalition for a Drug Free America reported poll results that showed its campaign reaching New York teens successfully. The West Virginia branch of the American Federation of Teachers, a union for school teachers, surveyed their members on the desirability of including disabled students in mainstream classrooms. The Tourism and Convention Center of Massachusetts reported that a survey of state voters showed support for a new sports megaplex, while the Columbus, Ohio, based Council for Responsible Waste Solutions showed that Ohioans wanted to take care of disposal problems now rather wait for some future time. When poll results are announced by state or national groups with such innocuous names, it is always useful to try to find out which interest groups belong to or have partnered to establish such an alliance. In 1994, for example, the Kentuckians Against Casinos found that establishing new casinos ranked low on the list of Kentuckians' state priorities. The news report from *USA Weekend* (February 18, 1994) did note that the membership of Kentuckians Against Casinos included the Kentucky Council of Churches, the Southern Baptist Convention, and the Temperance League of Kentucky, all groups likely to oppose the increase of gambling in the state.

In each of these instances, the respective sponsor of the poll intended to use the poll results to buttress its own position with legislators and with the citizenry of the state. In addition, it hoped to get a good report in the media that would enhance its own reputation as being civic-minded.

USE BY THE MEDIA

The tracing of the first poll to the straw vote conducted by *The Harrisburg Pennsylvanian* in 1824 illustrates the close connection between polls and the media. In the early years of the 20th century, numerous media outlets, such as the *New York Herald,* the *Cincinnati Enquirer,* the *Boston Globe,* and the *Chicago Examiner,* conducted polls on candidates as well as polls on issues. By 1932 Robinson had identified 85 different polling operations in the United States, most of which were local or regional. One of the few with a national focus, and one of the largest and most prestigious, was that conducted by the *Literary Digest.*

Part of the intrigue surrounding the pre-election polls of 1936 involved Gallup's attempts to increase media subscriptions to his poll. Gallup was convinced that the sampling methods that he had been developing would produce a prediction of the election that was closer than that of the *Literary Digest,* and offered newspaper subscribers a money-back guarantee to that effect. While this gamble was successful, one can only imagine Gallup's anxiety as he awaited the election returns—a wrong prediction of which would have cost him about a quarter of a million dollars (Moore, 1992: 31–32). Following this election, Gallup continued to increase the number of newspapers that carried reports of his polls and also published in the popular press and in advertising trade magazines (J. Converse, 1987: 118).

After 1936, the number of independent polls declined and the media came to rely more on pollsters such as Gallup, Crossley, Roper, and later, Harris for their information on the public's views. By the 1960s, reports of the *Gallup Poll* and the *Harris Poll* represented the major uses of polls by the media (Moore, 1992: 275).

The use of survey data by the media changed dramatically when the major news organizations established their own polling operations. While CBS was the first to set up a polling unit in 1967, it temporarily halted its polling operations after 1970 (Moore, 1992: 273). However, after the 1972 election, the major news organizations felt a pressing need to establish a means to conduct their own polls. CBS/*New York Times* and ABC/*Washington Post* have maintained their own survey units, while NBC/*Wall Street Journal,* along with other major news organizations, rely on data commissioned from outside pollsters (Moore, 1992: 297). In charting the rise of poll reporting in the *New York Times,* Brehm (1993: 4) notes that while only a handful of polls appeared in the early 1950s, by the mid-1960s the number of stories cited jumped to more than one hundred per year and by the 1970s, this had "reached the current plateau of around 300 citations per year, or nearly one story a day."

Most of these news organizations conduct periodic polls on issues and now emulate the academic surveys by repeating standard questions over time. Foreign policy crises or major policy debates in the domestic arena evoke flurries of polling by the media organizations as they use the polls to cover the developing story and to increase readership. Operation Desert Storm may well have been the most polled-about event in American history, with hundreds of polls commissioned before the combat began. However, much of the media's efforts—and resources—are devoted to **trial heats** during presidential election years and to monitoring presidential approval in the years between elections.

Trial heats for the succeeding presidential contest begin almost immediately after an election and have become a part of the almost continual campaign for the presidency (the first poll for the 2000 election was conducted on election day 1996). [8] In the early stages of a campaign, good showings in the polls and the attendant media coverage can be critical factors in determining which potential candidates decide to run and how their showing in the primaries is interpreted (Graber, 1997: 250–253). While this **horse-race journalism** has been criticized (Wheeler, 1980), the "who's winning" aspect of an election campaign seems to be more interesting to the mass public than an in-depth probe of the issue positions of the candidates. Reporting of trial heat results remains an integral part of the media's campaign coverage.

This focus on trial heats culminates with another type of polling used almost exclusively by the media, the **exit poll.** Exit polling involves the sampling of precincts, with self-administered questionnaires completed by randomly selected respondents as they leave the polling place (Levy, 1983). The first exit polls were used as a check on the election projections made on the basis of key precincts, but over time exit polls have come to play a more prominent role in projecting election outcomes. They also provide a valuable source of information about the factors underlying voter choice. The interviewers who conduct exit polls begin sending their computer-tabulated results to the national office by noon. They are able to have their final exit interviews completed and transmitted within a few moments of the polls closing. By entering these data into sophisticated computer models, the network news organizations are able to project the winners of elections at the state level by the time the polls close.

After facing the huge cost of maintaining separate polling organizations for election day, CBS, ABC, NBC, and CNN combined their exit polling efforts in 1990, creating Voter Research and Surveys (VRS). On election day 1996, VRS conducted 71,093 interviews. Including the primary election campaign, they did more than 82,371 exit interviews during that year. [9] The consolidated VRS operation feeds data to each of the media partners so they can make independent predictions of the winners and losers. The technique of exit polling and prime-time predictions has led to tremendous controversy over whether "early calls" of elections discourage voters in western time zones from voting. Critics charge that the exit polls not only may impact final election results in western states but that they are "an impediment to the citizen's right to privately cast a ballot" (Cantrell, 1992: 414). From time to time, proposals have been made to limit the projection of elections before polls closed in the latest

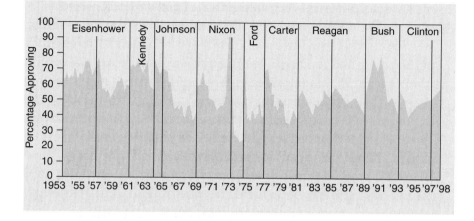

FIGURE 3.1 Presidential Approval Ratings Since 1953

SOURCE: *Public Opinion*, February/March 1988, pp. 36–39; and Gallup Polls, March 1992, through March, 1998.

time zone, but any such attempt to limit the media would probably be struck down as violating freedom of the press.

In polls conducted between elections, one of the key measures that is monitored is **presidential approval,** which has been termed "the most closely watched political indicator in the United States" (Erikson and Tedin, 1995: 109). The first general measurement of presidential approval was taken in 1938 when the Gallup Organization asked, "Do you approve or disapprove of the way President Roosevelt is handling his job as president?" Like many other aspects of the polling industry, use of this question has increased dramatically in recent years. It was asked 15 times during Truman's first term in office, but 110 times during the four years of the Bush presidency (Ragsdale, 1997: 229).[10]

As shown in Figure 3-1, presidential approval varies significantly over time. Having just been victorious, presidents generally come into office with a relatively high approval rating. As presidents take actions that displease certain groups and are subject to criticism, their approval rating experiences a natural erosion before stabilizing at a more natural level at the end of their first year. Presidential approval ratings are significantly related to Americans' perceptions of the economy (Kinder and Kiewet, 1979; MacKuen, Erikson, and Stimson, 1992). When foreign affairs becomes a salient concern to Americans, the effect is generally to produce at least a short-term increase in presidential approval in a "rally 'round the flag" effect (Mueller, 1973; 1992). For example, George Bush's approval ratings, boosted by Americans' support for U.S. involvement in the Persian Gulf War and the apparent success of these efforts, reached a record high of 89% at the end of February, 1991. During the next year, the country's economic problems and public perceptions of Bush's unwillingness to pay at-

---

What the Public Thinks?

One of the limits of call-in polls is that they are based on a convenience sample, that is, a sample in which respondents are selected not because they represent some larger population, but because of the ease of collecting data from them. In the case of call-in polls, respondents themselves choose to participate. If they are willing to take the time to make the telephone call and to pay the charges that are generally associated with such calls, their opinion is counted.

Two examples demonstrate the distortions that such procedures can produce. A poll conducted in 1990 by *USA Today* showed that Americans loved Donald Trump. A month after the poll results were released, *USA Today* reported that 5,640 of the 7,800 calls came from offices owned by Cincinanti financier Carl Lindner, whose employees apparently "admire Mr. Trump" (Crossen: 1991: A-1).

As part of its *Nightline* broadcasts, ABC frequently conducts call-in polls. In an effort to deflect some of the criticism of such polls as nonscientific, it will sometimes conduct a parallel survey of a representative sample of the American public. In a case dealing with the United Nations, 67% of 186,000 calls to the 900 number said that the United Nations headquarters should be moved out of the United States. The results to the representative telephone survey showed exactly the opposite result: 72% of these respondents wanted the U.N. to remain (Moore, 1992: 288-289)

---

tention to them or inability to deal with them effectively led his approval rating to drop 38%, returning exactly to the level recorded before the buildup for Operation Desert Storm. The patriotic fervor stirred by the successful military effort and the "rally" effect artificially inflated Bush's ratings across all groups in the population. As soon as the war faded from public consciousness, public perceptions returned to their earlier state (Ragsdale, 1997: 232; Parker, 1995).

While most polls conducted by the media are done "scientifically" —that is, with probability samples, a well-designed questionnaire, and appropriate attention given to the various aspects of data collection and processing—there is one type of poll used primarily by the media that has caused considerable controversy: the "900 number" call-in poll. As its name implies, call-in polls are ones in which respondents are not randomly selected and contacted by the polling firm, but rather ones in which participants select themselves by calling a 900 number.

The obvious problem with such polls from a scientific standpoint is that since respondents are self-selected there is no basis for claiming that the results are representative of some larger population. In fact, such "polls" are biased toward those people with intense opinions on the topic and those with the resources and time to make and pay for the call. At times, interest groups of the right or left or some other special public swamp such numbers, producing the results they want. For the most part, journalists are aware of the nonrepresentative character of such polls; Kathy Frankovic at CBS and ABC's Jeff

Alderman have commented on the difficulty of reporting on such polls in a way that presents them accurately (Moore, 1992: 289). To the general public—who may not be aware of these problems—a poll is a poll. The public often weighs the potentially misleading results of a nonscientific poll equally with polls done appropriately. Even worse, the public may see all polls as suspect.

USE BY ACADEMIC RESEARCHERS

Academic researchers use survey research to examine a variety of aspects of human behavior. As noted in Chapter 2, several ongoing programs of survey data collection provide the basis for a significant amount of research in the areas of political science, sociology, social psychology, and mass communications.

The American National Election Studies

One of the most significant of these programs is the American National Election Studies (NES), conducted by the University of Michigan. These surveys are based on representative samples of citizens of voting age, living in private households. Interviewing for this series was first done following the election of 1948, and has been conducted before and after all presidential elections since 1952, and after all congressional elections since 1958. The NES time-series encompasses 23 biennial Election Studies spanning five decades. Over time, there have been several variations in the basic design of this study. The 1956–60 surveys contained a four-year **panel** component in which the same individuals were interviewed in 1956, 1958, and 1960, as did the study conducted in 1972–76. Some respondents from the 1990 study were re-interviewed in 1992 as part of an examination of the political consequences of the Persian Gulf War. The 1980 study included a panel component that spanned the campaign, while a series of "continuous monitoring" surveys were incorporated into the 1984 study in order to examine more extensively the dynamics of the vote decision during the campaign.

These interviews are rather extensive, and many questions are replicated across studies, facilitating extensive **cross-time analysis,** that is, comparing results on the same question at different time periods (Miller and Traugott, 1989). The range of topics addressed in the NES includes expectations about the election outcome; perceptions and evaluations of the major parties and their candidates; information about politics; positions on social-welfare, economic, social, and civil rights issues; attention to campaign coverage in the media; and detailed demographic information.

Data from these surveys have also served as the basis for many of the most important investigations of American political behavior, such as *The Voter Decides* (Campbell, Gurin, and Miller, 1954), *The American Voter* (Campbell, Converse, Miller, and Stokes, 1960), and *The Changing American Voter* (Nie, Verba, and Petrocik, 1976). NES data have been used in studying topics such as mass belief systems (Converse, 1964), political participation (Milbrath, 1965; Bennett and Resnick, 1990), the effect of the media on mass political behavior (Erbring, Goldenberg, and Miller, 1980), political efficacy and trust in government (Miller, 1974), and political socialization (Campbell, Converse, Miller, and Stokes, 1960). Much of the data to be presented in later chapters is based on these surveys.

The General Social Survey

Another significant source of data concerning the public's views on a range of issues is the General Social Survey (GSS) done by NORC. The first GSS was conducted in 1972. Since that time, the GSS has been conducted 21 times, and by 1996 a total of 34,577 respondents had been interviewed. The GSS is also an extensive interview, and since 1988 there have been over 700 variables in each survey. As described by Smith (1997: 28), the GSS includes major batteries of items on topics such as "civil liberties, confidence in institutions, crime and violence, feminism, governmental spending priorities, psychological well-being, race relations, and work."

The large number of items that are replicated in the GSS surveys facilitates the study of social change and allows for cases to be pooled across surveys to provide sufficient cases for analysis among subgroups, such as blacks or the self-employed. The detailed and extensive set of demographic variables collected in the GSS allow in-depth analysis of the influence of background characteristics on attitudinal differences. The 1996 Annotated Bibliography lists 3,771 uses of the GSS, and more than 300 new uses are occurring each year (Smith, 1997: 29).

Although not as large as the NES or GSS, the economic behavior program at the University of Michigan has since the late 1940s conducted an ongoing survey of the American public designed to measure consumer confidence. Academic economists have long been interested in this measure of consumer behavior, which has only recently become a topic of discussion in the news media. As the American economy grew steadily in the late 1990s, the Michigan consumer confidence measure became a point of commentary for the media and others who were trying to explain daily stock market fluctuations.

In addition to these major ongoing studies, academic researchers conduct special purpose surveys (often funded by the federal government through grants or by private foundations) designed to investigate specific topics. A myriad of topics have been examined with survey data ranging from attitudes toward health policies to the development of political views in children and their parents (Niemi and Jennings, 1974). It would be impossible to suggest a topic of public relevance that has not been suggested for study using survey research. In the chapters that follow, the results of many of these academic studies will be used to illustrate how Americans think about public issues.

Much of the survey-based research done by academic researchers involves analysis not of data that they have collected but rather a **secondary analysis** of data collected for some other purpose. Much of the research published using the NES or GSS was done not by the principal investigators for these surveys, but by other researchers who were provided the data through the Inter-university Consortium for Political and Social Research (ICPSR). In addition to the NES and GSS data, many other national, regional, and local surveys are archived by the ICPSR, which provides them to the larger research community. The consortium, which is a partnership of hundreds of colleges and universities, publishes an annual catalog (and online listing) of the datasets available to member institutions for teaching and research purposes. Nonmembers may purchase the datasets as well. The entries include national crime studies, health studies, the election studies, European and other foreign national studies, foreign policy studies, the CBS/*New York Times* datasets, and hundreds of others.

Data from the 1996 National Election Study, or any of the other studies in the **archive,** are available to both undergraduate and graduate students for their research. There are other archives of data, including the Roper Center at the University of Connecticut, which operate in the same fashion. As these examples illustrate, surveys represent an important source of data for academic researchers. The results and analysis of these data, together with information from national, state, and local surveys, the media, and other sources, provide the basis for much of what we know about the American mind.

Polls, Polling, and the Internet

Most of the university survey and research organizations have excellent web sites that can be accessed by students as well as researchers. As mentioned in this chapter, two of the most prominent university studies are:

The National Election Study conducted by the Center for Political Studies at the University of Michigan:

   http://www.isr.umich.edu/~nes/

and the General Social Survey conducted by the National Opinion Research Center (NORC) at the University of Chicago:

   http://www.norc.uchicago.edu/gss/homepage.htm

NOTES

1. Frequently the results from the last two or three days of interviewing are combined to form a "moving average" based on a larger number of cases, which is less likely to be influenced by day-to-day fluctuations that may be the product of sampling error.

2. Much of the polling done for candidates is done by commercial organizations, some of which do only political polling while others do political polling plus market and product research. The tremendous growth in marketing and survey research is illustrated by the fact that of the top ten survey companies in the United States, all but one was founded after World War II (Honomichl, 1986: 175). By one estimate, the top survey organizations had gross revenues in 1984 of $1.2 million (Honomichl,1986: 223); this figure has increased steadily and by 1996 had reached an estimated $5.0 billion.

3. In response to an increase in the use of push polling, several states have taken action to limit this activity. See for example New Hampshire 1997 Session House Bill 443 at the following Internet location: http://www.state.nh.us, and then go to Statute Section 664: 16-a.

4. The information in this section is derived from the U.S. Department of Commerce, Bureau of the Census, *Statistical Abstract of the United States 1996* (Washington: Government Printing Office, 1996), Appendix III.

5. State governments use survey research for many of the same purposes as the federal government. While states do not have as many large-scale or on-going survey projects as the federal government, state agencies use surveys for monitoring quality of life, program evaluation, needs assessment, and determining the public's views on policy issues.

   Local governments have similar needs for survey data as the states and the federal government. While the use of surveys by local governments varies considerably, such data collection efforts have been shown to be valuable in monitoring citizen satisfaction with services, determining voters' budget priorities, and evaluating programs.

6. The federal government has a history of resistance to the collection of attitudinal or opinion data. For example, despite the Census Bureau's long-term efforts in gathering data on population characteristics, it was not until 1967 that it agreed to collect data on the subjective indicator of asking women how many children they expected to have, even though such measurements were thought to be useful in making population projections (DeMaio, Marsh, and Turner, 1984: 31).

7. An example of the federal government's continuing focus on collecting data on background and quasi-factual characteristics while increasing the number of subjective indicators is the Census Bureau's American Community Survey. This survey is now in its demonstration period and is scheduled to be fully implemented in 2003. As part of this survey, information will be collected that will be used to evaluate programs such as welfare and workforce diversification, and to monitor and publicize program results. For additional information about this effort, see the Census Internet site at:
http://www.census.gov/acs/www

8. The earliest 2000 poll was conducted on election day 1996 by John McLaughlin and Associates. As reported in *The Polling Report* (1996), voter preferences four years before the election were: Al Gore, 42%; Jack Kemp, 33%; Ross Perot, 15%; and undecided, 11%.

9. As an indicator of the extent to which media resources are devoted to survey data, it is estimated that combining their exit polling operations saved the three major networks $9 million each over a four-year period (Moore, 1992: 265).

10. The question that Gallup first used in the 1930s, "Do you approve or disapprove of the job (name of president) is doing as president?" is generally considered the standard method for measuring presidential approval, and is used by a number of other organizations including the CBS News/*New York Times* Poll and the ABC News/*Washington Post* Poll. Other organizations, such as the Harris Poll, use ratings of the president, that is, "How would you rate the overall job President (name of president) is doing as president . . . excellent, pretty good, only fair, or poor?" rather than "approval" in measuring presidential performance. In addition, many Gallup Polls, as well as other surveys, contain additional questions that measure how the American public feels about the president, such as whether the public has a favorable or unfavorable opinion of him and whether or not a number of different characteristics (for example, "can get things done," "honest and trustworthy") apply to the president. While these data are used in describing the public's overall perceptions of the president, it is the question "Do you approve or disapprove of the job (name of president) is doing as president?" that is generally referred to in describing presidential approval.

4

How Are Opinions Measured?

Questions to Consider:

How are people selected to be surveyed?

Why are telephone polls considered scientific?

Do the survey questions influence the answers?

What is sampling error?

In the previous discussion of public opinion in American history, a number of ways by which policy makers are made aware of what "the public" thinks were described. Attending functions in the area they represent, meeting with individuals or groups, talking with other policy makers as well as other influentials, obtaining information from the media, talking with contacts from interest groups, and reading correspondence all provide some idea of what the public is thinking on an issue. While policymakers generally take information from each of these sources into account in their decision making, such considerations are not commonly what is meant by "public opinion." Recall that public opinion has been defined as "the combined personal opinions of adults toward issues of relevance to government." Given this approach to public opinion, the methods used to measure such opinion must represent those of some population, whether it is the voting age population of the United States, women in the State of Illinois, or low-income residents of an American city.

As noted in Chapter 2, the method used to provide public opinion data is survey research, which involves systematic data collection about a sample drawn from some larger population. In a properly designed and executed survey, information collected from a relatively small number of people can be used to represent accurately the views of some larger group. This chapter discusses the ways in which the data used in describing the American mind are collected.

MODES OF SURVEY DATA COLLECTION

There are three basic ways in which survey data are collected: face-to-face interviews, telephone interviews, and self-administered questionnaires. While these modes have relative advantages and disadvantages, they each involve certain common characteristics, including identifying a population of interest, selecting a sample, designing a questionnaire, and processing and analyzing the data collected. In describing the major steps involved in the survey process, the following sections present some of the elements that are common to these different approaches and that must be considered in identifying the views of some public. Later we describe some of the advantages and disadvantages of these modes of data collection.

Populations of Interest

A **population of interest** is an identifiable group of individuals whose opinion on some issue or set of issues is important to a policymaker. From the perspective of public opinion, the number of potential "populations of interest" is almost limitless. For example, the President of the United States might be interested in how "the American public" feels about some issue; in this case, the American public—typically defined as those age 18 and older—would constitute the population of interest. Similarly, a governor may want to know whether the electorate in the state approves of the way he or she is performing in office; in this case, registered voters in that state would comprise the population of interest. A council member may wonder how the town's residents feel about building a new sewer line, in which case these residents form the population of interest.

Other subgroups can also constitute populations of interest. On certain issues, policymakers may be particularly interested in the opinions of African-Americans, women, or those between the ages of 30 and 45. Political party officials often have an interest in how members of groups such as the AFL-CIO or the Right-To-Life Society feel about particular issues. The opinions and experiences of those who are unemployed and looking for work are important to officials charged with evaluating programs designed to reduce unemployment. How physicians, hospital administrators, insurance company representatives, and members of other groups feel about potential changes in the health care system and their impact on service delivery is an important consideration to both federal and state officials considering health care reform; each of these groups is a "population of interest" on this issue. In sum, any group whose opinions are of interest to a policy maker is a potential population of interest.

The wide range of potential characteristics of different populations can affect the choice of mode for data collection. As noted in Chapter 2, in the early history of survey data collection, the in-person method was generally considered the only way to gather reliable information. Developments in survey research have made it possible to collect data effectively by telephone and through self-administered surveys. In most cases, an in-person survey will cost more to conduct than a comparable telephone or self-administered survey, and resource considerations are an important part in the choice of mode of data collection. In addition to resource considerations, the characteristics of the group from which data are being collected, the ease of identifying and contacting individuals in the population, and the types of information being collected will affect the decision on means of gathering information.

Selecting a Sample

Once a population of interest has been identified, it is possible to collect information from all members of this group. While this approach may be appropriate if the population is extremely small, for most groups of interest to policy makers, gathering information in this manner would be not only very time-consuming, expensive, and inefficient, but also unnecessary. The principles of probability theory allow those interested in public opinion data to collect information from a small, but carefully selected, subset of the population—known as a **sample**—and to make inferences about the entire population with a high level of confidence.

There are two major types of sampling methods, **probability sampling** and **nonprobability sampling.** In a probability sample each individual or combination of individuals in the population has some known probability of being selected, while nonprobability samples are based on human judgment. The problems with the *Literary Digest* poll of 1936 and the incorrect forecasts of the election of 1948 were a result—at least in part—of the use of nonprobability samples.

When a sample is selected from a population, the interest is not in the opinions of the sample members, in and of themselves; rather they are of interest because they *represent* the characteristics of the population. In order to be confident that the sample does represent the population, some type of probability sampling must be employed. The key to any type of probability sample is random selection. In a probability sample, each element or individual in the population has some known, non-zero probability of selection.

There are several types of probability samples. The most notable of these—and the one which is assumed by the body of statistics typically used by survey researchers—is **simple random sampling** (SRS). In a simple random sample, each element in the population is listed and assigned a number, and a sample is drawn using a computer program or a random number table to generate the selected elements. While a simple random sample represents the "ideal" probability sample, in practice such samples are seldom used. For unless the population is small, it is not practical to identify all members of a population, much less to assign them each a unique identification number for selection.

Systematic random samples are similar to simple random samples in that they are generally drawn from a list of elements. They differ, however, in that while each number in a simple random sample is randomly generated, a systematic sample involves randomly selecting a single number, then taking every kth element in the list (for example, every 25th) until the desired number of elements has been selected. For example, if we wanted to select a sample of 80 individuals from a list of 2,400, we would take every 30th person, with the first one randomly selected from the first 30 on the list. If number 27 were initially selected, then numbers 57, 87, 117 … 2,397 would be included in the sample.

In a **stratified sample,** the elements of the population of interest are divided into groups (or strata), and independent samples (either simple random or systematic) are selected within each stratum. The advantage of a stratified sample is that it provides a greater degree of accuracy in the sample for those characteristics on which elements have been grouped.

Take as an example a study in which your population of interest is undergraduates at State University. Of the 20,000 undergraduates, 5,500 are freshman, 5,200 are sophomores, 4,800 are juniors, and 4,500 are seniors. Selecting a simple random or systematic sample of 1,000 would provide you with close to, but not exactly, 275 freshman, 260 sophomores, 240 juniors, and 225 seniors. If the list of the population were stratified by class and a systematic sample chosen, you would select exactly the correct proportion from each class.

A stratified sample ordinarily yields more reliable results than a simple random sample, and since stratification is a relatively simple process, it should be considered in deciding the type of sampling procedures to be used. To select a stratified sample, however, requires knowing something in advance about the characteristics of the population. Variables such as age, race, sex, or location generally are used as a basis for stratification.

The final type of probability sampling is known as **cluster sampling.** It is often used in surveys in which the population of interest is spread over a wide geographical area, or for which compiling a list of elements may be prohibitively expensive. In a cluster sample, the population is divided into groups, or clusters, often on the basis of geography. Cluster sampling is less costly than other types of sampling; unfortunately, from a research perspective, cluster samples have a larger potential for error due to sampling. Cluster sampling is used for most of the major face-to-face surveys conducted in the United States today, including the National Election Studies and the General Social Surveys, which provide much of the data to be presented in later chapters.

A properly designed and executed cluster sample can be very complex. To give some indication of how cluster sampling works, take an example in which the population of interest is residents of the county in which you live who are 18 years of age or older. Potential lists, such as telephone directories or driver registration records, are likely to be incomplete and somewhat out-of-date. Attempting to compile a list of all individuals or households in the county would be time-consuming and require considerable resources. In situations such as this, cluster sampling provides a cost-effective way of selecting a probability sample.

In this case, the county could be divided into clusters based on **census tracts,** and a random sample of census tracts selected. Within each of the selected tracts, a random sample of **blocks** could be selected, and an interview conducted with a selected individual at each household in the selected block. In this process, rather than having to list all households in the county, only those households in the selected tracts and blocks would need to be identified. In addition, the interviews to be conducted would be *clustered* in a relatively small number of blocks rather than spread throughout the county, thus saving interviewer time and travel expense. A cluster sample usually involves several steps in which lists (for example, census tracts; blocks within selected tracts; households within selected blocks) are compiled and a sample selected. At each of the points, some type of probability sample must be selected in order for the results to be representative of the population of interest.

You may encounter situations in which nonprobability sampling procedures have been used. In **pilot investigations** or **purposive studies,** such samples are often used for generating hypotheses or for obtaining information about individuals with unique characteristics. The limitation of data collected through nonprobability techniques is that the results cannot be used to make inferences about some larger population of interest. Virtually all of the studies of public opinion in which we are interested are based on some type of probability sample.

Random-Digit Dialing

Random–digit dialing (RDD) is a technique for selecting a probability sample in telephone surveys. Because of its importance in the history of public opinion research (see Chapter 2) and its extensive use in current survey practice, we will describe it here in some detail.[1]

In selecting an RDD sample, all of the working telephone exchanges in the area in which the population of interest resides have to be identified. For example, if the population of interest consisted of adults living in the state of Louisiana, then all exchanges in use in the state would have to be determined. Once these exchanges have been identified, one of them is randomly selected, and a second random number between 0000 and 9999 is generated to complete the telephone number. The same process is used to select a second telephone number, and is repeated until a sufficient quantity of numbers has been generated to produce the desired number of completed interviews.

The telephone numbers produced by these procedures will be not all be household residences. The sample will include numbers that are not in service as well as numbers for businesses and institutions, and several refinements to these procedures have been developed (for example, Waksberg, 1978). The result of these refinements has been to increase the efficiency of RDD samples by reducing the number of "unproductive" calls, that is, calls made to business and not-in-service or otherwise ineligible numbers; the underlying principles of RDD are the same. It should also be recognized that some type of stratification, particularly by area, is possible with an RDD sample. Ultimately, the means chosen for selecting a sample will depend upon the characteristics of the population of interest, the purposes of the study, and the resources available for carrying out the research.

Sampling Error

One of the most important concepts in surveys and public opinion research is **sampling error.** If you have seen or read reports of public opinion polls, you may be familiar with the statement, "the error due to sampling could be plus or minus three percentage points for results based on the entire sample." This statement refers to the sampling error. The term "error" does not imply that the data are wrong or that mistakes were made in the way they were collected; rather, all samples are subject to such potential error resulting from the fact that data are not obtained from all members of the population.

As noted earlier, when data are collected from a sample, the interest is not in the characteristics of the members of the sample themselves, but rather the characteristics of some larger population whom they represent. If a properly designed survey conducted close to an election found that Candidate X would receive 52% of the vote, then we would expect that this candidate would receive close to, but not exactly, 52% of the ballots cast. Probability theory provides us with a means for estimating how closely the sample estimate is to the true population value, given that we are willing to take a certain risk that the findings of the study are incorrect. The level of risk most commonly used is the .05 level (or the 95% **confidence level**). When survey results are reported, this means the researcher is confident that 95% of the intervals reported will contain the percentage for the population. So when you hear or read a report from a survey that "Candidate X has the support of 52% of those interviewed" and that "the potential for sampling error for this survey is ± 4%," you can be 95% confident that the true percentage for this candidate is between 48% and 56% (assuming, of course, that there were no other factors such as sampling bias, nonresponse, question-wording, or interviewer effects that influenced the results). For surveys in which approximately a thousand people are interviewed, the sampling error would be about ± 3.1. The larger the number of people interviewed, the smaller the sampling error.[2]

Sample Size

In designing any survey, an important consideration is the number of individuals from whom data should be collected. There is no ideal **sample size,** and the number of cases in any survey depends upon the study's purpose, the precision needed, and the resources available. As noted above, the larger the sample size, the smaller the sampling error, and in most instances a survey researcher will attempt to collect data from as many individuals as possible in order to increase the precision of the estimates of the population characteristics. The obvious trade-off, however, is that each additional individual from whom data are collected requires some added cost, whether it be postage and clerical time in a mail survey, interviewer time and telephone charges in a telephone survey, or interviewer time and travel expenses in a face-to-face survey.

Another consideration in determining the sample size is the purpose of the study. In some studies, the estimates based on the survey are required to be very precise; in such cases, data must be collected from an extremely large number of people. For example, the Current Population Survey, conducted by the United States Census Bureau, is designed to provide estimates of the employment, unemployment, and other characteristics of the general labor force and the U.S. population as a whole. As part of this survey approximately sixty thousand interviews are conducted each month! As Bradburn and Sudman (1988: 131) note, as a result of this large sample size, "... sampling variation between repeated samples is only about one-tenth of one percent; therefore, policy makers are assured that changes of more than one-tenth of one percent up or down reflect real changes in the economy and are not caused by sampling."[3]

A study in which the researcher is interested in examining differences among groups will also generally require a larger sample size than one designed solely to estimate the characteristics of the population. For example, if one were interested in differences in attitudes of individuals with varying amounts of education (such as among those with less than a high school education; high school graduates; those with some college; and college graduates), a larger sample size would be required in order to make accurate estimates for each of these groups. In general, the larger the sample, the more detailed the analysis that can be conducted.

In other cases, a very small sample size may be sufficient for the purpose of the study. For example, if one were interested in the opinions of the members of a regional professional association that consisted of 150 members, it would be possible to select a sample of as few as 30 individuals and still be fairly confident in your results. In situations where you are dealing with a very small population of interest, however, it is generally possible to attempt to collect information from each individual.

Many of the more publicized polls, such as those of Gallup, Harris, and the major media polls, typically conduct interviews with about a thousand people. The number of people interviewed in the American National Studies has ranged from 662 in 1948 to 2,705 in 1972. Most statewide or regional polls are based on between 500 and 800 interviews, and the average local survey consists of between 200 and 500 cases. The decision about the number of cases for which data will be collected depends largely on the resources available and whether the benefits of greater precision and more detailed analysis justify the increased costs.

Questionnaire Design

The basic data collection instrument in survey research is a questionnaire that may include items that ask people about their opinions, experiences, or background characteristics. The form of the questionnaire is essentially the same for each of the three modes of data collection. Questions are presented to respondents in either **closed-ended** (respondents select their answer from a list pro-

---

Sample Selection for Different Modes: Some Examples

In this chapter we have described various modes of data collection and different methods of sample selection. The following examples illustrate the use of different types of samples.

Face-to-Face Interviewing, Cluster Sampling: The American National Election Studies are studies of citizens of the United States who live in the 48 contiguous states and are of voting age on or before election day. Data are collected in face-to-face interviews conducted in the households of selected respondents. Selecting a representative sample of this population involves a relatively complex process in which sampling is done of (1) Standard Metropolitan Statistical Areas and counties; (2) area segments within the selected SMSAs and counties; (3) housing units within the sampled area segments; and (4) a single respondent within selected housing units.

Telephone Interviewing, Random-Digit Dialing: The Ohio Poll is a survey of 800 adult residents of Ohio that is conducted by telephone. The sample for this survey is selected by RDD. In generating this sample, all the working area code and telephone exchanges in the state are identified. A computer program randomly selects one of these exchanges and then adds to to it a randomly generated number between 0000 and 9999. This process is repeated until enough telephone numbers have been selected to achieve the desired number of completed interviews. Using this method, individuals who live in households without telephones are excluded from the sample.

Mail Survey, Stratified Random Sample: A survey on the uses of alternative and complementary medicine done with physicians in the State of South Carolina provides an example of a mail survey using a stratified random sample. A list of licensed physicians in the state was provided by the South Carolina State Data Center. Physicians on this list were stratified according to their speciality. A random sample within each of these strata was drawn and a questionnaire mailed to the selected physicians.

Self-Administered Questionnaire, Cluster Sampling: The Monitoring the Future Study, which has been conducted each year since 1975, consists of surveys of high school seniors that explores changes in important values, behaviors, and lifestyle orientations of contemporary American youth. Cluster sampling for this study involves three stages: (1) geographic areas; (2) schools (or linked groups of schools) within the geographic areas; and (3) students within sampled schools. Selected students are then asked to fill out a questionnaire that consists of about three hundred questions on a range of topics, including drug use, attitudes toward government, social institutions, race relations, and background characteristics.

---

vided) or **open-ended** (respondents provide their own answers to the question) format and responses are either recorded by interviewers (face-to-face and telephone surveys) or completed by the respondents (self-administered).

Survey researchers have long been aware that the way in which questions are asked can have an effect on the results of a study, and there are a number of considerations involved in developing any question and designing a questionnaire (Payne, 1951; Schuman and Presser, 1981). The following examples illustrate some of the decisions that must be made in crafting a questionnaire.

Type of Question. There are two basic question types, open-ended and closed-ended. In an open-ended question, respondents are asked to provide their own answers to the question, while in a closed-ended question they are provided with a list of alternatives from which to choose. The item, "What do you feel is the most important problem facing this country today?" is an example of an open-ended question; "In general, how satisfied are you with the services provided by your city government . . . very satisfied, somewhat satisfied, not too satisfied, or not at all satisfied?" demonstrates a standard closed-ended item.

The advantage of open-ended questions is that they do not restrict respondents to alternatives provided by the researcher, while closed-ended questions are more efficient in terms of data collection, coding, and analysis. Because of these efficiencies, most survey questions are closed-ended. For example, of the substantive questions included in the 1996 General Social Survey, 615 were closed-ended and 40 were open-ended, while a CBS/*New York Times* Poll conducted in April 1998, consisted of 40 closed-ended and two open-ended items. While the type of question asked should be determined by the purpose of the study, the advantages of closed-ended questions have led survey researchers to use this type predominantly (Converse and Presser, 1986).

Filter Questions. Once the type of question has been determined, another consideration is whether to include a **filter question** or not. That is, is it appropriate for everyone in the sample to be asked the question or is there a reason to exclude some respondents? When some respondents are to be excluded, the question would include a filter.

Filter questions are most frequently used with opinion questions. If you are interested in opinions on an issue, do you want to ask everyone or do you only want answers from those people who are more interested in or have thought about the issue? Those who feel that filter questions should be used argue that asking those who are ill-informed or have not thought much about an issue to give an answer artificially creates opinion and provides a misleading impression of "the combined personal opinions of adults toward issues of relevance to government." Those who believe that filters are not needed contend that "many people act or react on a wide variety of subjects where they have no specific knowledge" (Mitofsky, 1989: 618).

In survey questions that include a filter, respondents are typically read a statement on some issue and then "filtered" on the basis of their knowledge or interest. Commonly used filter questions include: "Do you have an opinion on this issue?" "Have you been interested enough in this issue to favor one side over the other?" "Have you thought much about this issue?" and "Where do you stand on this issue or haven't you thought much about it?" Examples of survey questions with different types of filters are presented in Table 4-1.

Another argument for using filter questions in surveys is based on the demonstrated tendency of about one-third of respondents to give opinions on issues that are obscure, such as the Agricultural Trade Act (Schuman and Presser, 1981: 196), or fictitious, such as the 1975 Public Affairs Act (Bishop,

Table 4.1 Examples of Different Survey Questions with Various Types of Filters

Some people don't pay much attention to the political campaigns. How about you? Would you say you have been very much interested, somewhat interested, or not much interested in following the political campaigns so far this year? (NO FILTER)

The government ought to help people get doctors and hospital care at low cost. **Do you have an opinion on this or not?** (IF YES): Do you agree that the government should do this or do you think the government should not do it?

Some people feel that if black people are not getting fair treatment in jobs, the government in Washington ought to see to it that they do. Others feel that this is not the federal government's business. **Have you had enough interest in this question to favor one side over the other?** (IF YES): How do you feel?

Some people feel that the government in Washington should see to it that every person has a job and a good standard of living (they would be at point 1). Others think that the government should just let each person get ahead on their own (they would be at point 7). And, of course, other people have opinions somewhere in between. Where would you place yourself on this scale, **or haven't you thought much about this?**

SOURCE: American National Election Studies 1948–1994 Continuity Guide (Ann Arbor, MI: Interuniversity Consortium for Political and Social Research, 1995).

Oldendick, Tuchfarber, and Bennett, 1980). If the use of a filter question can deter respondents who do not have an opinion from providing an answer, then the results should be more reliable and provide a more accurate reflection of the public's views. While the use of filter questions has been shown to increase the percentage of "don't know" or "no opinion" responses compared to asking the same question without a filter, such questions generally have little effect on the division of substantive opinion and have mixed effects on the relationships between items (Schuman and Presser, 1981: 196; Bishop, Oldendick, and Tuchfarber, 1983).[4] There is, then, no right or wrong answer to the question of whether survey items should include a filter; the decision should be based on the purpose of the research.

Tone of Wording. It should be obvious that the words used in survey questions can make a difference in the results. The conclusions reached from a question that asks respondents whether they favor "killing babies" are likely to be quite different from those based on a question of support for "a woman's right to choose." Several less extreme examples demonstrate how seemingly minor changes in wording can make a considerable difference in the conclusions one would reach about the public's views.

For instance, Smith (1987) found that percentage of the public who felt that the government was spending too little on "assistance to the poor" was consistently about 40% greater than the percentage who thought the government was spending too little for "people on welfare." Likewise, Schuman and Presser (1981: 276–285) demonstrated that the percentage of the public who felt that the United States should "not allow" public speeches against democracy was about 25% higher than the percentage who thought that the U.S. should "forbid" such speeches. Similarly, asking about approval of expenditures

Table 4.2 Examples of Tone of Wording Effect

Speeches Against Communism			
Do you think the United States should forbid public speeches in favor of communism?		Do you think the United States should allow public speeches in favor of communism?	
Yes (forbid)	**39.3%**	**No (not allow)**	**56.3%**
No (not forbid)	60.1%	Yes (allow)	43.8%
Sending U.S. Troops			
If a situation like Vietnam were to develop in another part of the world, do you think the United States should or should not send troops?		If a situation like Vietnam were to develop in another part of the world, do you think the United States should or should not send troops to stop a communist takeover?	
Send troops	**18.3%**	**Send troops**	**33.2%**
Not send troops	81.7%	Not send troops	66.8%

SOURCE: Howard Schuman and Stanley Presser, *Questions and Answers in Attitude Surveys* (New York: Academic Press, 1981), pp. 281–285. Reprinted by permission of the publisher.

of "public funds" produces different results than expenditures of "tax money," and "sending troops" is supported by a smaller number of people than "sending troops to stop a communist takeover" (Table 4-2).

You should recognize that the words used in a question—the **tone** of the question—will have an effect on the results. In constructing a survey question it is important to be aware of this consideration and not to use words that are emotionally laden or that will tend to lead respondents in one direction or another. For a survey question on an issue to be informative to policy makers, the item must reflect the substance of the issue as well as the choices to be made. In evaluating survey questions, you should consider how the tone of wording of the question may have influenced the results. As Smith (1987: 83) has noted, failure to consider such effects can lead to ". . . the possible policy and scientific misapplication of survey data."

Middle Alternatives. Another consideration in designing survey questions is whether or not to include a **middle alternative.** While many survey questions ask respondents to choose between two alternatives, there is frequently a logical middle position that people might prefer. Those who feel that such survey questions should be presented without a middle alternative argue that the middle alternative provides an "easy out" for those who do not have a strong position on an issue or who have not thought much about it, and that for many issues a policymaker must make a choice between two "extremes"; presenting a middle choice limits the ability to determine which alternative the public prefers. Arguments for including a middle choice include the points that many people actually prefer a position somewhere between the two extremes and that if results show a large majority with this view, policymakers might be encouraged to compromise or to stake out some middle ground.

As an example, consider a legislator in a state facing a budget crisis. The legislature is faced with the choice of increasing taxes or reducing state services. The legislator is interested in the public's will on this issue: Are people willing to pay increased taxes or would they prefer a reduction in state services? One way to ask this question, which is taken from the Ohio Poll, is: "Like most states, Ohio faces the problem of not having enough tax money to pay for the various services and programs that the state government provides. One way to solve this problem is to raise taxes. Another way to resolve the problem is to reduce state services and programs. Which do you prefer?" When asked in this way, 52% of those surveyed preferred reducing services, 35% supported raising taxes, and 13% were undecided.

In a later poll, however, the issue was posed somewhat differently, this time with a middle alternative. Respondents were asked, "Suppose the state of Ohio's budget problem is serious. In that situation the state could make major cuts in state funding for elementary and secondary schools, colleges and universities, and most other state services, or it could pass a major tax increase. Would you prefer: (1) major cuts for schools and other services; (2) a major tax increase; or (3) a combination of a tax increase and budget cuts?" The results of this survey found 13% favoring major cuts, 17% supporting a major tax increase, 12% undecided, and 58% favoring a combination of budget cuts and a tax increase.

A legislator would draw different conclusions from the results of these two questions. The question of the right way to ask a question cannot be answered as a purely technical matter, since questions can appropriately be asked either with or without a middle alternative. The decision about how to ask a question should be guided by the substantive issue for which the public's opinion is being sought. If a "middle alternative" is a viable option, the question should include this alternative; if the issue is a matter of choice between two extremes, including a middle alternative in the question would be less useful. In this example, the Ohio legislature adopted a combination approach for addressing the state's budget crisis (Tuchfarber, Oldendick, and Bishop, 1984).

A second example of how presenting a middle alternative might affect results is provided by questions on defense spending. A commonly asked survey question involves whether the United States should increase or decrease spending on defense. In this case, the middle alternative, "keep spending about the same as it is now," is a viable option and should be offered as part of the question. As the following data demonstrate, a policymaker might come to different conclusions about the public's feelings on defense spending as a result of whether or not the question included a specific middle alternative:

No Middle Alternative		Middle Alternative Offered	
Increase	52%	Increase	23%
Decrease	40%	Decrease	17%
Keep About the Same (Volunteered)	8%	Keep About the Same	60%

In general, the effects of including an explicit middle alternative in a question are to: (1) increase the percentage of respondents choosing the middle alternative; (2) have little effect on the division of substantive opinion; that is, if you take out those people who chose the middle response, the remaining division between those on either side of the issue is generally the same; and (3) have mixed effects on the relationships among items. As with the other decisions that must be made in developing a survey question, the choice of whether or not to include a middle alternative should be guided by the substantive purpose for which the results are to be used.[5]

Response Format. Another element that can effect the results of survey questions is the **response format,** or the way in which choices are presented to respondents. The previous description of middle alternatives illustrated some of the consequences of variations in question forms, and response formats generally can influence respondents. One commonly used response format asks subjects to choose between two alternatives, such as "favor/oppose," "agree/disagree," or "yes/no." Another form of this **forced-choice format** presents respondents with two sides of an issue and asks them which one comes closer to their point of view (see Table 4–3).

Another commonly used question format is the **"agree-disagree" format,** in which respondents are read a statement and asked whether they agree or disagree with its content. Frequently additional choices of "strongly agree" and "strongly disagree," along with a middle ("neutral") alternative, are included to create a five-point **Likert-type item** (Selltiz, Jahoda, Deutsch, and Cook, 1959: 366). Agree-disagree items suffer from **acquiescence response set,** which is the tendency of respondents to agree with a statement regardless of its content. Because of this, forced-choice items are generally preferred over agree-disagree questions (Converse and Presser, 1986: 38).

One of the limitations of forced-choice items is that presenting only two alternatives (or extreme positions) does not allow for differentiation in opinion or moderation for those whose views lie between the extremes. The **seven-point forced-choice format** attempts to overcome this restriction by placing the alternatives at points "1" and "7" of a scale and leaving the remaining points for respondents who have an opinion that falls between the extremes. This format is used frequently in the American National Election Studies.

Rating scales are regularly used in public opinion surveys in evaluating performance or citizen satisfaction. In a typical rating question, respondents are asked to make judgments along a scale varying between two extremes, such as from excellent to poor, extremely satisfied to extremely dissatisfied, and the like. The following illustrates a common rating scale question: "How would you rate the job ———— is doing as Governor . . . Would you say she is doing an excellent job, a good job, a fair job, a poor job, or a very poor job?"

In **ranking scales,** respondents are presented with a list of items and are asked to rank them along some dimension, such as importance, desirability, or

Table 4.3 Examples of Various Types of Response Formats

[YES/NO FORMAT]: Now thinking about health care: Can you (and your family) afford to pay for the health care that you need?

1. YES
2. NO

[AGREE/DISAGREE (2-POINT) FORMAT]: Sometimes politics and government seem so complicated that a person like me can't really understand what's going on. Do you agree or disagree with this statement?

1. AGREE
2. DISAGREE

[AGREE/DISAGREE (5-POINT) FORMAT]: This country would have many fewer problems if there were more emphasis on traditional family ties. Do you agree strongly, agree somewhat, neither agree nor disagree, disagree somewhat, or strongly disagree?

1. AGREE STRONGLY
2. AGREE SOMEWHAT
3. NEITHER AGREE NOR DISAGREE
4. DISAGREE SOMEWHAT
5. DISAGREE STRONGLY

[FORCED CHOICE (2-POINT) FORMAT]: Some people are afraid that the government in Washington is getting too powerful for the good of the country and the individual person. Others feel that the government in Washington is not getting too strong. What is your feeling . . . do you think the government is getting too powerful or do you think the government is not getting too strong?

1. THE GOVERNMENT IS GETTING TOO POWERFUL
2. THE GOVERNMENT IS NOT GETTING TOO STRONG

[FORCED CHOICE (7-POINT) FORMAT]: Some people feel that the government in Washington should see to it that every person has a job and a good standard of living. Others think that the government should just let each person get ahead on their own. And, of course, other people have opinions somewhere in between. Suppose people who believe that the government should see to it that every person has a job and good standard of living are at one end of the scale—at point 1. And suppose that the people who believe that the government should let each person get ahead on their own are at the other end—at point 7. Where would you place yourself on this scale?

1. GOVERNMENT SEE TO JOB AND GOOD STANDARD OF LIVING
2.
3.
4.
5.
6.
7. GOVERNMENT LET EACH PERSON GET AHEAD ON THEIR OWN

[RATING FORMAT]: Some people don't pay much attention to political campaigns. How about you . . . would you say that you have been extremely interested, very interested, somewhat interested, not too interested, or not at all interested in the political campaigns so far this year?

1. EXTREMELY INTERESTED
2. VERY INTERESTED
3. SOMEWHAT INTERESTED
4. NOT TOO INTERESTED
5. NOT AT ALL INTERESTED

[RANKING FORMAT]: Different types of government services are provided by the federal government, by state government, and by local government. If government is to be reduced, which of these levels of government do you feel should be reduced first . . . the federal government, state government, or local government? And which should be reduced second? And which should be reduced third? (RECORD "1" FOR LEVEL OF GOVERNMENT MENTIONED FIRST, "2" FOR THE LEVEL MENTIONED SECOND, AND "3" FOR THE LEVEL MENTIONED THIRD).

_____   FEDERAL GOVERNMENT
_____   STATE GOVERNMENT
_____   LOCAL GOVERNMENT

[MULTI-PART QUESTION]: Generally speaking, do you usually think of yourself as a Republican, a Democrat, an Independent, or what?

(IF R CONSIDERS SELF REPUBLICAN): Would you call yourself a strong Republican or a not-very-strong Republican?

(IF R CONSIDERS SELF DEMOCRAT): Would you call yourself a strong Democrat or a not-very-strong Democrat?

(IF R CONSIDERS SELF INDEPENDENT, NO PREFERENCE, OTHER): Do you think of yourself as closer to the Republican Party or to the Democratic Party?

1. STRONG DEMOCRAT
2. WEAK DEMOCRAT
3. INDEPENDENT—LEANS TOWARD DEMOCRATS
4. INDEPENDENT—DOES NOT LEAN TOWARD EITHER
5. INDEPENDENT—LEANS TOWARD REPUBLICANS
6. WEAK REPUBLICAN
7. STRONG REPUBLICAN

SOURCE: Adapted from items in the *American National Election Studies 1948–1994 Continuity Guide* (Ann Arbor, MI: Inter-university Consortium for Political and Social Research, 1995).

preference. Ranking scales are more difficult for respondents, particularly if they involve more than four or five items, and are especially unwieldy in telephone interviews. As a result, rating scales are much more commonly used than are rankings.

Another format with which you should be familiar is the **"feeling thermometer."** As its name implies, this format uses the concept of a thermometer, generally ranging from zero degrees (very negative) to 100 degrees (very positive), in measuring reactions to political figures, countries or groups.

The formats described here are those commonly used in gauging public opinion. As with each decision made in designing questions, the type of format used should be that which is most appropriate for the substantive question of interest. Question format, like other question attributes, can have an effect on results.[6]

Order of Alternatives.   The order in which alternatives are presented to respondents is another factor that can affect survey results. In some instances, the alternative that is given to the respondent first is selected more often, simply because it is presented first. This is known as a **primacy effect.** In other cases, the choice that is presented last is selected more frequently due to its position in the list. This is known as a **recency effect.** Such effects do not occur in all cases and survey researchers do not yet know enough about them to be able to specify when they might occur (Schuman and Presser, 1981: 58). The possibility of primacy and recency effects is an element that must be considered in developing survey questions.

Context Effects.   The **context** in which a question is asked can have a significant effect on the results. The proceeding questions in a survey provide the setting in which the subject responds to an item, and changing these circumstances can make a large difference in the survey results and in how a policymaker might interpret what "the public thinks" about an issue.

A frequently cited example of such context effects involves public opinion on communist and American reporters. As shown in Table 4-4, when respondents in a 1948 survey were asked a question on whether the United States should let communist newspaper reporters from other countries come in and send back to their papers the news as they saw it, 37% more said "yes" when this question was asked after an item on whether Communist countries should let American newspaper reporters go into Communist countries and report the news as they saw it than when the question concerning Communist reporters was asked first.

A similar example of how the context in which a question is asked can affect survey results is provided by research on Americans' "interest in public affairs" (Bishop, Oldendick, and Tuchfarber, 1984). When survey respondents were asked about "how much you follow what's going on in government and public affairs" 18% more said they followed it "most of the time" when this question was asked as the first question in the survey than when it was asked after questions on whether the person remembered anything special their U.S. representative had done for their district and how their congressman/congresswoman had voted on any legislative bill. Since most people did not remember anything their representative had done for their district or how they had voted, they said "don't know" to these items. When they were then asked how often they followed government and public affairs, they were less likely to say "most

Table 4.4 Example of Question Context Effects

Communist reporter item: Do you think the United States should let communist reporters from other countries come in here and send back to their papers the news as they see it?

American reporter item: Do you think a communist country like Russia should let American newspaper reporters come in and send back to America the news as they see it?

	% "YES" TO COMMUNIST REPORTER ITEM	% "YES" TO AMERICAN REPORTER ITEM
Communist reporter item asked first	36.5%	65.6%
American reporter item asked first	73.1%	89.8%

SOURCE: Howard Schuman and Stanley Presser, *Questions and Answers in Attitude Surveys* (New York: Academic Press, 1981: 31). Reprinted by permission of the publisher.

of the time." The "hard knowledge" questions had provided a different context for what the interviewer meant by "following government and public affairs."

The debate over the issue of abortion has been ongoing in the United States for a fairly extended time, and this is an issue on which many people have strong feelings. Even in such a prominent issue area, question context can have an effect on survey responses. As Schuman and Presser (1981: 37) have demonstrated, a "general" abortion question[7] receives support from 61% of the public when it is asked before a more specific abortion item[8], but is supported by only 48% when it comes after the specific item. If a policymaker were presented with the results from a survey in which the general question were asked first, he or she would conclude that a solid majority of the public *favored* making it possible for a woman to obtain a legal abortion; if presented with results from a survey in which the same question had been asked after the specific abortion item, the conclusion would be that a majority *opposed* this position. In interpreting survey results, policy makers need to be conscious not only of the way in which questions were worded but also the context in which they were asked.

A number of practical considerations, such as avoiding "double-barrelled" items, not framing questions in such a way as to bias respondents, asking relevant questions, and not assuming behavior or knowledge on the part of respondents need to be kept in mind when developing survey questions. A good list of such specific suggestions is provided in Frey (1989: 178–179).

Data Analysis

The techniques used in analyzing survey data are also common to the three modes of survey data collection. Typical survey analysis consists of **univariate description,** or the description of one variable at a time; **bivariate analysis,** in which the relationship between two variables is examined, generally by constructing some type of table or correlation; and **multivariate analysis,** which involves examining relationships among three or more variables. Techniques appropriate for analyzing survey data are applicable to information collected by face-to-face interviewing, telephone interviewing, or self-administered questionnaires.

ADVANTAGES AND DISADVANTAGES OF DIFFERENT MODES

While the preceding considerations are common to data collection for either face-to-face, telephone, or self-administered surveys, each mode has certain advantages and disadvantages. The greatest difference among the three modes is cost. Face-to-face household surveys are generally most expensive, followed by telephone surveys, then mail and other self-administered surveys. The magnitude of the difference among these modes depends to some extent on the population of interest. In a national face-to-face survey, for example, the personnel (interviewer and supervisor) costs, together with travel costs, are much greater than those for a similar survey conducted by telephone or by mail.[9] As a general rule, the cost of conducting face-to-face interviews is from three to five times more expensive than collecting the same information by telephone, and a properly designed and executed mail survey can be done for approximately half the cost of data collection via telephone.

Although face-to-face surveys are more expensive than other forms of data collection, they have a number of advantages over other modes, including **population coverage, response rates,** and the types of information that can be collected. The extent to which the population of interest can be reached through these various modes is to some extent dependent on the population. In a survey of adult residents of a state, for example, it is possible to identify virtually all households, and only a small percentage of the population (for example, those institutionalized, the homeless) would be excluded from the sample. In a telephone survey, these same groups would be excluded with the addition of those individuals who live in households without telephones. As noted in Chapter 2, this was once a more serious disadvantage for telephone surveys than it is today, although it must be considered if the population of interest is likely to include a high percentage of individuals without telephones.

Face-to-face surveys also generally have higher response rates—that is, more of those selected in the sample participate in the survey—than do telephone or mail surveys. Low response rates are the principal disadvantage of mail surveys, and while this approach can be effective with specialized populations, it is generally not employed when a large segment of the general public is the population of interest (Krysan, Schuman, Scott, and Beatty, 1994).

Another advantage of face-to-face surveys is the amount of information that can be collected. Many face-to-face surveys, such as the General Social

---

How Much Does It Cost?

The cost of conducting a survey depends on a number of factors including the population of interest, the length of the questionnaire, and the number of completed interviews. Cost is not the only criterion for selecting a mode of survey data collection, and other factors such as population coverage, the type of information needed, and the representativeness of the sample must be considered. The following are cost estimates to conduct a statewide survey of 800 adults with a questionnaire that contains 50 closed-ended and five open-ended items:

Face-to-Face Interviews:	$140,000
Telephone Interviews:	$ 24,000
Mail Questionnaires:	$ 8,400

Survey or the American National Election Study, contain several hundred questions and require an hour or more to complete. Telephone survey researchers generally try to limit their questionnaires to about twenty minutes, although there are examples of telephone surveys averaging forty-five minutes or more. Mail surveys generally contain fewer questions than either face-to-face or telephone surveys and, in general, the shorter the mail survey, the higher the response rate. The maximum length for a mail survey of a non-specialized population is about twelve pages if an acceptable response rate is to be achieved. Face-to-face surveys and mail surveys also allow for the presentation of visual materials, which is not feasible in a telephone survey. Interviewers in face-to-face situations are able to develop a greater rapport with the respondent, which is generally considered an advantage in obtaining reliable information. In addition, face-to-face interviewers can use visual cues to detect if a respondent is having difficulty understanding a question and to probe responses more effectively.

It is possible, of course, to combine various modes of survey data collection in order to gather information more effectively (Dillman, 1978). For example, in a mail survey, those individuals who had not returned a questionnaire after several follow-ups can be contacted by telephone in an attempt to obtain the information. Similarly, if the basic design of a survey involves telephone interviews, an attempt can be made to collect information by mail or face-to-face from those individuals who do not have phones.

While each of the modes has certain advantages, telephone surveys are presently the most frequently used mode of survey data collection, particularly for the types of public opinion and evaluation research information that are the focus of much of this text. The significantly higher cost of face-to-face interviews makes this approach prohibitive for all but a few surveys, such as the National Health Interview Survey, the Survey of Income and Program Participation, and the National Crime Survey. The generally low response rates for mail surveys, particularly when the general public is the population of interest, make this mode less effective as a source of data for most public opinion studies. Telephone surveys provide a balance between cost, acceptable response rates, and ability to collect sufficient information that makes them most appropriate for many studies of public opinion.[10]

THE TECHNOLOGY OF MEASURING THE AMERICAN MIND

As noted in Chapter 2, the development of random-digit dialing sparked a change from face-to-face to telephone interviewing that has produced a tremendous growth in survey research. Technological developments have also produced some rather dramatic changes in the way survey data are collected.

The traditional face-to-face interview consisted of an interviewer asking questions of a respondent and recording his or her answers on a paper questionnaire. These questionnaires were later edited, information on open-ended questions was coded, and data were entered into some type of machine-readable format. These **paper-and-pencil interviewing** (PAPI) methods were also used in telephone surveys.

Movement beyond traditional PAPI methods began in the early 1970s with the development of **computer-assisted telephone interviewing** (CATI). CATI uses "interactive computing systems to assist interviewers and their supervisors in performing the basic data collection tasks of telephone surveys" (Nicholls, 1988: 377). While individual CATI systems vary in their capabilities, the most comprehensive can assist in the full range of survey tasks, from sample management through preparation of datasets and analysis.

The development of CATI allowed not only more efficient collection of data for fairly straightforward questionnaires, it also facilitated more complex questionnaire designs that could not be readily accomplished with paper-and-pencil methods. These included applications such as randomization of questions and response choices, arithmetic calculations and logical checks, and the use of data from prior interviews or dependent interviewing without disclosing the data to the interviewer in advance (Nicholls, 1988: 380–381). Virtually all telephone interviewing facilities—whether commercial, government or academic—now use some type of CATI system.

The advantages which CATI interviewing was found to have over traditional PAPI methods in terms of data quality, the capacity to perform complex tasks, and the speed with which data were prepared for analysis, together with the decreased cost and increased use of portable laptop computers, led to the development of **computer-assisted personal interviewing** (CAPI) for field surveys involving face-to-face interviews. The first national household survey in the United States to use CAPI for at least part of its data collection was the 1987 National Food Consumption Survey (Weeks, 1992: 446). Many of the benefits of CATI over PAPI for telephone interviews are also evident in face-to-face interviews, including more complicated routing patterns, on-line consistency checking, and greater flexibility in presenting questionnaire items.

In addition, the use of CAPI can be extended for those face-to-face survey situations in which respondents are asked sensitive questions utilizing a self-administered format. With paper-and-pencil methods, interviewers generally give respondents a booklet containing the sensitive items and ask them to complete the booklet and return it to the survey organization in a return mailing envelope. Such self-administered questionnaires must necessarily be simpler and more straightforward than those involving an interviewer. But in a CAPI situation, the interviewer can give the laptop computer to the respondent who, after some brief instruction, can complete the items as a **computer-assisted self interview** (CASI). Since question administration is under program control, the interview can be much more complex than the typical paper-and-pencil questionnaire, without the respondent being aware of the complexities (Weeks, 1992: 452–453). Adding an audio component in which respondents can listen to the questions through a headset at the same time they are presented on the screen (**audio–CASI**) overcomes the problem of respondents who may be illiterate. Evidence suggests that CASI and audio-CASI methods increase the accuracy of responses to sensitive questions (O'Reilly, et al., 1994: 209–211).

Other technological developments that have changed the way survey data are collected include **prepared data entry** (PDE), in which the survey organization provides respondents with an electronic questionnaire that they complete using their computer; **touchtone data entry** (TDE), in which the respondent calls a computer and responds to questions using the telephone keypad; and **voice recognition entry** (VRE), in which the respondent calls a computer, but rather than key entering the data, the respondent simply speaks the digits (Weeks, 1992: 447–449). In recent years, there has also been an increasing use of the Internet for collecting survey data.

As computers continue to become more affordable and more universally accessible, new technological innovations such as these will affect the way survey research is done. While these changes will lead to improved data quality and more efficiency in the gathering of survey information, the basic steps in the survey process—from identification of a population on interest through data analysis—will remain unchanged.

Polls, Polling and the Internet

If you are interested in the scientific basis of polling, a good site to visit is that of the American Statistical Association:

http://www.amstat.org/

For more information about the programs at the Institute for Social Research at the University of Michigan, look at the site located at:

http://www.isr.umich.edu/src/isrcenter.html

There is information regarding graduate training in survey research methodology at the site of the Joint Program in Survey Methodology at the University of Maryland:

http://www.jpsm.umd.edu/home

NOTES

1. For a more complete discussion of RDD, see Alfred J. Tuchfarber and William R. Klecka, *Random Digit Dialing: Lowering the Cost of Victimization Surveys* (Washington: The Police Foundation, 1976); and Robert M. Groves and Robert L. Kahn, *Surveys by Telephone: A National Comparison with Personal Interviews* (New York: Academic Press, 1979).

2. A discussion of probability theory underlying the concept of sampling error is beyond the scope of the current text, but can be found in most social statistics or survey methods texts (see, for example, Kalton, 1983; Babbie, 1990). You should be aware, however, that the sampling error is based on the standard error, which is calculated by the formula:

$$S = \sqrt{\frac{P \times Q}{N}}$$

Where S = the standard error;

 P = the percentage of the population having a given characteristic;

 $Q = 1 - P$; and

 N = the number of cases in the sample.

Probability theory demonstrates that certain proportions of the sample estimates will fall within specified increments of standard errors from the population value. Approximately 95% of the samples fall within two standard errors of the population value.

While increasing sample size will reduce sampling error, the relationship is not a straight-line one. For example, to cut your sampling error in half, you would need to collect data on four times as many individuals.

3. This survey has also been called the "best United States Survey" (Bradburn and Sudman, 1988: 130). The high degree of precision of this survey, however, comes at a price: the current annual cost of the Current Population Survey is more than twenty million dollars.

4. For an extensive discussion of attitudes and non-attitudes, see Converse (1970).

5. Converse and Presser (1986: 37) suggest another alternative for dealing with the question of whether to offer an explicit middle alternative or not. In their view, the solution is to "... not explicitly provide the middle category and thereby avoid losing information about the direction in which people lean, but follow the question with an intensity item, thus separating those who definitely occupy a position from those who only lean toward it."

6. One of the most significant controversies in American electoral behavior—the extent to which the mass public exhibits consistent attitudes—centers on changes in question wording and format. Briefly, this controversy involves whether changes in the American electorate which were noted in the 1960s were a result of "true" changes in mass behavior or were a result of changes in the format used for measuring opinions. For more on this controversy, see Converse (1964); Nie, Verba, and Petrocik (1976); Bishop, Oldendick, Tuchfarber, and Bennett (1978); and Bishop, Tuchfarber, and Oldendick (1978).

7. The wording of this question was, "Do you think it should be possible for a pregnant woman to obtain a legal abortion if she is married and does not want any more children?"

8. The wording of this question was, "Do you think it should be possible for a pregnant woman to obtain a legal abortion if there is a strong chance of a serious defect in the baby?"

9. In one of the most comprehensive comparisons of face-to-face and telephone interviews, Groves and Kahn (1979: 188) reported that the cost of conducting a face-to-face survey was approximately 2.5 times greater than carrying out the same data collection effort by telephone, while Tuchfarber and Klecka (1976: 19) estimated that the cost of personal interviews was 3.4 times that of those done by telephone. While these studies were conducted almost twenty years ago, they remain among the few large-scale studies in which extensive comparisons were made between these modes. More recent experience

with cost comparisons of face-to-face and telephone surveys indicates that the magnitude of these differences remains similar today.

10. To illustrate this point, of the studies reported in *Survey Research* in 1997, data for 114 were collected by telephone, 31 were done face-to-face, and 21 were collected by mail. As noted above, there are situations in which the need to gather a large volume of information or to present visual materials will dictate face-to-face data collection and others where limited resources or a small, easily identifiable population make a mail survey most effective. In most cases, however, a telephone survey represents the most cost-effective means of collecting public opinion data.

Part III

What Do
Americans Believe?

5

The Sources of Opinions

Questions to Consider:

How do children learn about politics and government?

Do families "pass on" party identification?

What do schools teach about politics?

Does religion or ethnicity influence politics?

How does the media influence opinions?

When pollsters call to survey opinions, most often people are quite prepared to answer their questions about politics or policies with opinions and perceptions reflecting their views. One of the questions that most intrigues students of public opinion is how individuals come to hold opinions on such a wide range of issues. At what point in a person's life does he or she "learn" the answer to the question, "Do you consider yourself to be a Republican, a Democrat, or an Independent?" When do people decide to be liberals or conservatives? Part of that learning process begins, it appears, in childhood.

In 1996, millions of school children, their parents and teachers participated in a project called "Kids Voting USA." Using prepared curricula tailored to each grade level, teachers led children in discussion of the upcoming presidential election and the meaning of voting. According to the sponsors of the project, the intent of the project was to "plant seeds for democracy,"[1] or, in other words, to learn to be active voting citizens. Studies have shown that if people vote soon after becoming eligible at the age of 18, they are much more likely to participate in elections for the rest of their lives. On election day, thousands of parents and community members volunteered to conduct mock elections at the same polling places where voters cast their ballots. More than two million children cast "ballots" for president under the auspices of Kids Voting. The project was widely acclaimed to be a success in preparing children for their future role as voters. In an unanticipated outcome, research conducted by Steven Chaffee of Stanford University showed that the project actually had a "trickle up" effect, stimulating the parents of the children to participate in the election. Chaffee found that the Kids Voting curriculum motivated families to discuss politics and provided a "second chance at socialization" for parents at the lower end of the socioeconomic scale (Evans, 1996). Kids Voting was intended to involve school children in the political system at an early age as a way to increase participation later. This project raises two issues for us as students of public opinion. First, why is it necessary to teach citizens to participate in the system, and, secondly, how do children learn about politics at such an early age?

The process of learning about the political system is generally called **political socialization.** As defined by Roberta Sigel, political socialization is "the process by which people learn to adopt the norms, values, attitudes, and behaviors accepted and practiced by the ongoing system" (Sigel, 1970: xii). According to this definition, the goal of political socialization is to teach the appropriate behaviors and attitudes to citizens so that they will support the political system. Investigating this process became a very important thrust of research in political science in the late 1960s as part of the drive to discover the processes by which democratic societies could be sustained. Work by a number of authors was based on the assumption that, "The operation of the political system is seen as dependent on the political outlooks of the citizenry." (Dawson, Prewitt and Dawson, 1969, 1977; and Jaros, 1973). The alternative approach to political socialization focuses on the growth and development of the individual personality of the citizen rather than the needs of the system, defining the process more broadly as "the acquisition of political attitudes, values, and behaviors," regardless of whether they support the current system or not. Scholars who work from this "psychological" perspective are interested not only in how the citizen acquires values and behaviors that may support the system, but where the process of learning about politics fits into the development of human personality and ongoing human relationships. (See the work of Hyman, 1959; Greenstein, 1965; Hess and Torney, 1967 for the origins of this approach.)

For the purposes of this book, it is helpful to consider political socialization from both perspectives—the needs of the political system and individual development—because the two processes interact continually. Through educational systems and public policy, the larger political system tries continually to influence individuals to exhibit certain attitudes and behaviors, such as being law-abiding and voting. The individual, however, is engaged in a lifelong journey of learning and development. The political socialization of childhood will be affected through the lifespan by a range of influences that are beyond public influence.

As we begin to look at the process of political socialization in children and adults, it is useful to think about why certain groups and institutions such as parents and schools can act as agents of socialization. Paul Allen Beck has suggested that in order for an individual to be influenced, three conditions must be met: exposure, communication, and receptivity (Beck, in Renshon, 1977: 117). In other words, for the Kids Voting USA project to have influence over the future opinions and voting habits of schoolchildren, the students had to be exposed to the project, receive communications from their teachers and parents about it, and, most importantly, be motivated by some force to be receptive to the messages about voting. Obviously, the success of the project will only be known many years in the future.

THE POLITICAL LEARNING OF CHILDREN
AND ADOLESCENTS

To the surprise of the first researchers who studied the political attitudes of children, kindergarten students were able to identify major political figures such as the current and past president and to express, in many cases, an identification with a political party. Undoubtedly, elementary school children carried such identification into the Kids Voting project. How do small children gain such identifications and attitudes? Clearly, the influence of the family is paramount in the political socialization of young children. To recall Beck's conditions, mothers and fathers have maximum *exposure* with children, *communicate* with the child frequently, and, most importantly, experience maximum conditions of *receptivity*. Children are extremely dependent on the approval of their parents and other family members for the development of emotional and intellectual maturity and stability. When a child points at the televised image of President Clinton and says, "I like his smile," and the parent responds approvingly, whether with a smile or verbal agreement, the child's predisposition to share the mother's opinion is reinforced. Negative attitudes toward individuals or political views are also reinforced by parental actions. Behavior is influential as well: a child who is raised in a family where both parents actively participate in campaigns and elections is likely to participate regularly as an adult.

In their seminal work on political socialization, David Easton and Jack Dennis proposed four psychological processes that characterize children's views of politics and the political system (1969: 391). In the first stage, **politicization,** children become aware of the existence of authority figures and institutions beyond their parents, adult relatives, and teachers. They seem to be aware that there exists some form of power in terms of government and laws beyond their immediate social circle. When children begin to think about **political authority,** they are likely to think in terms of individuals or persons instead of institutions such as the courts. Easton and Dennis found that children saw both the police officer and the president to be representatives of government. As they put it, "As representatives of political authority for the child—the policeman is seen as working for the government and the president *is* the government—both figures . . . have some psychological importance for the child." (152) This process, which is epitomized by the child's admiration of Abraham Lincoln or Martin Luther King, is termed **personalization.** The third process is named **idealization,** referring to the child's identification of political authority as generally benevolent and trustworthy. One suspects that children would expect a parallel between the loving relations with the family and with these other authority figures. The classic example of political socialization is the visit by the firefighter to the kindergarten class for a discussion of fire safety. Children are seeing an example of authority beyond the family in the person of the firefighter and they are asked to see this professional as their friend and protector. Indeed, Easton and Dennis's surveys of children showed that younger children saw both the president and the policeman as helpful to their families. Later in the development of children's ability to conceptualize, the process of **institutionalization** takes place and the firefighter or police officer then can become part of the concept of local government. Not until this process of institutionalization begins are children able to conceptualize such institutions as the Congress or city government.

The earliest studies of political socialization of children found remarkably positive feelings among children toward the political system. As Hess and Torney concluded from their studies in the 1960s, "The young child perceives figures and institutions of government as powerful, competent, benign, and infallible and trusts them to offer him protection and help" (1967: 213) To some extent these feelings may have been generated by the political atmosphere of the 1950s and early 1960s when the children were studied. However, other research showed that the children selected for these studies were enrolled in mostly middle class schools with largely white populations. The question then became whether the strong positive feelings that children expressed toward government were based on the socioeconomic class of their families or were reflective of all children. (See also the classic work of Greenstein, 1965.)

Several different studies were conducted during the late 1960s in large industrial cities, focusing on the political attitudes of nonwhite children (Dennis, 1969; Rodgers and Taylor, 1971). Some of the studies showed high levels of support for authority figures such as the police officer and the president among very young children but less support for the government among older black children. Greenberg (1970), among others, reported consistent differences in levels of support for government figures even among younger children. The research of Jaros, Hirsch, and Fleron (1968), who replicated the research in schools that enrolled poorer minority and Appalachian children, demonstrated the possibility of cultural differences in these patterns of socialization. Where the middle class white children demonstrated positive attitudes toward political figures and institutions and showed considerable trust in the democratic systems, Jaros's subjects expressed much more negativism in their feelings toward political figures and pessimism about how the system worked. The results of such studies of subgroups suggest that for some children, the idealization phase of development may be replaced by such antipathy toward government that the phase becomes one of **hostilization.** This contrast in outcomes clearly underlines the power of the family as a primary influence in the adoption of political attitudes.

Studies conducted by researchers in the 1970s also demonstrated that the political cynicism of the period was transmitted by parents to the children. For example, the study conducted by Dennis and Webster in 1974 found that children were less likely to idealize government than those studied in the early 1960s. In 1974, only 25 percent of sixth grade children said that the president keeps his promises, compared to almost 71 percent who answered positively in 1962. Arterton's study of children's attitudes during the Watergate period showed an increase in general cynicism among third and fifth graders and a startling decline in children's feelings of approval for the president (1974). Such comparisons over time provide strong indications of the parents' influence over their children's basic outlook on government. Of course, it is also important to note that older children may be influenced by sources outside of the family, including the media, peers, and other authority figures.

What is clear from the research is that families are most successful at influencing children in their identification with a political party and much less successful at transmitting views on particular political issues. Much of the knowledge about these processes is drawn from a longitudinal study conducted by Niemi and Jennings, who surveyed adolescents and their parents in 1965 and then re-surveyed these groups in 1973 and 1982. The first results of the Niemi and Jennings study underscored the ability of parents to influence their children's political party identification (1968). As shown in Table 5-1, in the 1965 study, 59% of the high school students chose the same political party identification as their parents. Agreement on political issues was much lower, and in a finding that Niemi and Jennings say indicates the positive environment of schools, adults were more cynical about politics than their children. The results of the first Niemi and Jennings survey raised a number of issues for students of public opinion: Why is partisanship transmitted so successfully to children? What other variables intervene to keep political attitudes and preferences from being transmitted as well? What will happen to the partisanship of these students as they age?

All of the studies that look at the political socialization of children eventually come to the question of persistence. Will the views and behaviors expressed by children in the fifth or twelfth grade persist into adulthood? How long-lasting are the effects of the family or the school system? The Niemi and Jennings survey of high school seniors and their parents was repeated in 1973 and in 1982 to try to ascertain the degree to which attitudes persisted or changed over time. By 1973, the students showed much less agreement with their parents' partisan preference: only 45% of the students and parents agreed (1975). While a larger percentage of children were declaring themselves to be Independent voters, only a modest number expressed an identification with a different party than that endorsed by their parents. On some political issues, preferences expressed by children and their parents seemed to be converging, while on others, they were farther apart. Children and their parents were all

Table 5.1 Parent versus Student Partisanship

	PARENTS		
STUDENTS	**Democrat**	**Independent**	**Republican**
Democrat	66%	29%	13%
Independent	27%	53%	36%
Republican	7%	17%	51%
Number of cases	(914)	(442)	(495)

SOURCE: M. Kent Jennings and Richard G. Niemi, *The Political Character of Adolescence*, Princeton, NJ: Princeton University Press, 1974, p. 41.

more cynical than they had been in the mid-1960s. The 1982 wave of the panel found that Democratic party identification had weakened among parents and their children, but the children seem to have stabilized their partisan identification with age (Jennings and Markus, 1984). What does this tell us about the persistence of childhood political socialization? Jennings and Niemi interpret the results to say that these families certainly show **life cycle effects,** meaning changes in political views that are attributable to stages in life, and perhaps some examples of **generational effects,** which can be attributed to events taking place for a particular generational cohort. They conclude, however, that more forces seem to be bringing the generations together than pushing them apart (1975:1335).

THE INFLUENCE OF FORMAL EDUCATION

Every society, whether primitive or highly structured, has struggled with passing on its cultural values and rules of behavior to its children. While the process of political socialization always begins within the child's family, societies have often turned to formal processes of schooling to carry on the socialization process. Primitive societies may rely on sex-segregated processes for educating boys and girls to their adult duties. During the formative years of the American republic, schooling followed the patterns set in Western Europe. Adolescent boys of upper class families were often sent to formal schools, with only the children of the elite enrolling in what we would now call a post-secondary education. In the late 17th and early 18th centuries, girls (and young boys) were educated only at home, first by their mothers and, if wealthy, by private tutors. The importance of the woman's role in inculcating appropriate democratic values into their sons and daughters was often cited in the years following independence as evidence of women's value to the nation (see Kerber, 1980). As the principle of universal suffrage (for men) spread across the American states, it became evident to the political leaders that some provision should be made for increasing the civic education of future citizens. Thus, public education systems were devised at the elementary and secondary level. Most publicly supported colleges and universities came into being after the Civil War with the establishment of land grant universities through the Morrill Act (1862).

There can be no doubt that public education in the United States was driven first by the need to produce citizens who could support this radical democratic system and secondly by the need to develop skills for individuals. The question that has challenged scholars, however, is whether the extensive public education system of this country has had its desired impact on the process of political socialization. The data from a number of studies, including the National Civics Test, reported in 1990, are decidedly mixed.

If the goal of the school system is to produce citizens who will participate in the system in an informed way, what tools do the schools have to influence children? Obviously, school systems attempt to socialize children through the curriculum, including the selection of textbooks and the requiring of specific courses for graduation. In some states, courses such as American Government or Texas Government (to name only one state) are mandated in public universities. As noted by Dawson, Prewitt, and Dawson (1977), schools may be engaging in civic education or, in the more extreme case, in political indoctrination (144). Secondly, schools shape students' attitudes through the activities that Dawson calls "classroom ritual life," including the daily salute to the flag and Pledge of Allegiance, the annual celebration of the Pilgrim feast, and the study of American heroes such as Washington and Lincoln. The third force cited by most scholars is the influence of the classroom teacher. Does the teacher teach his or her own political values to the students or is the teacher an effective instructor of the school system or community's chosen values and behaviors? The final component of the school's influence is the classroom behavior that is encouraged or discouraged, whether by the individual teacher or by the community in which the school is located. Students may, it has been hypothesized, learn as much from the encouragement of debate and dialogue or a strict code of obedience to authority as from the actual subjects taught in any grade.

The Curriculum

A number of different scholars have looked at the impact of the curriculum on political socialization with fairly negative results. In a pioneering study, Edgar Litt compared the effects of civics instruction in three school districts, each using a different type of text and having a different socioeconomic makeup. Generally, Litt found that there was some influence on the civic learning of the students when texts were used that tried to influence participative values, but in no case were more than one quarter of the students affected (1963). Langton and Jennings reported on a comparison of students who had taken a traditional American government or history course versus those who had enrolled in a more contemporary (and supposedly more engaging) American Problems course. As they summarize the study, "An overview of the results offers strikingly little support for the impact of the curriculum" (Jennings and Langton, in Jennings Niemi, 1974, p. 190). It did not appear to matter which curriculum or course students took, in terms of their level of political knowledge or orientation. Indeed, the most important effect seemed to be one of **recency:** if the students had just completed the course, their recall was better. Jennings and Langton, did, however, find quite significant differences between white and African American youth. The civics curriculum did seem to change the orientations of black students on number of dimensions, increasing their feelings of loyalty to the system while decreasing trust and participation (202).

As part of their conclusions, Jennings and Langton suggest that the ineffectiveness of the curriculum may be due to several factors, including the redundancy of the material presented, the training and pedagogy of the teachers, and the general environment of the class and school. Hess and Torney's study of the influence of school on younger children comes to much the same conclusions. As they note, "The young child's attitude toward authority or institutions, however, seems not to correspond directly to the amount of emphasis on these topics reported by the teacher. Compliance to rule and authorities is a major focus of civic education in elementary schools" (217). They suggest that while the school is an important factor in political socialization, it is most effective at teaching obedience and relatively ineffective at teaching the responsibilities of citizenship or the actual political processes of the system.

Ritual and Ceremony

American school systems consciously adopt rituals and practices designed to instill patriotism and loyalty in children. Besides the Pledge of Allegiance and the learning of American history, schools provide avenues for participation through elected student councils. While these practices may instill a sense of loyalty among students, most researchers who have studied these activities believe that they may instill passivity rather than political knowledge or interest in participation. At the elementary school level, students see elections as important, but, with little knowledge of political parties or election processes, "children wish to minimize conflict" (216). It is suggested by these authors that what might be happening in the elementary grades is the setting up of an idealized view of the citizen, one who is nonpartisan and whose individual vote makes a difference. If this idealization is internalized by children, they may become even more cynical and alienated from the system when they realize the role of conflict and interest groups in the system (216).

The Teachers

Elementary and secondary school teachers, as well as college professors, are often recalled by their former students as having a dramatic impact on their lives. In fact, teachers may become the object of community disapproval if their influence appears to be greater than that of the parents or the community. Thus, as Jennings, Ehrman, and Niemi put it, [teachers] "are criticized both for being too effective and too ineffective" in the area of social science (226). Since the curriculum seems to have little impact on students, perhaps it is because of a lack of teacher preparation or interest. On the other hand, if students become activists on a particular topic, teachers or college professors are likely to blame. Although it is quite difficult to study the impact of teachers on their classes apart from the curricula and the community's social mix, Jennings, et al. suggest that the same principles apply to teacher-student-parent relationships as to those of students and their parents. If the teacher is reinforcing the views of parents, the students tend to be pushed toward homogeneity of views. If parents and teachers hold conflicting views, the students tend to adopt a middle position.

After comparing the curriculum, district climate, teacher preparation and attitudes, and other characteristics of two school systems, Richard Merelman suggests that teachers may not be very influential over children's views because they are themselves "political ingenues." By this he means that teachers are not drawn into the profession by their political views, nor do they have very well-defined ideas about politics. While Merelman found that teachers had little reluctance to have discussions about political issues in their classrooms, they were woefully uninformed about political issues in their own community and had few political predispositions. The exception to this finding involved male social science teachers who tended to exhibit lower morale and more dissatisfaction than other groups of teachers. They were often the ones to encourage students in discussion but, perhaps because of their own alienation, they did not convey higher support for democratic values to their students (Merelman, 1971: 197).

School Behaviors

Since the curriculum, the teachers, and the rituals of the playground do not seem to have a great impact on the civic-mindedness of children, what other kinds of learning take place within the educational institutions? Although it is quite difficult to study, researchers suggest that the climate of the classroom—whether students have significant chances to participate in discussions or decisions—might impact their holding of democratic values. In addition, the diversity of the classroom in terms of the student body seems to have an impact on students. Peer influence, another major agent of socialization, also plays a role within formal schooling. Several studies (Langton, 1969; Newcomb, 1958) show that children will tend to conform to the dominant ideology or viewpoints of their classmates.

It is worth noting the work by Talcott Parsons on this subject. Parsons, in his "The School class as a social system," reminds us that children adopt social roles within the classroom. Although the gender of students is fixed, children can become leaders or valued teammates within the classroom setting. They may be well rewarded for their efforts by teachers or by their classmates. Parsons believed that "the elementary school class is an embodiment of the fundamental American values of equality of opportunity." (Quoted in Dawson, Prewitt, and Dawson, p. 155). In addition, students may learn the rules of competition, cooperative behavior, and fairness in the classroom, or they may learn the opposite. Dawson et al. remind us that children may become aware of the tension between the democratic values being taught in the curriculum and the emphasis placed on passivity and orderliness by school authorities. (155)

The School as a Sorter Mechanism

It is important to note that schools and the educational system operate both to educate all the children sent to them and to sort out children as they move through the educational ladder of success. Given the generally lackluster success of the school system in conveying political knowledge and civic behaviors to students as documented by these many studies, it should not be a surprise to find out that those students who come from homes where the parents have college educations or have a higher socioeconomic status are more interested in political events, pay more attention to the news, perform better on tests of civic knowledge, and generally have higher levels of participation in politics. What we may see in terms of the impact of schools on political socialization is a reinforcement of the family's political involvement.

As a part of a Congressionally mandated program to test student achievement on a wide range of subjects, the National Civics Awareness Test was administered to a nationally representative sample of students in 1976, 1982, and 1988. The results of these tests were reported in *The Civics Report Card* (1990) published by the U.S. Department of Education. The 1988 tests showed a slight increase in knowledge about government and civics among 13-year-olds and a slight decrease in achievement by the 17-year-olds. However, the Report Card also showed that levels of achievement continue to be lower among Hispanic and African American youth as well among youth who have fewer advantages in family income and educational achievement. Tables 5-2 and 5-3 show the results on the National Civics Awareness test for children from different types of socioeconomic backgrounds. It is clear that children whose parents are college-educated score higher at every level on the civics questions. In addition, students show strong differences in achievement depending on their future educational plans and the type of secondary program in which they are enrolled. The data presented in Table 5-4 shows the wide gap between those who are college-bound and those who plan to enter the workforce after high school.

What do all of these studies tell us about the impact of formal education on the political opinions and behaviors of Americans? It appears that while the school system may be successful at instilling loyalty and patriotism in children as well as obedience to the law, it has much less impact on the formation of attitudes toward political institutions and processes in this country. The impact of the family and the community in which the child is raised may be reinforced by the civics curriculum for children from upper socioeconomic levels, but may have little impact on the political opinions and outlook of children from other backgrounds. The comparison between college-bound students and those who are not suggests strongly that schools may not have as much impact on students' opinions as the children's families and their ambitions to enroll in institutions of higher education.

Table 5.2 National Civics Proficiency Test Average Scores
National Average and by Region and Demographic Factors

	Grade 4	Grade 8	Grade 12
National Average Score	214	260	296
Gender			
Male	215*	259	299
Female	213	261	294
Race/Ethnicity			
White	220	266	302
Black	198	244	274
Hispanic	200	241	280
Region			
Northeast	216	263	294
Southeast	210	254	291
Central	218	264	300
West	212	258	299

*Average score.
SOURCE: Adapted from *The Civics Report Card: Trends in Achievement from 1976 to 1988 at Ages 13 and 17; Achievement in 1988 at Grades 4, 8, and 12.* Washington, DC: U.S. Department of Education, 1990, p. 42.

Table 5.3 National Civics Proficiency Test Average Scores
By Characteristics of the Child's Home Environment

	Grade 4	Grade 8	Grade 12
National average score	214	260	296
Parents' Education Level			
Less than High School Level	208*	238	273
High School Degree	211	253	285
Some College	221	264	299
College Degree	223	272	307
Parents at Home			
Both Parents	217	265	301
One Parent	207	251	288
Neither	184	238	278
Reading Materials at Home			
0 to 2 Items†	202	241	272
3 Items	215	256	292
4 Items	223	270	303

*Average score.
†*Items* means the following group of materials: newspaper, magazine, encyclopedia, and dictionary.
SOURCE: Adapted from *The Civics Report Card: Trends in Achievement from 1976 to 1988 at Ages 13 and 17; Achievement in 1988 at Grades 4, 8, and 12.* Washington, DC: U.S. Department of Education, 1990, p. 52.

Table 5.4 National Civics Proficiency Test Average Scores At Grade 12 by High School Program and Post-High School Plans

	Percent	Average Score
High School Program		
Academic	58	309
General	34	282
Vocational	8	272
Post-High School Plans		
Four-Year College or University	54	311
Two-Year College, Technical School, Vocational School	21	284
Full-Time Work	17	277
National Score at Grade 12		296

SOURCE: Adapted from *The Civics Report Card: Trends in Achievement from 1976 to 1988 at ages 13 and 17; Achievement in 1988 at Grades 4, 8, and 12.* Washington, DC: U.S. Department of Education, 1990, p.55.

The Influence of Ethnic Identity

Americans hold widely varying opinions on public issues ranging from abortion to air pollution. However, on many issues, the divisions within public opinion are linked to the ethnic background or ethnic identification of the respondents. How do a person's ethnic origins come to influence his or her views? Obviously, the earliest source of ethnic identification comes from the family. For white Americans, ethnic identity is most likely transmitted to children through the practice of family traditions or the telling of the family history. For children of color, ethnicity and physical characteristics are shared with parents and siblings. In the case of Hispanic families, the major source of ethnic identity may be the use of Spanish as a primary language in the home or the Spanish surname, rather than their shared physical traits. The family may transmit a clear sense of ethnicity or group membership to the children, or that identity may be de-emphasized. In most second or third generation white families, the ethnic origins of the child may be so mixed as to have little or no meaning. Recent immigrants are, naturally, more closely tied to their native culture and heritage.

The ethnic background of individuals, while first transmitted by the family, is likely to be either reinforced or modified by later socialization processes. As noted in the discussion of formal schooling, African American and Hispanic children demonstrate less positive support for the political system and, after exposure to civics education, may respond by becoming more disaffected with the system. Learning about racial issues seems to increase the cynicism of African American high school students. As they grow older, children absorb messages about how their own ethnic group is perceived by others through personal experiences and through the media. They may become more aware of their own identity and the experiences of their group than they were within the nuclear family. According to Conover (1984), those individuals who have the strongest group identity are more likely to express distinct political views and preferences linked to their group's interests or values.

African Americans

In general African Americans are much more liberal on domestic policy issues than virtually any white ethnic group, with the exception of Jewish voters. Given the history of slavery and discrimination that effectively barred African Americans from participation in the political life of the country until after the Civil War in the North and until the 1960s in the South, it is not surprising that African Americans express much stronger support for affirmative action programs, for government enforcement of civil rights, for government action to assist poor Americans, and for a strong federal government than do whites. There is also considerable support within the African American community for redistributing income through the tax system and for a national health care system. The support for national social welfare policies extends throughout the African American community regardless of income level, education, or social class. Although African Americans mostly identified with the Republican party as the party of Lincoln after the Civil War, they changed their allegiance to that of the Democrats during Roosevelt's New Deal. Since the 1940s, almost 90% of African American voters regularly cast their ballots for the Democratic candidate for president.

There are other areas where the distribution of opinions within the African American community is somewhat different from that within the white community, but the difference is not as strong as it is on civil rights and social welfare issues. Since the Vietnam War, which saw a disproportionate number of African Americans serving in the army and suffering casualties, this ethnic group is somewhat less likely to support the use of military force involving American soldiers overseas. African Americans are also less likely to support open access to abortions for women, although African American women are just as likely as white women to undergo the procedure.

Perhaps some of the most striking differences between black and white Americans are found in their extremely disparate perceptions of racism and opportunity for people of color in this country. African Americans are much more likely to perceive society as racist and discriminatory than are whites. Research by Sigelman and Welch (1991) also showed that more than 40% of blacks thought that racism seemed to be getting worse nationally, although only 25% believed that conditions were worsening in their own community. A recent study (*Time*/CNN poll, 1997) showed that there are generational differences within the public on the question of racism: the study showed that both white and African American teenagers are less likely to see racism as responsible for the problems of African Americans than are adult Americans. This generational difference suggests that the views of parents are being modified by their children's experiences in the world in a way that reduces some of the gap in opinions between black and white Americans.

Hispanic, Asian and Native Americans

Hispanic Americans have also suffered discrimination and lack of opportunity in the United States, especially in the southwestern region of the nation. However, it is much more difficult to define a national pattern of opinions distributed by Hispanic people because of the strength of ties to their respective countries of origin. Cuban Americans, most of whom immigrated after Castro's rise to power, tend to be middle class and to hold opinions very similar to other groups of white ethnic Americans, except for their views on whether the U.S. should try to overthrow the Castro regime. In contrast, Mexican Americans and Puerto Ricans, who have been among the poorest groups in the United States, tend to express support for social welfare programs and antidiscrimination measures at levels similar to those seen in the African American community. There are other, smaller communities of Hispanic people scattered throughout the country, including immigrants from all the nations of Central America and South America.

There are some aspects of Hispanic cultures, however, that tend to cross the national origin boundaries. Hispanics are largely Catholic in their religious affiliation and are strongly anti-abortion in their views. With a somewhat more traditionalist culture, Hispanic communities strongly value religion, the church, and the family.

The influence of the family is probably strongest in the maintenance of Spanish as the language of the home for many Hispanic families. At least one study has shown that children whose primary language is Spanish demonstrate less attachment to the political system than do children who are bilingual or whose primary language is English. (Lamare in Niemi, 1974) Of course, those children who are facile in English are more likely to come from households with better educated parents and higher household income. Since those characteristics are also associated with stronger attachment to the institutions of government for all young people, it is not easy to sort out the effects of being raised in a Spanish-speaking family.

Asian Americans make up only 5.3% of the U.S. population. Like Hispanics, there are many countries of origin for Asian Americans and, thus, many varieties of opinion among the communities. Opinions are more distinct in areas where there is an enclave of similar ethnic peoples, as in some California communities, but there is very little research available on the distribution of opinions among Asian Americans across the nation.

Another ethnic group that undoubtedly conveys its ethnic identity to its children is that of native Americans. Again, this community is fragmented by tribal identity, but the overall poverty and lack of education among native Americans has tended to depress interest in politics and public issues among these communities. Another factor that has led to considerable cynicism and distrust of government among native Americans has been the long history of federal government control of many aspects of these people's lives.

RELIGION AND PUBLIC OPINION

For many Americans the source of religious affiliation is the family of their birth. Just as a little girl does not know that she is Irish or German until someone tells her, small children have no idea of religious affiliation other than what they learn from their parents or other family members. For some of the groups that immigrated to the United States, religious affiliation is closely linked to ethnic identity. Among those groups would be Hispanic Americans, Italians, and many Eastern European and Irish families that are most likely Catholic in affiliation. Other ethnic groups such as the German Americans descended from Protestant, Catholic, or Jewish immigrants.

For some Americans, religious affiliation is more a family characteristic than a source of political attitudes or opinions. For others, the important influence is not as much the affiliation as the basic principles of the faith that guide their lives. These principles may have a great influence on their political and social views. In the course of studying the distribution of opinions among religious denominations, researchers have found that affiliation with a religion is not a very good predictor of opinions for many individuals. It is true that Catholics are, in general, more likely to vote for Democratic candidates than for Republicans and may be more liberal on some social issues than the general public, but the differences are declining. Members of the mainstream Protestant denominations show no pattern different from the majority of Americans in their views. Looking more closely at the way that religion influences an individual and his or her opinions, scholars have looked for other indicators of how religion influences opinions. With the growth in political strength and activity among conservative or fundamentalist Protestant groups, it has become clear that holding a certain set of religious beliefs is linked to a particular set of political views and opinions for this subgroup.

The Evangelicals

Over the last 20 years, a number of Protestant denominations and independent churches began to take political action and attempt to influence public policy. In fact, at least one of the television evangelists, Pat Robertson, became a Republican candidate for the presidency. The adherents of these churches tend to be quite conservative on social issues, including strong opposition to abortions, and to be Republican in partisanship. Since some of the churches taking a more political stand were within mainline Protestant denominations, looking at opinions by denominational affiliation "hid" these groups from analysis. Scholars tried various survey questions to tease out those individuals who held this more evangelical perspective. In general, it has been possible to identify this group by asking a series of questions, including whether they view the

Bible as inerrant, whether they consider themselves to be "born again," and whether one can be saved by faith alone. Individuals who answer affirmatively to all three are generally considered to be evangelical Protestants (Jelen, 1989). About 20% of Americans could be considered evangelical or fundamentalist Protestants.

In terms of their beliefs, these conservative Christians are more likely than mainstream Protestants to oppose social-welfare programs and big government programs, to oppose easy access to abortions, to support prayer in the schools, and to oppose the inclusion of gays in the military. They are much more likely to identify themselves as Republicans than as Democrats, and only 23% voted for Bill Clinton in 1992, as compared to 43% of the national electorate.

The Catholics

As pointed out by Leege and Welch (1989), there are also evangelical groups within the Catholic church who may hold some similar religious beliefs. They differ considerably from the Protestant evangelicals because their views are considerably more liberal, especially on social welfare issues. Leege's work confirmed the general trend for Catholics to be more liberal than the general public, but looked more closely at the beliefs that are deeply held by individuals to see if these predicted political views. Specifically, Leege and Welch focused on the degree to which Catholics held individualistic or communitarian beliefs, that is the degree to which they were closely tied to parish and community life. They found evidence that communitarian indicators were linked to certain more traditional views, including the importance of the male breadwinner, opposition to abortion, and concerns about changes in society. Religious individualism is associated with more liberal social views. What Leege and Welch make clear is that the American Catholic community includes individuals with different beliefs and that those differences will be reflected in different political views. In addition, they note that the more assimilated the individual is into mainstream society and the higher the income and educational attainment, the less likely it is that the person will be strongly Democratic and liberal.

Jewish Opinions

Like Catholics, Jewish Americans have long been considered to be very liberal in their views on social and political issues. They have been highly identified with the Democratic party and its more liberal candidates. In a recent study of Jewish voters, Cohen and Liebman (1997) examined a number of possible explanations for the liberal record of these Americans. They tested explanations ranging from a theology that specifies charity and good works, to the independent and relatively secular lifestyle of most American Jews, to their history as an oppressed minority. While the results of this study showed that Jews are, in general, more liberal on a range of positions than are non-Jews, when the data are controlled for equal levels of educational attainment, it appears that Jews are only more liberal than non-Jews on a particular subset of issues. Specifically, Jews are far more likely to identify with the Democratic party (72%) than are non-Jews. They are also strongly supportive of civil liberties, of the separation of church and state, of permissive social norms including abortion, and of spending on some domestic programs. Cohen and Liebman conclude from their research that Jews are liberal and highly identified with the Democratic party because they have been a minority group needing the protections of the government, and that their liberalism on this set of issues is probably not related very clearly to religious beliefs or practices.

GENDER AND OPINIONS

Over the last two decades, there has been growing evidence of a **gender gap** in voting for the presidency. By the 1992 election, Bill Clinton received 46% of the women's vote but only 41% of the men's vote. The gender gap first appeared in a significant way during the 1980 election when women cast their votes against Ronald Reagan (Frankovic, 1982). Since that time they have looked at the distribution of opinions within gender groups and tested various explanations for the gender differences that they have found.

Some of the early students of political socialization did notice that there were differences between boys and girls at the elementary school level, particularly with respect to their interest in politics and political issues (Greenstein in Dennis, 1974). Girls were less interested in political issues and the topic of government than were boys, and this margin of disinterest stayed about the same across age groups. Thinking about other work on gender differences in achievement in school, it might by hypothesized that girls become less interested in politics because they are not encouraged to be so, in much the same way that young adolescent girls are now known to lose interest in science and mathematics because they are not expected to be interested in those topics and future careers. Another hypothesis would suggest that since there are relatively few role models of women holding high political office, girls, like young people of color, see little reason to pursue an interest in politics, since the likelihood of holding political office is slim.

Although there is not enough evidence to validate either of those hypotheses, it is clear that women continue to exhibit less interest in politics and to possess less information about political topics than do their male counterparts (Della Carpini and Keeter, 1992, 1996, Ch. 4). A recent study by Verba, Burns, and Schlozman (1997) examines the gender gap between men and women in political knowledge, political efficacy, and political interest. As indicated in Table 5-5 it appears that women are less likely than men to know the answers to a number of political questions and to care much less for discussion about politics. Both genders are equally likely to know about local politics, to pay attention to local politics, and to pay attention to the news.

According to Verba, Burns and Schlozman, the difference in interest and engagement in politics and political issues, especially beyond the local level, remains even among men and women of equal education, equal occupations, and

Table 5.5 Gender and Political Information and Interest

Measures of Political Information	Women	Men
Name of one U.S. Senator	51%*	67%
Name of second U.S. Senator	30%	43%
Name of Congressional Representative	32%	42%
Name of state representative	18%	22%
Name of head of local school system	30%	27%
Meaning of civil liberties	77%	84%
Measures of Political Interest	**Women**	**Men**
Very interested in politics (screen question)	24%	29%
Very interested in national politics	29%	38%
Very interested in local politics	21%	22%
Discuss national politics nearly every day	20%	31%
Discuss local politics nearly every day	16%	22%
Enjoy political discussion	26%	36%

*Percent giving the correct answer.
SOURCE: Adapted from Sidney Verba, Nancy Burns, and Kay Lehman Schlozman, "Knowing and Caring about Politics: Gender and Political Engagement," *The Journal of Politics,* 59 (November, 1997), p. 1055.

equal access to extensive personal resources that might support political activity. They also found, however, that in some states, having a female governor or U.S. Senator seemed to greatly increase the sense of engagement among women. Thus, they wonder whether the lack of having more women in positions of political power does discourage women from following politics more closely.

Regardless of the gender gap in interest and engagement, there are issues on which women seem to take different positions from those of their male counterparts. Within the last 20 years, as noted above, women are more likely to vote Democratic for president than are men. There also is a tendency for women to be more opposed to the use of force in foreign policy situations: women were less supportive than men of U.S. intervention even in the Gulf War, which commanded extremely high levels of support in the populace. Some scholars have suggested that women are, in general, more risk-averse than men, leading to their increased opposition to nuclear power, to environmental pollution, and, similarly, to foreign policy stances that may lead to war. There has been no clear explanation as to why the genders differ on these issues, although evidence has been presented that traces the gender gap on the use of force back over more than 40 years of survey research (Shapiro and Mahajan, 1986). There are some theories about why women take different positions on these issues, but none provides a complete explanation. It is interesting that being a "feminist" does not differentiate men from women: men and women express the same range of views on abortion laws and on equal rights for women, as we will see in more detail in Chapter 9.

THE INFLUENCE OF PEERS

If the conditions for political socialization for children include *exposure, communication,* and *receptivity,* then it seems highly likely that an individual's opinions can be influenced by friends, neighbors, and, as adults, by colleagues or co-workers in the workplace. There is, surprisingly, very little research to confirm the degree of influence that might be exercised between friends or colleagues but, if the expression of opinions might increase an individual's acceptance within the group, peer influence must exist. Some students of behavior have suggested that the expression of opinions actually works as a mechanism of social adjustment for individuals, that is, to ease their relations with others. In addition, it is thought that individuals who aspire to join a particular group begin to model the behavior of their future career, including expressing the opinions appropriate to the new role long before they actually achieve this new status. For example, a young woman who aspires to become a business executive might begin dressing in business attire and discussing the stock market and economic conditions early in her college career, long before she begins the process of job interviews for her intended position.

Some of those scholars who looked at childhood socialization did examine the relationships between elementary and high school friends in terms of political opinions. The Niemi and Jennings study of parents and high school students also included the students' best friends of the same sex for some questions on party identification and issues. Considering the early age at which partisanship is transmitted by parents, it is not surprising that there was little agreement among peers on party identification. There was some evidence of peer agreement on political issues, most notably on those that affect younger people. A study by Langton (1969), however, produced stronger results. Studying children in the Caribbean, he found that when children of middle class families were attending school with mostly working class children, their views moderated toward those of their peers. The converse was also true. In European nations like Italy, where the political party structure is much more ideological, students are likely to have friends from the same social and political background.

These scant results confirm our common sense knowledge of adolescent behavior. Except during an election year, when there may be some activity that includes youth, political issues are not very important to young people, so why would we expect peer groups to try to influence their members on such issues? Peer groups are extremely powerful in transmitting the correct and accepted social norms and behaviors to their members, so one would expect that if political issues impacted their lives, peers would be agents of political socialization. Remember that in 1992, MTV for the first time took an active role in the political campaign, launching its "Rock the Vote" series to increase participation in the elections among young people. The campaign was generally evaluated as effective in increasing voting turnout in the 18 to 21-year-old age group.

The influence of peers among adults is theorized and sometimes assumed but there is very little research to report. There is some work that shows that husbands and wives tend to hold similar opinions, especially relative to their socioeconomic class and educational levels. In addition, the research on the impact of religion on individuals' opinions demonstrates that for Catholics and for evangelicals, high levels of formal religious observance are associated with the holding of opinions more reflective of the church and its leadership. Although one could speculate that those who are more active in church are internalizing the beliefs of the leadership, it is also possible that the influence of fellow worshipers who are also friends and social companions is quite pervasive. Certainly in the case of more cultlike religious groups such as the Church of Scientology, society believes that it is peer pressure that keeps members in strict conformance with church beliefs.

Similarly, in the case of beliefs shared by colleagues and coworkers, it is very difficult to ascertain whether working journalists or individual members of labor unions or stockbrokers share political viewpoints because of their self-selection into a particular career or because the contact with peers influences their opinions. What we know about political socialization and how it relates to the need for social approval by children might suggest that adult peer socialization is a more powerful effect than we recognize. One reason that we have so little evidence about the impact of peers is that it is difficult to measure through survey research. Most people are reluctant to admit that they hold certain opinions to "please others," and, in most cases, they may have internalized a viewpoint so firmly that it is now their own personal opinion. Finally, individuals who live in the same neighborhood, belong to the same church, or work in the same company may share opinions due to a recognition of the best interest of the neighborhood or company. What is good for the company may be good for the individual and, therefore, good for all of the coworkers in the firm. Such a complex set of influences is very difficult to disentangle so that the degree of peer influence can be measured.

GENERATIONAL INFLUENCES ON OPINION

Common sense and personal life experience lead us to expect differences in opinions between different generations of Americans. Grandparents rarely seem to approve of grandchildren piercing body parts, living together without benefit of marriage, or choosing a career in rock music. Yet, these are mostly personal, lifestyle decisions. Do the generations hold different views on current public issues? Does growing older tend to create a generation of conservative voters? There is evidence in the presidential vote patterns over time that older Americans are somewhat more likely to be Republican in their voting habits and, perhaps, more conservative on some issues. The rate of participation in elections rises steeply as cohorts age, with more than 70% of registered voters over the age of 45 turning out to vote, as compared to less than 40% for those 18 to 20 years old.

The tendency for older Americans to classify themselves more as conservatives than do the younger groups is a generational difference that we attribute to **life cycle effects.** As individuals age, they are more aware than ever of their own interests and will express opinions that support those interests, and they are probably more aware of changes in society that they do not approve or share. The oldest generation of Americans is less comfortable with change and unlikely to wish to participate in some of the changes taking place in society. Younger Americans, who are likely to vote and participate in politics at a very low level, are more interested in establishing their lives, pursuing a career, and finding companionship than discussing political issues. Interest in and engagement with politics definitely shows an increase for individuals after they turn 30, probably stemming from their interest in their communities, their economic prospects and their families' well-being. So, there are life cycle changes both in participation and in interest in certain public issues.

There are other types of differences between members of different age groups that can be identified as true **generational effects**. What is meant by that term is that a cohort of people who were born at a certain time demonstrate a similarity of political view or political attachment that is related to events that took place during the years in which they formed a political identity. As will be discussed in Chapter 6, research demonstrates that Americans who came of political age, that is, became engaged with politics, during the years of the Great Depression, are likely to still be strong Democratic voters. Americans who became adults before 1930 are likely to reflect the Republican attachment of their youthful years. Similarly, it appears that Americans who came of age during the years of the Reagan presidency may become identified with the Republican Party in greater numbers than other generations. Baby Boomers show much less proclivity towards one party or another perhaps because one party did not dominate during their formative years. Some evidence suggests that Americans who became adults during the period of 1960s protest movements demonstrate less attachment in general to the political parties as a result of their disagreement with the political system in their youth.[2]

The generational effect that brought so many Americans to the Democratic Party during the presidency of Franklin Roosevelt was also the period that persuaded many African American voters to move from a Republic affiliation to a Democratic one. One of the questions that remains unanswered for students of this phenomenon is whether any political event of the last 50 years has had such an enduring effect. Partisan identity, once fixed either by childhood socialization or a generational event, tends to persist for the rest of the individual's life if the attachment is strong enough. Independent voters tend to stay independent voters as well. As will be discussed in Chapter 6, the increase in independent voters may signal a general weakening of partisan identification unless a major political event places its imprint on a new generation of voters.

THE MEDIA'S INFLUENCE ON OPINION

The impact of the news media on public opinion is a vast topic, one which currently has its own extensive literature (Graber, 1997; Bennett, 1996; Davis, 1996), and one which is constantly changing as the mechanisms for delivering news and information undergo rapid change. At one point in this nation's history, the only medium for the transmission of news and political debate to the people was through local newspapers. Today, more than 90% of Americans use television for their major source of news. More than 30 million Americans tune in to primetime network broadcasts every evening. Those broadcasts, in turn, generate significant income for the corporations that own the networks through the advertising dollars generated by the news.

Before the advent of cable television and, more recently, satellite television, many commentators feared that the news was becoming too homogenized: all Americans would receive a sanitized, and, perhaps, biased version of the news from the three networks. The electronic revolution has certainly displaced that fear. Today, Americans choose between major networks including the FOX network, CNN and other cable news sources, and hundreds of sources of information available over the Internet. Instead of centralized news, political information today is fragmented and, in the case of the Internet, may be fraudulent or totally politicized, depending on the source.

In terms of influencing the opinions of Americans of all ages, the media performs three functions: supplying information about issues and candidates through broadcasting the news; setting the agenda for public debate through editorial decisions; and conveying a vast array of messages from the government, politicians, and major interests to the public.

Supplying Information

Americans readily admit their dependence on the media, and in particular, television, for news about their community, the nation, and the world. In terms of how much influence it has on their opinions about public issues, it is important to ask what kinds of information the news is supplying and how people actually process the news they receive. The question of whether the news is biased has occupied the attention of both liberal and conservative commentators for decades. Liberals claim that the editorial bias of media is conservative because all forms of the media, with the exception of public radio and public television, are actually part of corporate America, with a bias towards capitalism. Conservatives point to a 1996 study that showed that 61% of journalists surveyed identified themselves as liberals and that 89% voted for President Clinton in 1992[3]. In every election year, the media are studied to identify any such biases, with the result that there is little evidence to back up the claims of either liberals or conservatives. There is, however, a school of thought that charges the media with a form of **establishment bias.** Work by Graber, Exoo, and others finds that the question of which stories to cover and which sources to use is definitely slanted toward the government and known establishment sources. Bennett argues that what the media do is to *index* the degree of interest and conflict in the establishment and then, if there is debate within the elites, cover that story. What this means is that many issues that may confront ordinary Americans or the issues that truly impact minority or severely disadvantaged groups receive little or no news attention.

The other charge that is leveled against the media, both print and electronic, is that a premium is put on sensationalism and high interest stories. In the case of newspapers, the coverage of campaigns has become focused on the question of who is winning "the horse-race" rather than on the policy positions and character of the candidates. Increased polling by the media provides data for these stories. In the last few elections, the major national papers and network news organizations have attempted to provide more substantive information about the candidates, but there is still more headline news in the polls. Television news is particularly subject to the charge of putting entertainment first. In fact, a recent story in the *New York Times* said that the NBC nightly news seemed to be moving into first place in viewers because it had taken a "lighter," more peppy approach to the news. In part, the actual physical characteristics of television news push it into a show business format. Time is limited, and viewer interest is stimulated by short, tight stories with great video shots. The effect is that the news is sometimes dominated by available footage rather than complicated news stories.

What do people learn from the news that has an impact on their opinions?[4] A recent study by the Pew Center (the Pew Research Center, 1997) showed that people's interest in political news declined for the second straight year in 1997, with no domestic news story making the top ten list of news stories for the year. People watch the news in great numbers, but they actually pay attention to a subset of stories. Graber's year-long work with a panel of Chicagoans showed that people scan the news both on television and in newspapers, but remember only about half of the important news stories of a year. They paid close attention to less than one-quarter of all the major news stories, although they discussed many more with friends. The stories that people found most interesting were those with personal relevance, those with human interest, and those with societal importance. People also admitted to rejecting some stories because they were of no interest to them or because the issue was beyond their control (Graber, 1984: 86–87). Given the relative lack of new information presented on television news, Graber finds that people's learning from the news is quite sensible. As she concludes, " the findings indicate that people know how to cope with information overload, that they balance a healthy respect for their own pleasures with moderate willingness to perform their civic duties, and that they have learned to extract essential kernels of information from news stories while discarding much of the chaff" (97).

Setting the Agenda

Another function of the media for shaping public opinions is to shape the agenda of what is news. Part of that **agenda-setting** function is the identification of the important stories and debates to be covered as discussed above. Not only do the media identify the issues that will become "headline news," but their treatment of those issues may also have an effect on public opinion. Iyengar and Kinder (1987) suggested that media **priming,** the choosing of which issues to emphasize as important, shapes the political choices that citizens need to make. In addition, the media are responsible for **framing** the issue in terms of defining how responsibility is to be assigned for the problem.

The media also shape the agenda for the public through their choice of coverage for political campaigns and issues. Patterson has examined the media's blind emphasis on the daily events of the campaign and its treatment of campaigning as a type of national game over several election cycles. He suggests that the ordinary citizen is ill-served by the media during campaigns because the coverage actually leads the public away from thinking about the real issues that divide parties and candidates. It is not, he points out, the fault of the media, but a result of letting the media set the agenda for public discussion.

The media have actually formalized the process of setting the agenda for the public through their focus on the "most important problem" question that is asked by Gallup in its national poll and is repeated by polls sponsored by the media. A study by MacKuen (1981) compared the content of news stories with the responses to the most-important problem question over a period of 15 years. He found that the most important problem identified by survey respondents tended to follow an increased number of reports on that problem. For example, the "drug problem" rose to number one on the most-important problem list following two months of national stories about drug usage. Other stories have shown that media coverage of problems actually tends to peak after the problem itself has peaked in intensity. There is no question that people do tend to follow the lead of the media in determining which issues are most important to discuss. As noted earlier, however, this means that some problems do not make it to national prominence due to a lack of coverage, either because the political leadership does not want to address these problems or because the problem is too complex to cover.

Conveying Messages

Finally, the media conveys the messages of candidates, political leaders, and political interests to the people as part of the attempt by these message-senders to influence public opinion. This "manipulation" of the news media has reached new proportions in American political campaigns, with the sending of huge advance teams to the site of candidate speeches to assure that the most flattering and patriotic camera shots will be released to the news. The same kind of planning also takes place for presidential visits at home and abroad. The use of the media to send messages was probably perfected by Franklin Delano Roosevelt who used his "fireside" chats on radio to assure the nation during the Depression and World War II. Since that time presidents and other political leaders have learned to use television to grab the attention of the people. Politicians at every level have also learned to try to control news reporting through the practice of "spin control," which means that the politician explains on camera how an event or speech is to be regarded, thus preempting the comments of the journalists and editors.

Politicians are not the only practitioners of using the media for messages. Corporate America, interest groups, foreign leaders, nonprofit groups, and consumer advocates all try to get news coverage of their messages to try to influence public opinion. And, as the degree of sophistication increases, all of these players are more conscious of the public relations strategies necessary to convey a message via the media. During the United Parcel Service strike of 1997, the Teamsters Union was widely regarded as the public relations victor through its constant focus on the needs of the workers, the overuse of part-time employees, and the fairness of its demands. The success of the union in sending those messages to the public improved the image of that individual union and the labor movement as a whole.

To what extent are individuals influenced by these attempts at media manipulation? Research conducted by McClure and Patterson during a presidential election suggests that most people view campaign advertisements with considerably selectivity (1976; Patterson, 1980; also the early work of Lazarsfeld, et al., 1944). They watch the ads of the candidates they like and generally reject or ignore messages sent by candidates they have rejected. For all of the money spent on advertising for candidates, there is very little evidence that a voter will change his or her mind in response to the information in ads. The truly independent voter, and those voters with the least information about politics and the system, are those who are most likely to be influenced by the information received through the media. The impact of the media on non-campaign issues is also not as great as the message-senders think. Graber and others suggest that most people use the media as a supplement to information that they gain in other ways—from experience, from friends and colleagues, and from their own perceptions and memories.

As we have seen, certain influences act on the individual earlier in life, that is, the ethnicity of an individual and, possibly, his or her religious background are part and parcel of the family environment in which the child is raised. The formal educational system influences the child or, at minimum, mediates some of the family effects of socialization, as does the interaction with peers and the media during childhood. As an adult, socialization continues through peers, spouse and family, generational effects, and the impact of the media. In the chapters that follow, we will look at how these influences impact public opinion about the issues that have confronted the American electorate in recent years.

Polls, Polling and the Internet

To look at a site that is aimed at the political education of high school students, try Junior State of America:

> http://www.jsa.org

Another well-known site that caters to younger Americans is Rock the Vote:

> http://www.rockthevote.org/

Some sites encourage individuals to participate in "voting" on a particular issue. Of course, this constitutes a totally unscientific poll. One of these is VoteLink at:

> http://www.votelink.com

NOTES

1. The project was sponsored by major U.S. corporations, including J.C. Penney Co., Inc., America West Airlines, Ford Motor Company, Hilton Hotels Corp., and Knight-Ridder Inc., each of which provided contributions of more than $250,000.

2. Some studies suggest that there may also be a phenomenon known as *period effects,* which means that historical events influenced citizens of all age groups. It is possible that the Watergate scandal increased political cynicism throughout the electorate, not just in the generation that came of age during that period.

3. The data were published in the *Washington Post* on May 27, 1996. The poll was taken by the Freedom Forum and the Roper Center. Commentators criticized the poll on the ground that the survey only reached 139 Washington journalists.

4. There is some controversy within the scholarly community over the degree to which the media actually influences opinions. While many scholars, like Graber and others, find that people do "learn" from the media and pay attention to media stories that interest them, research on how people decide between candidates and how they formulate political opinions has shown limited media impact. This body of research is sometimes called the "minimal effects" model.

6

Political Orientations

Questions to Consider:

Do Americans think about politics as liberals or conservatives?

Are Democrats or Republicans more dominant among voters?

To what extent do Americans trust the government and its leaders?

Do Americans believe they can influence the government?

In the previous chapters we have outlined some of the ways in which public opinion is formed, how it is measured, and how such data are used. With this chapter, we turn to the distribution of public opinion on a variety of topics, and we begin with some broad orientations that are of particular import in American politics: political ideology, party identification, trust in government and political institutions, political efficacy, and the power of the federal government.

Political ideology is central to any discussion of public opinion. As Bennett (1995: 259) has noted, ideology among the American public "has been a staple of public opinion research over the past 30 years." In Jacoby's terms, "[V]irtually all political stimuli (candidates, parties, issue stands, etc.) can be described in ideological terms (1991: 202). Therefore, ideological thinking is likely to have multiple effects on public opinion. As argued by Neuman (1986: 18), "[t]he terms *liberalism* and *conservatism* have served for the last century as the fundamental yardsticks for measuring political life . . . political life is incomprehensible without some sense of its central continuum."

Similarly, party identification has consistently been shown to be "an important source of policy orientations in the American electorate " (Jacoby, 1988: 643) and to be strongly associated with positions on policy issues (Abramowitz and Saunders, 1998). The authors of *The American Voter* (Campbell, Converse, Miller, and Stokes, 1960) attributed a central role to party identification in influencing attitudes toward candidates and issues, and this role has been demonstrated to be more or less enduring over time (Miller, 1991: 566). As individuals develop a personal attachment to one of the parties, the party's position on a specific issue supplies a useful guide for the person's attitude on that issue. Party identification and political ideology are rated as overriding orientations in American politics because "previous research has shown that they have the strongest, most pervasive effects across a variety of issues" (Jacoby, 1991: 183). These orientations help determine individuals' positions on policy issues.

While ideology and party identification have generally been viewed as independent variables[1] and are significant for their role in shaping positions on other issues, orientations such as confidence in institutions, trust in government, and political efficacy are important in that they provide the context within which political opinions are shaped. As stated by Miller (1974: 951), "[A] democratic society cannot survive for long without the support of a majority of its citizens." When confidence in political institutions, trust in government, and political efficacy are low, the potential for change in the political and social system is enhanced. Diminished confidence in institutions raises questions about the legitimacy of government, making it more difficult for the government to remain effective without the leeway provided by diffuse support (Hetherington, 1998: 791). Without public support for institutions and the sense by the public that they are able to have some effect on the political process, "problems will begin, will become more acute, and if not resolved will provide the foundation for renewed discontent" (Hetherington, 1998: 804).

Finally, the issue of the power of the federal government is included as a "fundamental orientation" because divisions on this question run to the core of this country's history. Many of the key battles between the Federalists and the anti-Federalists during the ratification of the Constitution were over the amount of power that should rest with the central government. The question of the power of the federal government has been a source of conflict through such landmark events as the Supreme Court's ruling in the case of *Gibbons v. Ogden,* the Civil War and Reconstruction, the New Deal, World War II, and the Great Society programs developed in the 1960s. The recent trend toward increasing states' rights and the devolution of power from the central government reflects the continuing conflict between liberals and conservatives on the proper role for the government. The division on this basic issue of the federal government's role has an impact on the public's views on more specific policy issues.

POLITICAL IDEOLOGY

In the study of "the American mind" there has been considerable controversy over the extent to which the American public engages in ideological thinking about politics. A public that perceives political debate and policy issues in ideological terms would measure issues against a fairly strict philosophical standard, whether that is liberal, marxist, conservative, or libertarian. If voters are highly ideological, they are unlikely to vote against affirmative action in the same election in which they elect a very liberal senator who supports this policy. The authors of *The American Voter* (Campbell, Converse, Miller, and Stokes, 1960: 250) argued that only a small segment of the public thought about politics in ideological terms. As portrayed by Converse (1964), the typical American voter possessed low levels of information about public affairs, did not exhibit meaningful beliefs on policy issues, and voted more on the basis of social characteristics and party identification than because of any well-reasoned consideration of the parties and candidates.

In the almost 40 years since these findings were presented there has been a great deal of debate over the extent to which Americans engage in ideological thinking. Some have argued that the low levels of such thinking found among the mass public are more a result of measurement error in the survey questions used in examining this topic than a lack of sophistication among the public (see, for example, Achen, 1975; Erikson, 1979). Others, such as Norman Nie and his colleagues (Nie with Anderson, 1974; Nie, Verba, and Petrocik, 1976), maintain that the rather unflattering portrait of the mass public provided by *The American Voter* authors was largely a product of the time in which the research was conducted and that the increased salience of politics in the 1960s and 1970s led to more ideological thinking among the public. Critics of this research (for example, Bishop, Oldendick, Tuchfarber, and Bennett, 1978; Bishop, Tuchfarber, and Oldendick, 1978; Sullivan, Piereson, and Marcus, 1978) contend that this perceived increase in political sophistication was not a true change in the way the public thinks about politics, but rather an artifact resulting from the way in which these attitudes were measured. Another argument advanced in this debate is that while the public does not demonstrate the broad, overarching connectedness of opinion generally associated with ideological thinking, there are subgroups of individuals—issue publics—who are well-informed and exhibit consistent opinions across a more narrow range of issues (Natchez and Bupp, 1968; Kirkpatrick and Jones, 1974; Carmines and Stimson, 1980).

Despite the differing perspectives and conclusions of these studies, one common element is their use of the **liberal–conservative continuum** as the primary dimension underlying political thinking in the United States. Viewing issues in terms of this "left–right" political spectrum permits individuals to make sense of a broad range of events, and this dimension has proven to be a useful organizing principle for studying the beliefs of the American public.

As with the term "public opinion," there are a wide variety of definitions and uses of the term "ideology." Common to many of these uses—and central to our definition of this term—is the notion of a closely linked set of beliefs about the goal of politics and the most desirable political order that enables in-dividuals to interpret political events and provides a guide to decision making. Two relatively moderate ideological positions, liberalism and conservatism, have dominated the U.S. political system. While there are numerous distinc-tions between liberals and conservatives, their basic split is over the role of gov-ernment: liberals believe that government should take strong positive action to solve the nation's social and economic problems, while conservatives hold that individuals are primarily responsible for their own well-being. Conservatives are less supportive of government initiatives to redistribute income or to craft programs that will change the status of individuals (Mayer, 1992: 11–13).

To a large extent, the American public does not think about politics in an ideological manner. In their examination of this topic the authors of *The Amer-ican Voter* found that less than 5% of the public could be classified as ideologues, with another 9% being "near ideologues." Forty-two percent thought about politics in terms of "group benefits," 24% conceptualized it in terms of the "nature of the times," and 22% exhibited "no issue content" in their political thinking (Campbell, Converse, Miller, and Stokes, 1960: 249). Similarly, when the ideological character of the public's thinking is measured in terms of **con-straint** or consistency among idea elements, "there is virtually nothing in the way of organization to be discovered" (Converse, 1964: 230). Although varia-tions in the ideological character of the American mind have been reported (for example, Field and Anderson, 1969; Pierce and Hagner, 1980; Nie with Anderson, 1974; Nie, Verba, and Petrocik, 1976), the proportion of the citizens who exhibit consistent, well-integrated attitudes across a range of policy issues is rather small (Smith, 1989).

Despite these limitations, the liberal-conservative continuum has proven to be a valuable tool in the study of public opinion, and there is a general tendency for individuals to be fairly consistently "left," "right," or centrist in their politi-cal views (Zaller, 1992: 26). Although only a small segment of the public en-gages in the higher-order political thinking marked by an active use of ideolog-ical dimensions of judgment or high levels of constraint among idea-elements, a large majority of American citizens classify themselves as liberal, moderate, or conservative. While this ideological identification is distinct from ideological thinking, it has been shown to have an impact on issue attitudes (Jacoby, 1991: 202). One way to measure the ideological stance of the American public, which has been used in the American National Election Studies since 1972, is to ask:

> We hear a lot of talk these days about liberals and conservatives. Here is a 7-point scale (extremely liberal; liberal; slightly liberal; moderate, middle-of-the-road; slightly conservative; conservative; extremely conservative) on which the political views that people hold are arranged from extremely liberal to extremely conservative. Where would you place yourself on this scale, or haven't you thought much about this?

Responses to this question are shown in Table 6-1 and Figure 6-1.[2] These data show that, despite some minor fluctuations, the ideological composition of the American electorate has remained fairly constant during this period,

Table 6.1 Ideological Identification, 1972–1996

Ideology	1972	1974	1976	1978	1980	1982	1984
Extremely Liberal	2%	2	2	2	2	2	2
Liberal	10	15	10	11	9	9	10
Slightly Liberal	14	11	12	13	14	12	13
Middle-of-the-Road	37	36	38	36	31	35	33
Slightly Conservative	21	17	19	19	21	20	20
Conservative	14	16	16	16	20	19	19
Extremely Conservative	2	3	3	3	3	3	2

	1986	1988	1990	1992	1994	1996
Extremely Liberal	2	2	2	3	2	2
Liberal	8	8	11	12	8	9
Slightly Liberal	14	13	12	13	10	14
Middle-of-the-Road	37	31	36	31	33	30
Slightly Conservative	20	22	21	21	19	20
Conservative	17	20	15	17	24	21
Extremely Conservative	2	4	3	4	4	4

SOURCE: American National Election Studies.

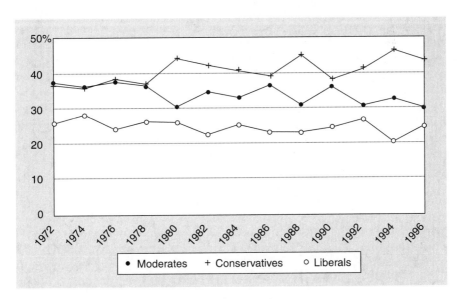

FIGURE 6.1 Ideological Identification, 1972–1996

SOURCE: American National Election Studies.

with liberals comprising about one-fourth of the public, one-third classifying themselves as moderates, and roughly 40% identifying themselves as conservatives. During this time, the percentage of conservatives has consistently been greater than that of liberals, and the difference has increased slightly over time. In 1972, for example, 26% identified themselves as liberals while 37% held conservative views; in 1996, the corresponding percentages were 25% and 44%.

Fluctuations in the percentage expressing liberal or conservative views also varied with the fortunes of the two major parties. In 1980, when Ronald Reagan was elected to his first term, the percentage of conservatives jumped by 7% from that found in 1978. Similarly, 1994, when Republicans gained control of the House of Representatives for the first time in 50 years, saw the highest percentage of self-identified conservatives, 47%. The lowest percentage of respondents identifying themselves as liberals, 20%, also occurred in this year, although this percentage was somewhat higher in 1992 (27%) and 1996 (25%) when Bill Clinton won the contest for the presidency.[3]

Table 6-2 shows the breakdown of ideological identification among various subgroups for selected years. The most consistent difference is between blacks and whites, with a higher percentage of blacks identifying themselves as liberals. In 1996, 33% of blacks considered themselves liberals, compared to 25% of whites, while 46% of whites and 31% of blacks said they were conservatives.

There are also consistent differences across age groups. In each year, the highest percentage of liberals is found among those 18 to 29. In 1996, more than half of those age 65 or older labelled themselves conservatives.

Across educational levels, there is a tendency for those with more education to identify themselves as either liberal or conservative, while those with less than a high school education are more likely to say their views are "middle-of-the-road." Across income levels, a higher percentage of low income individuals call themselves liberal, while those with higher family incomes are more likely to be conservatives. Although the differences between men and women are not large, this difference has increased over time with more men now identifying themselves as conservatives.

Political activists tend to be more ideological in their beliefs. Polls of convention delegates have consistently shown them to be more extreme in their ideology than average party members. In 1996, 15% of Democratic convention delegates (and no Republican delegates) classified themselves as "very liberal," while 35% of Republican delegates (compared to 1% of Democrats) considered themselves "very conservative" (Bennet, 1996: B-8). In later chapters in which differences in opinion on policy positions among ideological groups are reported, this variable will be shown to be a significant discriminator across a range of issues.

PARTY IDENTIFICATION

Party identification is one of the most important elements in the American political mind. Compared to other political attitudes it is relatively stable over time (Converse and Markus, 1979: 38) and has been shown to be highly

Table 6.2 Political Ideology by Demographic Characteristics, 1972–1996

	1972			1980			1988			1996		
	Lib.	Mid.	Con.	Lib.	Mid.	Con.	Lib.	Mid.	Con.	Lib.	Mid.	Con.
AGE												
18–29	39	35	27	31	28	41	30	32	38	34	34	32
30–44	23	37	40	25	30	45	26	27	47	28	28	44
45–64	17	41	42	22	31	47	16	36	48	23	29	48
65 and Older	21	37	42	22	35	43	20	34	46	14	36	51
Race												
Black	54	31	14	40	30	30	33	34	33	33	36	31
White	23	38	39	24	31	46	22	31	47	25	30	46
Sex												
Male	26	36	38	26	26	48	25	27	49	21	27	52
Female	26	38	36	25	35	40	22	35	43	30	34	36
Education												
Less Than High School	19	46	35	21	35	44	28	37	35	19	40	41
High School Graduate	20	43	37	20	38	42	21	35	43	16	43	41
Some College	33	32	35	31	25	44	21	30	49	26	27	47
College Graduate	39	19	41	31	20	48	26	24	50	34	21	45
Income												
Lowest Quartile	33	37	30	27	35	38	29	31	40	27	37	36
Second Quartile	26	40	34	26	33	42	24	31	45	24	37	40
Third Quartile	23	37	40	28	30	42	23	36	41	26	33	41
Highest Quartile	25	37	38	21	24	55	19	29	52	26	22	52

SOURCE: American National Election Studies.

Table 6.3 Party Identification, 1952–1996

Party Identification	1952	1956	1958	1960	1962	1964	1966	1968
Strong Democrat	23	21	28	21	24	27	18	20
Weak Democrat	26	24	23	26	24	25	28	26
Leaning Democrat	10	7	7	6	8	9	9	10
Independent	6	9	8	10	8	8	12	11
Leaning Republican	7	9	5	7	6	6	7	9
Weak Republican	14	15	17	14	17	14	15	15
Strong Republican	14	15	12	16	13	11	10	10
	1970	**1972**	**1974**	**1976**	**1978**	**1980**	**1982**	**1984**
Strong Democrat	20	15	18	15	15	18	20	17
Weak Democrat	24	26	22	25	25	24	25	20
Leaning Democrat	10	11	14	12	14	13	11	11
Independent	14	13	15	15	14	13	11	11
Leaning Republican	8	11	9	10	10	10	8	13
Weak Republican	15	13	14	14	13	14	15	15
Strong Republican	9	11	8	9	8	9	10	13
	1986	**1988**	**1990**	**1992**	**1994**	**1996**		
Strong Democrat	18	18	20	17	15	18		
Weak Democrat	23	18	19	18	19	20		
Leaning Democrat	11	12	13	14	13	14		
Independent	12	11	11	12	10	8		
Leaning Republican	11	13	12	13	12	11		
Weak Republican	15	14	15	15	15	16		
Strong Republican	11	14	10	11	16	13		

SOURCE: American National Election Studies.

correlated with other indicators of political behavior, political attitudes, and the vote decision (Weisberg, 1980: 33). As defined by Campbell, Converse, Miller, and Stokes (1960: 121), party identification is a "standing decision," perhaps made in childhood, to support one party or the other. It is "generally a psychological identification, which can persist without legal recognition or evidence of formal membership and even without a consistent record of party support." The measure of party identification used in the NES first asks respondents, "Generally speaking, do you think of yourself as a Republican, a Democrat, an Independent, or what?" Those who classify themselves as Republicans or Democrats are then asked, "Would you call yourself a strong (Republican, Democrat) or a not very strong (Republican, Democrat)?" Those who classify themselves as Independents are asked, "Do you think of yourself as closer to the Republican or Democratic Party?" The result is a 7-point classification scheme ranging from Strong Republican to Strong Democrat. The distribution of these responses from the NES data is shown in Table 6-3 and summarized in Figure 6-2.[4]

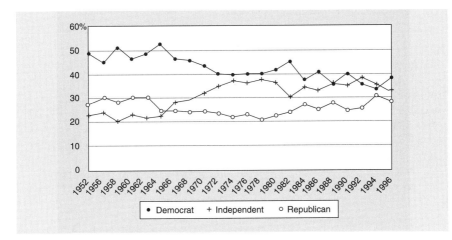

FIGURE 6.2 Party Identification, 1952–1996

SOURCE: American National Election Studies.

These data show a decline in identification with the Democratic party during this period. Prior to 1966, approximately half of the public called themselves Democrats. Since then, this percentage has declined, and today slightly more than one-third of Americans identify with the Democratic party. There has been less variation during this era in the percentage of the electorate identifying themselves as Republican. This percentage has hovered around 25%, ranging from a low of 21% in 1978 to a high of 31% in 1994. Corresponding to the decline in the proportion of self-identified Democrats has been the rise in the proportion of Independents. In 1952, fewer than one in four respondents considered themselves an "Independent"; over the past ten years, this proportion has consistently been about one-third.

Data from the Gallup Poll, going back to 1940, indicate that the increase in political independents has been even more striking than that portrayed in the NES data, and that there has been more distinct movement by adherents of the two major parties. In 1940, 42% of the electorate considered themselves Republicans, 35% were Democrats, and 18% thought of themselves as Independents. After 1940, the percentage of Democrats increased, reaching its highest level—as in the NES data—in 1964, while the proportion of Republicans declined fairly steadily, reaching its low point in 1979. During this time, the percentage of Independents continuously increased, and more recent Gallup Poll data show the public to be fairly evenly divided among Democrats, Independents, and Republicans.[5]

As was the case for ideology, there have been consistent group differences in party identification. As evidenced in Table 6-4, the largest and most consistent of these differences have been between blacks and whites. In 1952, 64% of blacks indicated they were Democrats, compared to 47% of whites. Over time, the percentage of blacks who are Democrats first increased, reaching 81% in 1964, before returning to 64% in 1996. Among whites, the percentage

Table 6.4 Party Identification by Demographic Characteristics, Selected Years, 1952–1996

	1952 Dem.	1952 Ind.	1952 Rep.	1964 Dem.	1964 Ind.	1964 Rep.	1980 Dem.	1980 Ind.	1980 Rep.	1996 Dem.	1996 Ind.	1996 Rep.
AGE												
18–29	51%	29	20	50	31	19	32	48	20	34	45	22
30–44	53	23	24	51	27	21	40	37	23	36	33	31
45–64	44	22	34	57	18	24	48	30	22	40	32	28
65 and Older	45	20	35	46	14	40	48	23	29	44	26	31
Race												
Black	64	21	16	81	13	6	75	20	5	64	32	4
White	47	23	29	50	24	27	37	37	26	35	33	32
Sex												
Male	48	26	26	51	25	24	38	40	22	32	35	33
Female	49	21	30	54	21	26	44	32	24	44	32	25
Education												
Less Than High School	54	22	24	63	20	18	55	30	15	45	39	16
High School Graduate	45	23	32	48	24	28	40	39	21	42	34	24
Some College	41	23	36	40	30	30	35	39	26	38	33	29
College Graduate	24	36	40	38	25	37	34	32	34	31	31	38
Income												
Lowest Quartile	56	17	27	62	18	20	49	33	18	48	33	19
Second Quartile	52	23	25	56	21	23	46	35	19	44	31	25
Third Quartile	48	27	25	51	25	24	37	41	22	36	35	29
Highest Quartile	40	25	35	40	27	34	33	34	34	26	34	40
Ideology												
Liberals	—	—	—	—	—	—	54	36	9	65	29	6
Moderates	—	—	—	—	—	—	44	37	18	38	42	20
Conservatives	—	—	—	—	—	—	25	34	41	17	27	56

SOURCE: American National Election Studies.

Vive La Difference?

Not only is the American public fairly evenly divided between Democrats, Independents, and Republicans, it is also split in its view as to which party would do a better job of handling different problems. There are, however, issues on which one of the parties is perceived as able to do a better job than the other. The following are responses to questions from the 1996 NES, which asked respondents, "Which party do you think would do a better job of handling (this problem), or wouldn't there be much difference between them?"

Issue	Democrats	Wouldn't Be Much Difference	Republicans
Handling the nation's economy	32%	37	31
Handling foreign affairs	27	35	38
Making health care affordable	51	32	17
Welfare	38	24	38
Solving the problem of poverty	46	35	19
Deficit	27	40	33
Environment	44	43	13
Crime	24	45	31
Cut social security	11	40	50
Improve race relations	37	55	8
Raise taxes	35	35	30
Keep out of war	12	69	19

These data show that on most issues 30%–40% of the public believes there is not much difference in how well the parties would handle these issues. This percentage reaches a majority in the case of improving race relations and more than two-thirds on the issue of keeping this country out of war. These figures also indicate that—at least in 1996—the Democrats were thought to be the party that could do a better job in making health care affordable, solving the problem of poverty, protecting the environment, improving race relations, and not cutting Social Security, while more of the public thought Republicans would be the better party for handling the problem of crime, dealing with the budget deficit, and keeping the country out of war.

Other polling data from the 1996 campaign showed that the Democrats were also more likely to be seen as the party that would do a better job on issues such as helping people achieve the American dream and caring more about the needs of women. Republicans were more likely to be perceived as the party that does a better job promoting strong moral values and controlling government spending (Ladd, 1996b: 30–31).

identifying themselves as Democrats has declined during this period, while the number of Independents has increased.

Education and family income show similar and consistent relationships with party identification over time. Identification with the Democratic party is greatest among those with less than a high school education and decreases as level of education increases, while the highest percentage of Republicans is found among college graduates and declines as educational attainment decreases. Similarly, individuals with lower family incomes are more likely to be affiliated with the Democratic Party, with the percentage of Democrats decreasing across income levels, and the highest proportion of Republicans is consistently evident among the highest income group.

There is also a significant relationship between age and party identification, although the nature of this relationship changes somewhat during this time. Throughout this period, younger people are less likely than older people, particularly those age 65 or older, to call themselves Republicans (Converse, 1976: 10). In the 1950s, there was a tendency for those under age 45 to identify with the Democratic Party. As the percentage of Independents has risen over time, the increase has been particularly evident in the youngest age group. In 1996 the percentage of Independents among those 18–29 was almost 20% higher than the percentage of those 65 or older who did not identify with either of the major parties.

This period has also seen a change in the relationship between gender and party affiliation. Through the 1970s, there was little distinction between the partisan views of men and women. In 1980, slightly more women than men considered themselves Democrats, with men more likely to be Independents. By 1996, this **gender gap** in party identification had widened, with a higher percentage of women than men calling themselves Democrats (44% to 32%) and men more likely than women to say they are Republicans (33% to 25%).

These data also demonstrate the consistent relationship between ideology and partisanship. In 1980, more than half of those who considered themselves liberals also identified with the Democratic Party and less than 10% identified themselves as Republicans, while 41% of conservatives said they were Republicans and 25% were Democrats. By 1996, the split was even greater, with Democrats outnumbering Republicans among liberals, 65% to 6%, and Republican identification more evident among conservatives by a 56% to 17% margin.

CONFIDENCE IN INSTITUTIONS

In addition to political ideology and party identification, the public's general feelings toward government, its institutions, and the political process are significant components of the American mind. As Arthur Miller (1974: 951) has noted, "[A] democratic political system cannot survive for long without the support of a majority of its citizens. When such support wanes, underlying discontent is the necessary result, and the potential for revolutionary alteration of the political and social system is enhanced." If a country experiences a prolonged loss of confidence in its institutions, it can lead to a significant loss of legitimacy that reduces the country's chances of withstanding a crisis of effectiveness (Lipset and Schneider, 1983). Orientations such as confidence in institutions, trust in government, political efficacy, and views on the power of the federal government are each important elements in the public's general estimation of government and the political process.

The confidence which Americans place in their institutions provides a backdrop against which positions on more specific policy issues can be viewed. The data reported in Table 6-5 show the percentage of the public who reported having "a great deal of confidence" in the people running various institutions. In their analysis of similar data, Lipset and Schneider (1983: 42) noted that in 1966 a majority of the public had a great deal of confidence in the people running "medicine," "the military," "education," "major companies," and "the United States Supreme Court," and more than 40 percent had confidence in "the Congress," "organized religion," and the "executive branch of the federal government." Between 1966 and 1971, however, "confidence had declined in the leadership of every institution named in the surveys." The generality of these trends, they conclude, indicates that this "was not a period of declining confidence in just business or government or labor, but a loss of faith in institutional leadership generally: a trend of public alienation, in varying degrees from the leaders of all major institutions" (Lipset and Schneider, 1983: 43).

With the exception of "organized religion" in 1974, the level of confidence in the leaders of any of these institutions never reaches the level of the 1966 survey. While there have been brief periods of modestly increasing or decreasing confidence in the leaders of these various institutions since 1971, they do not compare to the stark and consistent drop found between 1966 and 1971 (Lipset and Schneider, 1987).

The trends for the governmental institutions—Congress, the executive branch, the Supreme Court, and the military—are shown in Figure 6-3 and summarized in Table 6-6. As shown in Table 6-5, all four of these institutions experienced a substantial drop in confidence between 1966 and 1971. Since that time, overall evaluations of the executive branch and the Supreme Court have remained fairly constant, while those for Congress have continued to decline and those for the military have increased, driven primarily by the public's positive response to the military success achieved in Operation Desert Storm.

As a whole, these data indicate that Americans have become increasingly distrustful of all major institutions in society. In the two most recent years, approximately 10% of the American public expressed a great deal of confidence in the leaders of the executive branch and less than 1 in 10 felt great confidence in Congress. As Patterson and Magelby (1992: 539) have noted, such data raise concerns about the health and vigor of the institutions of democratic governance.

TRUST IN GOVERNMENT

Closely related to confidence in institutions is the concept of **trust in government.** As described by Arthur Miller (1974: 952), the dimension of trust in government "runs from high trust to high distrust or **political cynicism.**

Table 6.5 Confidence in Institutions, 1973–1996

							Percentage saying "great deal of confidence"						
	Mil.	Bus.	Rel.	Edu.	Exec	Fin.	S.C.	Lab.	Con.	Med.	Pres.	Sci.	T.V.
1966	62%	55	41	61	41	—	50	22	42	72	29	—	—
1971	27	27	27	37	23	—	23	14	19	61	18	—	—
1973	33	31	36	37	29	—	32	16	24	54	23	41	18
1974	40	32	45	50	14	—	34	19	18	62	26	50	23
1975	36	20	26	32	13	32	32	10	14	52	24	42	18
1976	42	22	32	38	13	40	36	12	14	55	29	48	18
1977	37	28	41	41	28	43	37	15	20	54	25	45	18
1978	30	22	32	28	13	32	30	12	13	46	20	39	15
1980	29	28	36	30	12	33	26	16	9	54	23	45	15
1982	30	24	33	34	20	27	32	14	13	46	19	43	14
1983	31	25	30	29	14	24	28	9	10	53	18	47	13
1984	38	32	32	28	19	31	35	9	13	51	18	47	13
1986	32	26	26	28	22	21	31	9	17	47	19	42	15
1987	37	32	30	35	19	28	39	11	17	53	18	48	11
1988	36	26	21	30	17	28	37	11	16	53	20	42	14
1989	34	26	22	30	22	19	36	10	18	48	17	45	14
1990	34	26	24	27	25	17	36	11	16	46	15	41	14
1991	62	21	26	30	27	12	39	12	18	48	16	43	15
1993	42	22	23	23	12	15	31	8	7	41	11	41	12
1994	38	27	26	26	12	18	32	11	8	43	10	41	10
1996	38	24	26	23	10	25	30	12	8	45	11	43	10

Key:
Mil.: the military
Bus.: major companies
Rel.: organized religion

Edu.: education
Exec.: executive branch
Fin.: financial institutions

S.C.: Supreme Court
Lab.: organized labor
Con.: Congress

Med.: medicine
Pres.: press
Sci.: scientific community

T.V.: television

SOURCES: 1966, 1971: Louis Harris and Associates; 1973–1996: NORC General Social Survey

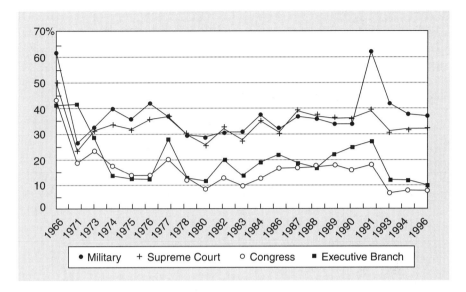

FIGURE 6.3 Confidence in Leaders of Governmental Institutions, 1966–1996

SOURCE: General Social Surveys

TABLE 6.6 Trends in Confidence in Leaders of Governmental Institutions

	Congress	Executive Branch	Supreme Court	Military
1966	42	41	50	62
1970s	21	19	32	35
1980s	14	18	33	32
1990s	12	17	35	43

Cynicism thus refers to the degree of negative affect toward the government and is a statement of the belief that the government is not functioning and producing outputs in accord with individual expectations." As such, we would expect trust in government to be related to confidence in institutions.

In the NES, there are five questions that are regularly used to measure trust. Trends for these items are shown in Figure 6-4.[6] In examining the data from the early part of this period, Miller (1974: 952) concluded that "the data reveal a strong trend of increasing political cynicism for the general population between 1964 and 1970," a trend that he attributed to dissatisfaction with the policy alternatives that the major parties offered as solutions to contemporary problems. Similarly, Lipset and Schneider (1983: 16) noted "a virtual explosion

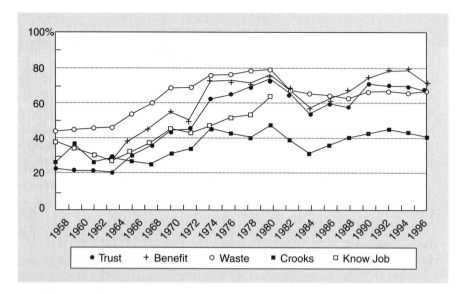

FIGURE 6.4 Trust in Government, 1958–1996 (percentage giving "distrustful" response)

SOURCE: American National Election Studies

in antigovernment feeling" between 1964 and 1970, with mistrust increasing an average of 8% between 1964 and 1968 and another 9% from 1968 to 1970.

The dramatic impact of Watergate is evident in the 1974 data. The percentage of distrustful responses on each of these items rose between 1972 and 1974, with the increase ranging from 4% on the question of whether government employees "know their jobs" to 20% on the question of whether the government is "run for the benefit of a few big interests." This relatively high level of cynicism toward government continued through 1980, and it was data of this type that led President Carter's pollster Patrick Caddell (1979: 2) to declare a "crisis of confidence" that resulted in Carter's "malaise" speech of 1979 (see Chapter 3).[7]

These indicators of trust in government rebounded slightly during the presidency of Ronald Reagan. The percentage who believed that the government can be trusted only some of the time, for example, decreased from 74% in 1980 to 59% in 1988. Similarly, the percentage who felt that the government wastes a lot of tax money declined from 80% in 1980 to 64% in 1988, and the percentage who thought the government is run for the benefit of a few big interests dropped from 77% to 67% during this period, reflecting an increase in trust resulting from an improving economy and the absence of a crisis atmosphere during much of this time (Lipset and Schneider, 1987).

The rebound in trust during the Reagan years, however, did not approach nearly the magnitude of the decline of the preceding two decades and the 1990s have seen a slight reversal of the Reagan era gains. Each of the four measures that have been asked in the 1990s shows an increase in the proportion of "distrustful" responses.[8] Moreover, despite some minor fluctuations over these

**Table 6.7 "Trust Government to Do What Is Right"
By Demographic Characteristics, 1958, 1964, and 1996**

	Percentage saying "only some of the time"		
	1958	1964	1996
TOTAL SAMPLE	24%	22	68
AGE			
18–29	21	17	67
30–44	21	20	72
45–64	27	26	64
65 and Older	32	27	66
Race			
Black	33	25	67
White	24	22	68
Sex			
Male	23	20	66
Female	25	24	69
Education			
Less Than High School	31	27	59
High School Graduate	20	18	69
Some College	16	19	68
College Graduate	16	20	70
Income			
Lowest Quartile	36	27	61
Second Quartile	22	25	68
Third Quartile	18	19	70
Highest Quartile	19	18	70
Party Identification			
Democrats	27	20	60
Independents	24	24	70
Republicans	18	27	74
Ideology			
Liberals	—	—	64
Moderates	—	—	66
Conservatives	—	—	73

The question asked was, How much of the time do you think you can trust the government to do what is right—just about always, most of the time, or only some of the time.

SOURCE: American National Election Studies.

40 years, the overall conclusion must be that for the past three decades, the American mind has exhibited a distrustful disposition toward government. It appears that the significant events of this period—Vietnam, Watergate, the energy crisis, recession, hyperinflation, campaign fund raising scandals—have produced increasingly cynical public attitudes.

As might be expected given the magnitude of these changes, this decline in trust has been evident across all subgroups (see Table 6-7). The change in the percentage who felt that the government could be trusted "only some of the time" was 44% among all respondents, and ranged from 25% among the lowest income group to 56% among Republicans. In 1958, it was those with lower family incomes, less education, Democrats, blacks, and older people who were least trustful of government. By 1996, the least educated and lowest income groups exhibited the highest levels of trust (although these groups, like all others examined, became much less trustful of government during this period), Republicans were the least trustful, and there were only minor differences in trust between blacks and whites or across age groups.

POLITICAL EFFICACY

A related broad orientation that is a significant in understanding the American mind is an individual's sense of **political efficacy.** As defined in *The Voter Decides* (Campbell, Gurin, and Miller, 1954: 187) political efficacy is "the belief that individual political action does have, or can have, an impact on the political process." As measured by these authors, the index of political efficacy consisted of responses to four agree-disagree items: (1) I don't think public officials care much what people like me think; (2) Voting is the only way that people like me can have any say about how the government runs things; (3) People like me don't have any say about what the government does; and (4) Sometimes politics and government seem so complicated that people like me can't really understand what's going on.[9] Responses to these questions over time are presented in Figure 6-5.

While these data indicate a decline in political efficacy among the American public, the changes are neither as large nor as consistent as those found for trust in government. Between 1952 and 1960, the proportion of inefficacious responses to these four items decreases slightly, a pattern consistent with an "education-driven" model in which the increasing average level of education of the population leads to increased efficacy (Converse, 1972: 326). After 1960, inefficacious responses on three of these four questions (the exception being the "voting is the only way" item[10]) increase and, with minor fluctuations, remain at a high level through 1996.

Examining the individual items, the picture that emerges is one of a public that does not feel that the means of influence is available to it or that those in power will be responsive. Over the past 25 years, close to 70% of the public has felt that politics and government are too complicated for them to understand, and the percentage of Americans who believe they have no say in what the government does now approaches about half. The proportion of the public who thinks that public officials don't care what people like them think has risen from one-fourth in 1960 to seven out of ten in 1996.

From 1968 through 1980, the NES asked two additional political efficacy items related to the "external" component of this concept: (1) Generally speaking, those we elect to Congress in Washington lose touch with the peo-

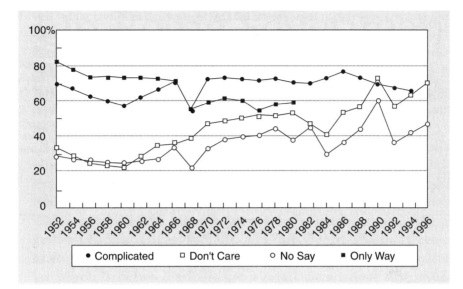

FIGURE 6.5 Political Efficacy, 1952–1996

SOURCE: American National Election Studies

Table 6.8 External Efficacy Items, 1968–1980

Congress Loses Touch

	1968	1970	1972	1974	1976	1978	1980
Agree	55	62	68	71	72	74	75
Disagree	45	38	32	29	28	26	25

Parties Only Interested in Votes

	1968	1970	1972	1974	1976	1978	1980
Agree	48	56	59	61	64	65	62
Disagree	52	44	41	39	36	35	38

SOURCE: American National Election Studies.

ple pretty quickly; and (2) Parties are only interested in people's votes, but not in their opinions. Results for these two items are provided in Table 6-8.

Trends on these two questions are similar to those for the "public officials don't care" item. The percentage of inefficacious responses increases over time, and by 1980 75% felt that Congress loses touch with people pretty quickly and 62% maintained that the parties were only interested in votes, not the opinions of the public. Both internal and external efficacy have fallen over time, with external efficacy—which refers more to perceptions of the political system—declining more rapidly (Converse, 1972: 334; Miller, 1979: 12). These data reinforce the view that the American mind has experienced a declining faith in governmental institutions.

POWER OF THE FEDERAL GOVERNMENT

As noted in the description of ideology, beliefs about the power of the federal government are a major feature distinguishing liberals and conservatives. Fearing the rise of an all-powerful leviathan on the Potomac, conservatives have traditionally opposed almost any proposal that would enlarge the role of the central government in American society. Liberals, on the other hand, are inclined to see government as a vehicle for promoting what they feel to be social justice; hence, they advocate programs that expand Washington's power (Bennett and Oldendick, 1977).

As described by Bennett and Bennett (1990), the public's view on the power of the federal government can be traced to this country's origins, and has changed in response to social and economic conditions. The battle over the ratification of the Constitution was, in large measure, one over the role the central government should play, with the Federalists desiring more federal power and the anti-Federalists wary of an increasing role of the central authority. Some of the earliest public opinion polls on this issue showed Americans to be slightly in favor of the growth in the power of the central government that occurred during the New Deal, and suggested that this country's involvement in World War II solidified this judgment (Bennett and Bennett, 1990: 21–24). While the issue of Washington's power was not a significant factor in the 1950s and early 1960s, it increased in salience in 1964 with the candidacy of Barry Goldwater, who had declared the federal government to be "... out of touch with the people, and out of their control" (Goldwater, 1960: 20).

It was in 1964 that the NES began asking the following question to assess public sentiment on the power of the federal government:

> Some people are afraid the government in Washington is getting too powerful for the good of the country and the individual person. Others feel the government has not gotten too strong for the good of the country. Have you been interested enough in this to favor one side over the other? [IF YES]: What is your feeling, do you think the government is getting too strong or the government has not gotten too strong?

Responses to this question are displayed in Table 6-9.

In 1964, the public was about evenly divided between those who thought the government had gotten too powerful and those who thought it had not.[11] The balance moved slightly to the side of side of those who thought the government was getting too powerful in 1966 and 1968, returned to equilibrium in 1970, and moved back to a 60-40 split in favor of those who thought the government was becoming too strong in 1972. Between 1972 and 1976 there

Table 6.9 Power of the Federal Government, 1964–1992

	1964	1966	1968	1970	1972	1976	1978	1980
Getting Too Powerful	46	59	57	48	61	72	76	76
Not Gotten Too Strong	54	41	43	52	39	28	24	24

	1984	1988	1992					
Getting Too Powerful	59	63	71					
Not Gotten Too Strong	41	37	29					

SOURCE: American National Election Studies.

was a significant increase in the perception that the government had gotten powerful, and this increase continued through 1980. Citing this and other survey results, Bennett and Bennett (1990: 31) conclude that "the early 1980s may have marked the height of a quarter-century-long shift away from support of a powerful central government."

President Reagan's first term in office appeared to calm some of the public's fears about increasing federal power. Between 1980 and 1984, the percentage who felt the government had gotten too powerful declined from 76% to 59%, and this increased only slightly (to 63%) in 1988. By 1992, however, the proportion of those with an opinion on this item who believed that the government had gotten too strong returned to seven out of ten. While the pattern of responses to this item is not as stark as some of the others examined in this chapter, the overall picture is one in which a large and increasing percentage of Americans believe that the federal government is getting too powerful. Such a finding is consistent with beliefs about the government that are less trusting and a system in which Americans feel a diminished sense of political efficacy.

Opinions about the power of the federal government among subgroups and how these opinions have changed over time provide some insight into the dynamics of the American mind on this issue. The data in Table 6-10 demonstrate that in 1964 there was a division of opinion along race, class, and party lines and, to a lesser extent, among age groups. An overwhelming majority of blacks felt that the government had not gotten too powerful, and those with more education or with higher family incomes were more likely to say the government had gotten too strong. More than twice as many Republicans as Democrats were wary of the federal government's power, and those under 30 years of age were least concerned that the government was getting too strong.

As noted by Bennett and Oldendick (1977: 9), by 1972 "... differences that had been substantial, and in some cases huge, had shrunk into insignificance." Differences across education levels and income groups as well as among age groups were no longer significant, and the gap between black and white

**Table 6.10 Power of the Federal Government
By Demographic Characteristics, 1964–1992**

	Percentage saying "government getting too powerful"					
	1964	**1970**	**1972**	**1980**	**1984**	**1992**
AGE						
18–29	42%	41	62	75	50	70
30–44	45	50	63	78	55	70
45–64	50	50	58	77	63	70
65 and Older	48	52	58	74	69	73
Race						
Black	7	24	49	49	46	59
White	50	51	62	79	60	73
Sex						
Male	48	51	63	77	62	74
Female	44	46	59	75	56	67
Education						
Less Than High School	38	44	61	67	72	70
High School Graduate	47	48	59	78	59	74
Some College	53	55	56	81	54	73
College Graduate	61	50	68	78	54	66
Income						
Lowest Quartile	38	43	58	70	65	65
Second Quartile	41	47	63	74	58	70
Third Quartile	47	53	60	78	61	75
Highest Quartile	56	49	61	80	52	68
Party Identification						
Democrats	31	41	58	62	60	60
Independents	47	49	65	82	59	76
Republicans	73	58	57	87	58	76
Ideology						
Liberals	—	—	59	65	49	59
Moderates	—	—	54	78	56	70
Conservatives	—	—	65	84	63	77

SOURCE: American National Election Studies.

attitudes had shrunk from 43% in 1964 to 13% by 1972, reflecting a large increase in the percentage of blacks who were skeptical of the government's power. Similarly, party identification, which had been a solid predictor of views on the power of the federal government in 1964, had become a less reliable divider of opinion by 1972. Differences in views by political ideology are somewhat more consistent, with a higher percentage of conservatives than liberals or moderates in each year believing that the government is becoming too powerful. By 1992, a majority of all groups examined felt the government was getting too powerful. There is some evidence that in 1964 the public's views on this question reflected policy positions and the fundamental liberal-conservative division over the proper role of the government. Over time, however, this question of "federal power" has come to reflect the public's trust in government, and the changes in opinion on this item provide another indicator of the increasing distrust of government that has developed in the American mind (Bennett and Oldendick, 1977: 23).

SUMMARY

In this chapter we have examined the more significant general orientations toward government that comprise the American mind. While there is some debate over the extent to which Americans engage in ideological thinking, the ideological composition of the American electorate—at least as measured by the number of people identifying themselves as "liberals," "moderates," or "conservatives"—has remained fairly constant over the past quarter century. About one-fourth of the public think of themselves as liberals, approximately 4 in 10 consider themselves conservatives, and a third classify themselves as "middle-of-the-road."

Party identification is one of the most important and more stable attitudes in American politics. There has, however, been significant change in the partisan composition of the American electorate over the period during which polls have measured this phenomenon. In 1940, 42% of the electorate considered themselves Republicans, 35% were Democrats, and 18% thought of themselves as Independents. The percentage of Democrats increased between 1940 and 1964, while the proportion of Republicans declined fairly steadily until about 1980. This period also saw the rise of political "Independents," and each of these three groups currently comprise about one-third of the national electorate.

The latter third of the twentieth century has also witnessed a major decline in trust in government and in the institutions of society. Recent surveys have indicated that only about 10% of the public have a great deal of confidence in the leaders of the executive branch or in Congress. Similarly, the extent to which the public exhibits trust in government has dipped sharply during this period, and this stark decline has been evident across all subgroups of the population. Paralleling this decline has been a decrease in the public's sense that its actions can have an impact on the political process.

Americans have also become increasingly concerned about the power of the federal government. While a majority of those with an opinion on this issue in 1964 believed that the government had not gotten too strong, in 1996, 70% felt that the government in Washington had become too powerful. This increase in the sense that the government was becoming too strong was also evident across all subgroups of the population.

The way in which the American mind views government and its institutions is vastly different than it was a generation ago. Americans today exhibit less psychological attachment to either of the two major parties, are less trustful of government and its institutions, fear the federal government's power, and are less certain that they can have an impact on the political process. The data presented in this chapter may not demonstrate unequivocally that a "crisis in confidence" exists in the United States, but the patterns presented here certainly should raise concerns about the stability and long-term health of the political system.

Polls, Polling, and the Internet

As you have noted from the data presented in this chapter, the foremost source of information about political partisanship and ideology are the National Election Studies, conducted by the Institute for Political and Social Research at the University of Michigan. To find information about the questions asked in each of the election year surveys, go to their web site at:

    http://www.umich.edu/~nes

For similar information from the General Social Survey, go to:

    http://www.icpsr.umich.edu/gss/

NOTES

1. Although much of the research involving these two variables has focused on their roles as independent variables (Jacoby, 1991: 202) there is also a line of research that demonstrates that they can be influenced by positions on policy issues (for example, Franklin and Jackson, 1983; Rice and Hilton, 1998).

2. While a large majority of the American public is able to place themselves along this continuum, it should be noted that a significant minority—generally around 30%—is not able or willing to place themselves on this scale. For this subset of the population, ideological identifications make little, if any, difference in their policy positions (Jacoby, 1991: 196).

3. While the questions used in other surveys differ somewhat from that used in the NES, the basic pattern of ideological identification is the same, with conservatives outnumbering liberals and the percentage of conservatives increasing slightly during this period. For the period 1973–1996, the percentage of liberals reported in the General Social Survey ranges between 23% and 30%, while the percentage of conservatives reached its height (37%) in 1994. The CBS/*New York Times* surveys (which ask, "How would you describe your views on most political matters? Generally do you think of yourself as liberal, moderate, or conservative?) consistently demonstrate that a higher percentage of the American public identifies itself as conservative than as liberal.

4. In grouping these data into three categories, the responses to the root question, "Generally speaking, do you usually think of yourself as a Republican, a Democrat, an Independent, or what?" have been used, as suggested by Warren Miller (1991). That is, those who identify themselves as "strong" or "weak" partisans are considered to be aligned with that party, while those who "lean" toward a party are treated as Independents. While there is some evidence that "leaners" behave more like partisans than true Independents (Weisberg, 1980; Smith, et al., 1995), using the distributions from the root question provides a more accurate measure of the stability and meaningfulness of an individual's identification with a party.

5. Data on party identification from other sources such as the General Social Survey show similar patterns of decline in the number of Democrats and the rise of Independents in the past 25 years. In the 1972 GSS data, for example, almost 50% of those responding identified themselves as Democrats, 28% were Independents, and 22% were Republicans. More recent GSS data have shown a fairly equal division among Democrats, Independents, and Republicans. Despite the consistent increase in Independents identified by various polling organizations, the data do not seem to indicate that Americans are "so strongly dissatisfied with the two major parties that they are actively seeking a third party to save them" (Moore, 1996a: 1).

6. The five items are: (1) How much of the time do you think you can trust the government to do what is right—just about always, most of the time, or only some of the time? (2) Would you say that the government is pretty much run by a few big interests looking out for themselves or that it is run for the benefit of all the people? (3) Do you think that people in the government waste a lot of the money we pay in taxes, waste some of it, or don't waste very much of it? (4) Do you feel that almost all of the people running the government are smart people who usually know what they are doing, or do you think that quite a few of them don't seem to know what they are doing? and (5) Do you think that quite a few of the people running the government are a little crooked, not very many are, or do you think hardly any of them are crooked at all?

7. It should be noted that Caddell's assessment was not universally shared. For a contrary view of the public's attitudes toward government during this period, see Warren Miller (1979).

8. The fifth item, involving whether "the people running the government know what they are doing," was dropped from the NES series after 1980 because some respondents offered the cynical response that "the people running the government know exactly what they are doing," implying deception and abuse of power rather than competence (Lipset and Schneider, 1983: 18).

9. It should be noted that considerable research into the concept of political efficacy has been conducted since the research reported in *The Voter Decides,* and several changes have been made in the items used to measure this concept. Among these are the division of this concept into two components: **internal efficacy**—the individual's belief that means of influence are available to him or her—and **external efficacy**—the belief that the authorities or the regime is responsive to influence attempts (Balch, 1974). Moreover, in 1966, 1968, and in each election study since 1988, these concepts have been measured not as simple agree-disagree items but as 5-point items with choices running from strongly agree to strongly disagree with "not sure; it depends" as a middle category. To maximize comparability across surveys, the middle category has been excluded in these years, the "strongly agree" responses combined with "agree," and the "strongly disagree" responses combined with "disagree."

10. In describing the distinct character of this item, Converse (1972: 329) has noted that this item "has pulled out of line rather markedly in response to phenotypic events" and should not be included with the other items in an efficacy scale. Lipset and Schneider (1983: 23) argue that the increases in this item when other indicators of political efficacy were declining "seems to reflect the growth in more active forms of political participation, particularly protest, during the 1960s."

11. Another aspect of the responses to this item involves the percentage of respondents who give "don't know" or "it depends" answers to this question. As Bennett and Bennett (1990: 28) caution, a fairly significant portion of the public does not have an opinion on this issue and "[F]ailure to determine who those without opinion are, or why one-quarter to two-fifths of the public take no position on the question, may lead to misinterpretation of public opinion on this issue." While this is important to an overall understanding of this issue, our interest is more in the division of "powerful" versus "not too powerful" responses among those with an opinion. Bennett and Bennett provide an excellent extensive discussion of the various dimensions of this issue.

7

Public Opinion on Social-Welfare Issues

Questions to Consider:

Do Americans want more government services?

Why is Social Security so popular?

What changes do Americans prefer in the health care system?

How do Americans feel about government programs for the poor?

Do liberals and conservatives truly differ on social policy issues?

In each era of American history certain issues have dominated political debate and, by so doing, have structured political campaigns and party platforms. The debate began with the struggle over ratification of the Constitution between the Federalists and anti-Federalists, and evolved to the battle between eastern commercial interests and western and southern agricultural interests, to the North-South battle over slavery, and to the sectional politics that characterized the era between the Civil War and 1920. American political culture has limited the success of left-wing political movements, and the fundamental belief in the separation of church and state has constrained the role of religion as a major dividing force in this country. In the era of modern polling, the major division in American politics has been socioeconomic (McSweeney and Zvesper, 1991).

Since 1932, the issues that have dominated discussion at the national level have involved the government's role in the economic sphere and in providing for the welfare of its citizens. Issues such as Social Security, welfare, government guarantee of jobs, civil rights, and protection of the environment reflect various components of this dimension.

Polls conducted during the early years of the New Deal showed that Americans were divided over President Roosevelt's policies during the 1930s and 1940s, favoring programs such as Social Security and wages-and-hours legislation, but opposing the National Recovery Administration and the Agricultural Adjustment Administration (Bennett and Bennett, 1990: 21). Since these early polls, surveys of the public's views on questions concerning the welfare state have reflected the central role that such issues play in American politics. In this chapter we examine a number of socioeconomic issues, including recent trends in opinion and differences in views across subgroups.[1]

SOCIAL-WELFARE ISSUES

In general terms, the public is divided on the question of the government's role in the area of social welfare. Since 1982, the NES has asked whether the government should "provide fewer services, even in areas such as health and education, in order to reduce spending" or "provide more services even if it means an increase in spending." The data in Table 7-1 show the division in opinion on this issue. If responses 1, 2, and 3 are treated as representing a "fewer services" position with 5, 6, and 7 representing a preference for "more services," the percentages holding these contrasting views have been fairly close, with the balance shifting several times during this relatively brief period. Throughout this time the percentage who held a middle position (category 4) on this issue has remained at about 30%. In 1982, those preferring fewer services outnumbered those desiring more, 41% to 31%. By 1986, the distribution had shifted in favor of those who felt the government should provide more services, 46% to 26%. The preference for more services was maintained until 1994, when the public was evenly divided. In 1996 the balance reverted to those preferring fewer government services—almost identical to the distribution at the beginning of this series. The American mind, then, is divided on the issue of whether the government should provide more or fewer services and is strongly influenced by the degree of economic well-being experienced by people. In good times, people prefer fewer government services; in bad economic times, people seek more services. In the following sections we shall see that this division can vary substantially by the specific type of service considered as well as by subgroups of the population.

Social Security

One topic that is of great interest to the American public in the area of social welfare is Social Security. This program has changed considerably since the passage of the Social Security Act of 1935, expanding from a single compulsory program, Old-Age and Survivors Insurance, to include Disability Insurance and Hospital Insurance (Part A Medicare), together with increases in benefits for its recipients (Penner, 1982: 17; Weaver and Max, 1995: 16). From its

Table 7.1 Government Provide More or Fewer Services, 1982–1996

Response Category	1982	1984	1986	1988	1990	1992	1994	1996
1. Provide Fewer Services	11%	7	5	6	5	6	7	7
2.	13	11	7	10	7	10	11	13
3.	17	16	14	16	14	15	16	19
4.	29	31	28	29	28	31	33	30
5.	14	17	19	18	18	19	18	17
6.	8	9	13	12	14	10	9	9
7. Provide More Services	9	9	14	9	13	9	7	6

SOURCE: American National Election Studies.

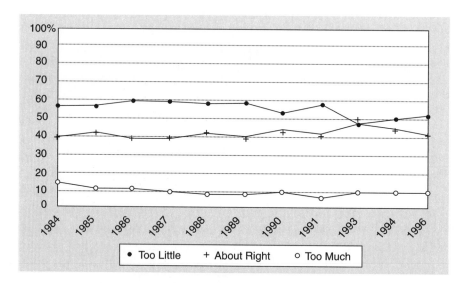

FIGURE 7.1 Government Spending on Social Security, 1984–1996

SOURCE: General Social Surveys.

inception, Social Security has been popular. As Page and Shapiro (1992: 118) report, in ". . . 1935, 89% of the public told Gallup interviewers that they favored 'old age pensions for needy persons'; 90%–94% favored such pensions according to Gallup questions asked in 1938, 1939, and 1941." While a number of questions were asked about this issue in the 1930s and 1940s, the early consensus that emerged made it of less interest to poll-takers, and there is a relative lack of appropriate cross-time data for tracking the American mind on this issue (Shapiro and Smith, 1985: 561).

The data in Figure 7-1 provide a description of the public's view on whether the government is spending too much, too little, or about the right amount on Social Security, a question that has been asked in the GSS since 1984. These data show continuing high levels of support for Social Security.

Between 1984 and 1991, a majority of the American public felt that the government was spending "too little" on Social Security. While this percentage has dipped slightly in recent years, the change has involved more people saying "about the right amount" is being spent on Social Security, rather than any sentiment that too much is being devoted to this program. Since 1985, consistently less than 1 in 10 Americans has felt that too much is spent on Social Security. Other polls demonstrate similar support for this program, with large majorities opposed to cuts in Social Security, and majorities believing that the government should do more to improve the program's benefits. Overall, the perception that Social Security is designed to benefit large numbers of people, that its targets are individuals in circumstances over which they have little or no control, and that workers put aside some of their wages for future benefits have contributed to the immense popularity of this program (Page and Shapiro, 1992: 120–121).

Education

Another area in which the public is largely supportive of government activity is education. Data from the NES conducted during the 1950s and early 1960s show that 60%–70% of the public agreed that the government in Washington ought to help cities and towns around the country if they needed help to build more schools (see Table 7-2A), and Gallup polls during this period showed substantial majorities in favor of "federal aid to help build new public schools"[2] (Page and Shapiro, 1992: 132).

Moreover, as the figures in Table 7-2B demonstrate, over the past 25 years a majority of Americans has thought that the government is spending too little on education, and this percentage is increasing. In the General Social Surveys of the 1970s, about 50% of the public felt too little was being spent on education. This increased to around 60% in the 1980s, and in the 1990s this percentage is approximately 70%. At no point in this period did more than 1 in 8 Americans believe that too much was being spent on education and in more recent surveys this percentage has been about 5%. The results from the NES on this question are consistent with these data. When asked whether federal spending on the public schools should be increased, kept the same, or decreased (Table 7-2C), slightly more than half of those surveyed in 1984 said it should be increased, with another 40% believing it should remain at the same level. The percentage who felt that spending on the public schools should be increased rose to about 65% in 1988 and remained at this level through 1996, while the percentage who thought such spending should be decreased never reached more than 7% during this period. The current state of public opinion toward funding education is substantially more liberal than it had been in earlier years (Mayer, 1992: 86).

While there is a public consensus favoring education, Americans do have some serious concerns about the performance of the country's public schools. For example, a 1994 Gallup poll found that 51% of those surveyed thought that children today get a worse education than they did, and 71% of respondents in a 1995 survey gave the public schools in the nation as a whole a grade of C, D, or F. Despite such concerns, the American public is, as Ladd (1995: 22–25) has

Table 7.2 Attitudes toward Education

A. If cities and towns around the country need help to build more schools, the
    government in Washington ought to give them the money they need.

Response Category	1956	1958	1960	1962*
Strongly Agree	53%	51	43	—
Agree	22	19	18	65
Not Sure; Depends	9	7	12	5
Disagree	6	8	9	30
Strongly Disagree	10	15	19	—

*Variant question wording.

SOURCE: American National Election Studies.

B. Are we spending too much money, too little money, or about the right amount on
    improving the nation's education system?

Response Category	1973	1974	1975	1976	1977	1978	1980
Too Little	51%	54	52	53	50	53	56
About the Right Amount	39	38	36	38	40	35	34
Too Much	9	8	12	9	10	12	10

	1982	1983	1984	1985	1986	1987	1988
Too Little	57	62	64	63	61	62	66
About the Right Amount	34	32	33	32	34	31	30
Too Much	9	6	3	5	5	7	3

	1989	1990	1991	1993	1994	1996
Too Little	69	74	71	70	72	70
About the Right Amount	28	23	24	24	22	24
Too Much	3	3	5	6	6	6

SOURCE: General Social Surveys.

C. Should federal spending on public schools be increased, decreased, or kept about
    the same?

Response Category	1984	1988	1990	1992	1996
Increased	54%	65	64	66	68
Same	40	30	32	30	26
Decreased	6	4	4	4	7

SOURCE: American National Election Studies.

noted, ". . . deeply committed to education. [They] say so every time asked, no matter how they are asked" and this support cuts across group lines.

Health Care

While the public is largely supportive of Social Security and education, it has more mixed views on the issue of health care. When the question involves government spending on health care, public support for medical care rivals that for Social Security (Page and Shapiro, 1992: 129). As shown in Table 7-3A and 7-3B, data from the 1950s and 1960s indicate that a majority of Americans believed that the government ought to "help people to get doctors and hospital care at low cost." Similarly, more people felt that the government in Washington should be responsible for seeing to it that people have help in paying for doctors and hospital bills than believe people should take care of these things themselves. Since 1973, the GSS has included a question on whether this country is spending too much, too little, or about the right amount on improving and protecting the nation's health (Table 7-3D). From 1973 through 1986, 60% of the public thought we were spending too little, and in the late 1980s and 1990s, this percentage reached 70%. At no point during this period did more than 10% of the public feel that too much was being spent on this concern.

When the question shifts to whether there should be a government insurance plan that would cover medical and hospital expenses or whether medical expenses should be paid by individuals and through private insurance, the public is more evenly divided. Treating responses 1, 2 and 3 in Table 7-3E as representing the "government insurance plan" side of the issue and points 5, 6 and 7 as the "private insurance" side, the split in public opinion on this issue was relatively even from 1970 to 1988, shifted to a majority support for a government plan during the first two years of the Clinton presidency, and moved back to balance in 1996.

The more mixed views concerning the health care system are evident in more extensive studies of this issue conducted in the 1990s. A number of analysts trace an upsurge in the salience of health care as an issue to a special senatorial election in Pennsylvania in 1991. Blendon and his colleagues (1992a: 3371) assert that in this race, "voter interest in reform of the American health care system played a central role in the come-from-behind victory of Democratic Sen. Harrison Wofford over Republican candidate Richard Thornburgh." Driven by factors such as spiraling health care costs, the number of uninsured Americans, and lack of access to adequate health care services, the United States health care system in the early 1990s was viewed as one "in crisis" (Blendon and Edwards, 1991).

A great deal of public opinion data supports the idea that Americans perceived a crisis in the health care system. For example, a 1991 Harris Survey found that 52% of the public thought that fundamental changes to the health care system were needed to make it work better, and another 35% felt that the system had so much wrong with it that it needed to be rebuilt (Blendon, Szalay, Altman, and Chervinsky, 1992: 19). Moreover, virtually any proposal to change

Table 7.3 Attitudes toward Health Care

A. The government in Washington ought to help people get doctors and hospital care at low cost.

Response Category	1956	1960
Strongly Agree	44%	54
Agree	17	12
Not Sure; Depends	9	13
Disagree	9	6
Strongly Disagree	21	16

SOURCE: American National Election Studies.

B. Do you think the government in Washington ought to help people get doctors and hospital care at low cost or do you think the government should not get into this?

Response Category	1964	1968
Government Help People	59%	61
Depends; Other	7	7
Government Stay Out of This	34	32

SOURCE: American National Election Studies.

C. In general, some people think that it is the responsibility of the government in Washington to see to it that people have help in paying for doctors and hospital bills. Others think that these matters are not the responsibility of the federal government and that people should take care of these things themselves. Where do you put yourself on this scale or haven't you made up your mind on this?

Response Category	1975	1983	1984	1986	1987	1988
1. Government Responsibility	37%	27	24	29	26	26
2.	13	20	20	20	21	22
3. Agree With Both	30	32	35	33	35	37
4.	7	11	13	12	9	9
5. People Care For Themselves	14	10	8	6	8	7

	1989	1990	1991	1993	1994	1996
1. Government Responsibility	32	32	33	29	26	28
2.	23	26	24	24	21	22
3. Agree With Both	30	30	27	32	32	33
4.	8	8	10	9	12	11
5. People Care For Themselves	7	4	6	6	9	7

SOURCE: General Social Surveys.

D. Are we spending too much, too little or about the right amount on improving and protecting the nation's health?

Response Category	1973	1974	1975	1976	1977	1978	1980
Too Little	63%	67	66	63	59	57	58
About the Right Amount	32	29	29	32	34	36	34
Too Much	5	4	5	5	7	7	8

	1982	1983	1984	1985	1986	1987	1988
Too Little	59	59	61	60	60	69	70
About the Right Amount	34	35	32	34	36	26	27
Too Much	7	6	7	6	4	5	3

	1989	1990	1991	1993	1994	1996
Too Little	70	74	71	74	67	68
About the Right Amount	27	23	26	18	24	24
Too Much	3	3	3	8	9	8

SOURCE: General Social Surveys.

E. There is much concern about the rapid rise in medical and hospital costs. Some people feel there should be a government insurance plan which would cover all medical and hospital expenses. Others feel that medical expenses should be paid by individuals and through private insurance like Blue Cross. Where would you place yourself on this scale or haven't you thought much about this?

Response Category	1970	1972	1976	1978	1984
1. Government Insurance Plan	28%	31	28	29	16
2.	9	7	9	9	10
3.	8	8	7	8	11
4.	15	14	12	13	21
5.	6	7	9	9	16
6.	10	6	10	10	14
7. Individuals/Private Insurance	24	28	25	22	12

	1988	1992	1994	1996
1. Government Insurance Plan	20	23	21	14
2.	11	15	14	10
3.	12	14	16	13
4.	19	20	18	21
5.	14	12	12	16
6.	11	9	9	14
7. Individuals/Private Insurance	13	8	10	11

SOURCE: American National Election Studies.

the health care system was supported by a majority of the public: 90% of the public favored a proposal that would make private insurance more affordable and available; 82% supported setting up a new public program to provide coverage for anyone who doesn't get health insurance through their employer; 71% favored requiring all employers, including small employers, to provide health care benefits for their employees; and 69% approved of expanding the Medicare system to cover all Americans (Jajich-Toth and Roper, 1990: 152). A 1991 *Los Angeles Times*-Gallup poll found that 91% of the American public thought there was a health care crisis in the United States (Blendon and Edwards, 1992: 2).

Public perception of the crisis in health care was one of the factors that led President Clinton to propose wide-reaching health care reform as one of key initiatives of his first term. When this plan was first introduced, it seemed to enjoy the support of the American public. As this plan was debated in Congress, however, its critics' claims that this plan "went too far" and would create too much bureaucracy raised concerns among the public. As Americans became concerned that Clinton's health care plan would create too much government involvement in the nation's health care system and would create a large and inefficient government bureaucracy, public support for this plan eroded (*Public Perspective,* 1994: 23–28), and the Clinton administration was forced to settle for only minor adjustments in health insurance coverage.

While Americans see problems in this country's health care system, are less satisfied with this system than are residents of other industrialized nations (Blendon and Donelan, 1991), and feel that more should be spent on improving and protecting the nation's health, they are not ready to support the substantial changes in the system that appeared possible under the Clinton health proposal (*Public Perspective,* 1998a: 36–39). The evidence of a perceived "crisis" in health care may be more one of a prospective crisis in which Americans fear that rapidly increasing health care costs or individual health problems might make it difficult for them to obtain adequate health care in the future (Oldendick, 1992a: 7). As a result, they are more likely to support gradual changes in this country's health care system.

Assisting the Needy

When the public's attention turns from those social-welfare programs that potentially benefit large numbers of people to a more specific focus on assisting those in need, its views become even more mixed. This is also an area in which the specific aspect of the issue addressed, as well as the way in which the question is posed, can make a significant difference in responses.

In discussing this issue, Shapiro, Patterson, Russell, and Young (1987: 120) have characterized programs for the poor as the most controversial social-welfare issue because "many Americans associate these policies with 'welfare' fraud and tangled bureaucracies and feel these programs provide disincentives for employment." Page and Shapiro (1992: 124) argue that, in principle, Americans favor government support for the needy, pointing to polls from the 1930s through the 1980s that show large majorities of the public favoring government action to "provide for all people who have no other means of making a living," or "who have no other means of subsistence" and "helping people who are unable to support themselves."

One specific aspect of government involvement in the economic arena concerns government's role in guaranteeing jobs. The data in Table 7-4 show that the public is divided on this issue, and that question wording can have an effect on opinions. In NES data from 1956 to 1960, close to 65% of respondents agreed with the idea that the government in Washington ought to see to it that everyone who wants to work can find a job. In 1964 and 1968, when seeing to "a good standard of living" was added to the government's role and "letting each person get ahead on his own" was posed as the alternative, the public was not as supportive, with slightly more than one-third feeling this should be the government's role and a majority believing that "the government should just let each person get ahead on his own."

From 1972 to 1996, the NES used a 7-point version of this question. Throughout the period the percentage on the "let each person get ahead on his own" side of the scale has been greater than that for the "government should see to it" position, and in 1996 a majority supported letting individuals get ahead on their own (responses 5, 6, and 7). The GSS measure of this question used during the same period asked not about jobs, but whether the government in Washington should do everything possible to improve the standard of living for all poor Americans as opposed to letting each person take care of himself. In 1975, the balance on this question was on the "government responsibility" side, with 40% saying this was the government's role, 24% feeling that people should help themselves, and 36% agreeing with aspects of both sides or otherwise adopting a middle position (Table 7-4D). Opinions shifted slightly in the 1980s, with the largest percentage holding a middle position and slightly more people believing this should be the government's role than asserting that people should help themselves. In 1994 and 1996, the middle position is still held most frequently, with a roughly equal number of proponents on either side.

Another GSS measure in this area asked respondents whether or not it should be the government's responsibility to provide a job for everyone who wants one (Table 7-4E). While this item was only asked in four years between 1985 and 1991, in each instance a majority leaned in the direction of saying this should not be the government's responsibility. These findings echo those of Shapiro, Patterson, Russell, and Young (1987b: 269) who concluded that "[E]mployment is much less thought of as an entitlement than Social Security or medical care." The public clearly has mixed feelings about the government's role in providing a job and a good standard of living for all Americans.

The issue of providing assistance to the needy is even more controversial in the public's mind. In each year since 1973 in which the GSS has asked

Table 7.4 Opinions on Government Guarantee of Jobs and Living Standards

A. The government in Washington ought to see to it that everybody who wants to work can find a job.

Response Category	1956	1958	1960
Strongly Agree	48%	49	52
Agree	15	14	13
Not Sure; Depends	8	8	9
Disagree	11	11	8
Strongly Disagree	18	19	18

SOURCE: American National Election Studies.

B. Do you think that the government in Washington should see to it that every person has a job and a good standard of living or should the government just let each person get ahead on his own?

Response Category	1964	1968
Government Should See To It	36%	35
Depends; Other	13	12
Let Each Get Ahead on His Own	51	53

SOURCE: American National Election Studies.

C. Some people feel that the government in Washington should see to it that every person has a job and a good standard of living. Others think the government should just let each person get ahead on his/their own. (1972–78: And, of course, other people have opinions somewhere in between.) Where would you place yourself on this scale, or haven't you thought much about this?

Response Category	1972	1974	1976	1978	1980	1982	1984
1. Government See To Jobs	16%	14	14	9	11	11	12
2.	7	6	6	4	8	7	8
3.	9	10	10	9	11	10	13
4.	23	25	22	24	21	23	23
5.	14	15	13	19	16	18	19
6.	8	10	13	14	19	15	15
7. Let Each Person Get Ahead	22	20	22	21	14	14	10

	1986	1988	1990	1992	1994	1996
1. Government See To Jobs	11	11	13	10	10	8
2.	7	7	10	8	7	8
3.	9	11	13	12	12	10
4.	23	21	21	23	21	21
5.	17	18	16	20	20	21
6.	15	16	14	14	16	20
7. Let Each Person Get Ahead	18	16	13	13	14	13

SOURCE: American National Election Studies.

D. Some people think that the government in Washington should do everything possible to improve the standard of living of all poor Americans; they are at Point 1 on this card. Other people think it is not the government's responsibility, and that each person should take care of himself; they are at Point 5. Where would you place yourself on this scale, or haven't you made up your mind on this?

Response Category	1975	1983	1984	1986	1987	1988
1. Government Responsibility	30%	17	17	19	17	17
2.	10	16	11	13	12	12
3. Agree with Both	36	41	48	46	46	46
4.	11	15	16	12	14	13
5. People Help Themselves	13	11	9	10	10	12

Response Category	1989	1990	1991	1993	1994	1996
1. Government Responsibility	17	20	17	12	13	13
2.	15	15	17	15	14	13
3. Agree with Both	44	44	44	49	45	47
4.	14	13	13	14	16	16
5. People Help Themselves	9	8	9	10	11	11

SOURCE: General Social Surveys.

E. On the whole, do you think it should or should not be the government's responsibility to provide a job for everyone who wants one?

Response Category	1985	1989	1990	1991
Definitely Should Be	14%	18	16	19
Probably Should Be	21	30	28	26
Probably Should Not Be	34	29	34	26
Definitely Should Not Be	32	23	22	29

SOURCE: General Social Surveys.

whether too much, too little, or about the right amount was being spent on welfare, the most frequent response has been "too much" (see Figure 7-2). The extent to which public sentiment slanted in the "too much" direction has varied somewhat during this period, starting from a majority in 1973, falling somewhat in the mid-1970s, increasing to more than 60% in the late 1970s, then falling back again during the 1980s. The most recent surveys (1993–1996) have seen a movement back in the conservative direction, with 57% in 1993, 62% in 1994, and 58% in 1996 expressing the view that "too much" is being spent on welfare.

As Smith (1987: 78-79) has shown, in GSS surveys that asked about spending on *assistance to the poor*, the number of Americans who felt that too little was being spent was about 40% greater than the percentage who felt too little was being spent on *welfare*. As he concluded, "the term 'welfare' obviously

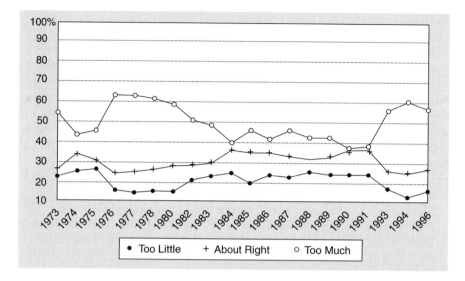

FIGURE 7.2 Government Spending on Welfare, 1973–1996

SOURCE: General Social Surveys.

carries more negative connotations than does 'poor,' " with welfare more likely
to conjure up images of "loafers and bums" and the poor more likely to be
thought of as the "truly needy."

In analyzing data similar to these, Page and Shapiro (1992: 126) reported
that the attitudes that the public expresses, while somewhat ambivalent, are not
inconsistent. Instead, they argue that the variations in opinion provided in the
answers to these differently worded questions reflect exactly the distinctions
the public wants to make on this issue. In their view, the public doesn't "like
the idea of welfare programs that give cash payments to people, some of whom
may not be truly helpless and may thereby be discouraged from helping themselves." Overall, they conclude that "these views are consistent with one another, form a coherent pattern, reflect the information made available to the
public, and fit with Americans underlying values—which combine generosity
with individualism" (127).

The Environment

Over the past quarter century the environment has emerged as an increasingly important issue in the American mind. Since the initial peak of the environmental movement in the early 1970s, this issue "has been a persistent
concern, prominent in the media and magnified by worldwide environmental
groups" (Gilroy and Shapiro, 1986: 270). As awareness of environmental is-

sues has increased, the American public have come to expect such things as cleaner air, cleaner water, more parklands, and the preservation of wildlife (Ladd, 1990: 11).

The public's commitment to the environment has been characterized as "genuine and substantial" and polling data have shown that Americans are willing to pay for cleaner air and water; they are not, however, willing to pay *any* price for greater environmental protection (Ladd, 1990: 11). The data in Table 7–5 support this conclusion.

The two General Social Survey questions on spending for "improving and protecting the environment" or "on the environment" show that over the past quarter century, a majority of the public has felt that too little is spent on the environment. Public support for environmental spending reached its peak at the beginning of the 1990s, when about three-fourths of those surveyed said that too little was being spent in this area. This percentage has declined slightly since that peak, and in the most recent (1996) survey 61% felt that too little was spent on the environment, 28% said "about the right amount," and 11% thought that too much was being spent in this area.

Data from the 1993 and 1994 GSS's also indicate that the public believes it is the government's role to protect the environment. About 90% of those surveyed felt the government should pass laws to make business protect the environment, even if this interfered with businesses' right to make their own decisions (Table 7–5C), and approximately three-fourths believed that government should make laws to protect the environment rather than letting ordinary people decide for themselves (Table 7–5D).

The public does not believe that protection of the environment necessarily involves a trade-off with the economy, and is less steadfastly pro-environment when the issue is presented in this way. About half the public feels that this country needs economic growth in order to protect the environment (Table 7–5E). Slightly more than half disagree with the idea that economic growth always harms the environment and another fourth of the public neither agrees nor disagree with this notion (Table 7–5F). A slightly higher percentage of people disagree than agree with the statement that people worry too much about human progress hurting the environment (Table 7–5G) and the public is fairly evenly divided on the issue of whether we worry too much about the future of the environment, and not enough about prices and jobs (Table 7–5H. The extent to which Americans say they are willing to make sacrifices to protect the environment also varies by the extent of the sacrifice requested. About half of those responding said they would be very willing or fairly willing to pay much higher prices to protect the environment (Table 7–5I). This percentage fell to less than 40% when sacrifice involved paying much higher taxes (Table 7–5J) and to one-third if protecting the environment meant accepting cuts in their standard of living (Table 7–5K).

Overall, while Americans are generally willing to support protection of the environment, they do not believe that this goal must come at the price of economic well-being, and there are limits to the public's willingness to pay for an attractive environment (Ladd, 1990: 11).

Table 7.5 Opinions on the Environment

A. Are we spending too much money, too little money, or about the right amount on improving and protecting the environment?

Response Category	1973	1974	1975	1976	1977	1978	1980
Too Little	65%	64	58	59	52	55	52
About the Right Amount	28	28	32	32	36	35	32
Too Much	8	8	10	9	12	10	16

	1982	1983	1984	1985	1986	1987	1988
Too Little	54	58	63	59	64	68	68
About the Right Amount	33	33	33	33	31	26	28
Too Much	12	9	4	8	5	5	4

	1989	1990	1991	1993	1994	1996
Too Little	76	76	71	59	61	61
About the Right Amount	20	20	24	31	30	28
Too Much	4	4	5	9	9	11

B. Are we spending too much money, too little money, or about the right amount on the environment?

Response Category	1984	1985	1986	1987	1988	1989
Too Little	58%	65	61	63	68	74
About the Right Amount	32	27	32	30	27	21
Too Much	10	8	7	7	5	5

	1990	1991	1993	1994	1996
Too Little	74	72	62	64	64
About the Right Amount	23	23	29	26	27
Too Much	3	5	9	9	9

C. If you had to choose, which one of the following comes closest to your views? Government should let businesses decide for themselves how to protect the environment, even if it means they don't always do the right thing, or government should pass laws to make businesses protect the environment, even if it interferes with business' right to make their own decisions.

Response Category	1993	1994
Government Let Businesses Decide	9%	11
Government Should Pass Laws	91	89

D. If you had to choose, which one of the following comes closest to your views? Government should let ordinary people decide for themselves how to protect the environment, even if it means they don't always do the right thing, or government should pass laws to make ordinary people protect the environment, even if it interferes with people's right to make their own decisions.

Response Category	1993	1994
Government Let People Decide	21%	27
Government Should Pass Laws	79	73

E. In order to protect the environment, America needs economic growth.

Response Category	1993	1994
Strongly Agree	5%	6
Agree	45	39
Neither Agree nor Disagree	23	26
Disagree	24	26
Strongly Disagree	3	3

F. Economic growth always harms the environment.

Response Category	1993	1994
Strongly Agree	2%	3
Agree	19	18
Neither Agree nor Disagree	26	27
Disagree	47	47
Strongly Disagree	6	5

G. People worry too much about human progress harming the environment.

Response Category	1993	1994
Strongly Agree	5%	5
Agree	28	32
Neither Agree nor Disagree	18	15
Disagree	41	41
Strongly Disagree	8	7

H. We worry too much about the future of the environment, and not enough about prices and jobs today.

Response Category	1993	1994
Strongly Agree	10%	11
Agree	30	31
Neither Agree nor Disagree	16	14
Disagree	34	33
Strongly Disagree	10	10

I. How willing would you be to pay much higher prices in order to protect the environment?

Response Category	1993	1994
Very Willing	11%	9
Fairly Willing	40	39
Neither Willing nor Unwilling	23	25
Not Very Willing	19	18
Not At All Willing	7	9

J. How willing would you be to pay much higher taxes in order to protect the environment?

Response Category	1993	1994
Very Willing	8%	6
Fairly Willing	32	29
Neither Willing nor Unwilling	21	22
Not Very Willing	25	27
Not At All Willing	14	16

K. How willing would you be to accept cuts in your standard of living in order to protect the environment?

Response Category	1993	1994
Very Willing	7%	4
Fairly Willing	27	28
Neither Willing nor Unwilling	24	24
Not Very Willing	26	29
Not At All Willing	16	15

SOURCE: General Social Surveys.

GROUP DIFFERENCES IN ATTITUDES

To this point, our discussion of "the American mind" on social-welfare issues has centered on the views of the entire adult population. You should recognize, however, that this overall attitude may not be shared by all subgroups, and that individuals with different background characteristics and political orientations may differ in their opinions on these issues.

The data in Table 7-6 are from four spending questions on the 1996 GSS (whether we are spending too much money, too little money, or about the right amount on (1) social security; (2) improving and protecting the nation's health; (3) welfare; and (4) improving and protecting the environment) and from two questions on the 1996 NES—whether federal spending on public

**Table 7.6 Opinions on Selected Social Welfare Issues
by Socio-Demographic Characteristics, 1996**
(percentage giving "liberal" response)

	Soc. Sec.	School	Health	Jobs	Welfare	Envir.
TOTAL SAMPLE	52%	68	68	25	16	61
Age						
18–29	54	80	69	35	17	74
30–44	57	70	71	23	14	64
45–64	50	65	68	24	17	58
65 and Older	42	54	71	23	15	39
Race						
Black	71	88	81	47	42	75
White	49	64	66	22	10	59
Sex						
Male	48	63	62	21	14	60
Female	55	71	73	29	16	61
Education						
Less Than High School	60	70	71	38	23	60
High School Graduate	58	68	69	28	14	58
Some College	57	72	72	22	14	63
College Graduate	34	61	61	20	14	62
Income						
Lowest Quartile	57	71	68	35	23	63
Second Quartile	58	68	74	28	15	63
Third Quartile	56	66	69	22	12	61
Highest Quartile	43	65	68	17	11	57
Party Identification						
Democrats	58	78	78	36	22	66
Independents	54	71	73	25	16	68
Republicans	41	49	52	10	7	46
Ideology						
Liberals	52	81	80	36	20	76
Moderates	56	69	73	25	16	65
Conservatives	47	53	56	12	11	46

SOURCES: 1996 American National Election Study and 1996 General Social Survey.

schools should be increased, decreased, or kept about the same, and whether government should guarantee jobs and a good standard of living. These figures provide a breakdown on the questions by subgroups.

As these data demonstrate, there are some fairly substantial and consistent differences across groups in their views on social–welfare issues. The largest of these differences are between blacks and whites, with blacks consistently more likely to adopt the liberal position on these issues. On the issue of Social Security, for example, 71% of blacks thought we were spending too little, compared to 49% of whites. Similarly, 88% of blacks, compared to 64% of whites, felt that federal spending on public schools should be increased and a much higher percentage of blacks (47%) than whites (22%) believed that the government in Washington should see to it that every person has a job and a good standard of living.

Differences in opinion across socioeconomic groups were not as large as those between blacks and whites, but an individual's level of education and family income did have an effect on several of these issues. The general pattern was that a smaller percentage of respondents with more education or from higher-income families took a liberal position on these issues. The percentage who felt that government should see to it that every person has a job and a good standard of living, for example, ranged from 38% among those with less than a high school education to 20% among college graduates, and from 35% in those lowest income group to 17% among those with the highest family incomes. College graduates and those with higher incomes were also much less likely than those in other groups to feel that too little was being spent on Social Security, while individuals with less than a high school education or in the lowest income group were more likely to believe that too little is being spent on welfare. There was little difference across education levels or income groups in their views on spending for improving and protecting the nation's health or improving and protecting the environment. Government spending on programs such as employment help and Social Security is likely to be of more benefit to those with less education or from lower-income families. It is not surprising, therefore, to find that such individuals are more supportive of government action in these areas.

The general pattern of opinion on these issues across age groups is for a higher percentage of younger people to give a liberal response. While these distinctions are not substantial for all issues, in several cases the variation across age categories is significant. The largest difference is on the question of spending to improve and protect the environment. Among those under 30, 74% thought that we were spending too little on the environment; this percentage declined to 64% among those 30–44, 58% among those 45–64, and 39% for those age 65 or older. Similarly, the percentage who felt that federal spending on public schools should be increased ranged from 80% among the youngest age group to 54% among those 65 or older. On other issues, such as spending to protect and improve the nation's health or welfare, there is little variation across age groups.

The differences between men and women on these issues, while generally not large, show a consistent pattern, with women more likely than men to take a liberal position. For instance, a higher percentage of women than men (73% to 62%) felt that too little was being spent on improving and protecting the nation's health; that federal spending for public schools should be increased (71% to 63%); that government should see to it that every person has a job and a good standard of living (29% to 21%); and that too little was being spent on Social Security (55% to 48%).

As noted in the previous chapter, the basic split between liberals and conservatives is over the role of government, with liberals believing in more government action and conservatives feeling that individuals are primarily responsible for their own well-being. Given this, we would expect significant differences in opinion on these social-welfare issues among those who identify themselves as liberals, moderates, or conservatives. The data in Table 7-6 show this to be the case.

For each of these six items, a higher percentage of those who classify themselves as "liberals" than conservatives take the liberal side of the issue and, in all cases but spending on Social Security, the percentage of moderates falls between the two. The extent to which the percentage of self-identified liberals exceeds the percentage of conservatives who adopt the liberal position on these issues is 30% for spending to improve and protect the environment, 28% on federal spending on public schools, and 24% on government guarantees of jobs and living standards and spending to improve and protect the nation's health. The positions of the public on these social-welfare issues clearly reflect its general political orientation.

Differences in opinion by party identification are also relatively large and demonstrate the more liberal views of Democrats and conservative attitudes of Republicans. For each of these items, the percentage giving the liberal response was higher among Democrats than among Republicans. For five the six questions—the exception being spending on the environment—the percentage of Independents voicing the liberal position fell between the two. The difference in the percentage taking the liberal stance on the items ranged from 29% (78% to 49%) on the question of federal spending on public schools to 15% (22% to 7%) on the issue of welfare spending. While the views of Independents generally fell between those of Democrats and Independents, the percentage of Independents who took a liberal position tended to be closer to the Democrats than to the Republicans.

Overall, these data illustrate some fairly substantial differences in the social-welfare views of various subgroups of the population. People's general political orientations are related to their views on these issues, with self-identified liberals and Democrats more likely to take a liberal position on these issues than conservatives or supporters of the Republican Party. Blacks, those with less education or lower family incomes, younger people, and women also tended to have more liberal views on these social-welfare questions.

SUMMARY

The views of the American public on social-welfare issues generally reflect the division in the American mind on the role of government in providing for the welfare of its citizens. The public is fairly evenly split on the general question of whether the government should provide more services or fewer, and support for government action varies significantly according to the nature of the program. Public support for a program like Social Security has been high since its inception and remains relatively strong. Americans also support spending for schools and feel that the government should help people get doctors and hospital care. The public is more divided, however, on the question of whether this country should have a government health insurance plan.

In recent years, Americans have shown themselves to be supportive of protecting and improving the environment. A consistent majority of the public believes that too little is being spent on the environment and the public generally supports actions, such as government regulation of businesses or individuals, that are perceived as promoting environmental quality.

Programs that find less support among the American public are welfare programs and those in which government attempts to insure that everyone has a good standard of living. While Americans are not opposed to helping people in need, they also believe in individual responsibility. They are, therefore, less supportive of government guarantees of living standards and of programs that they feel might discourage people from helping themselves.

Opinions on social-welfare issues vary significantly across subgroups of the population. Individuals who identify themselves as liberals or who support the Democratic Party are more likely to support an active role for the government in the social-welfare arena than are conservatives or Republicans. Whites are more likely to take a conservative position on these issues than are blacks, and those with more education or higher family incomes, older people, and men are also more likely to take a conservative position on questions involving the government's role in providing for the welfare of its citizens

Polls, Polling, and the Internet

One place in the United States that has gathered polling data and results from a multitude of academic and media sources is The Roper Center at the University of Connecticut. By accessing their web site, you can find cross-time trends for many of the social issues discussed in this chapter. To gain access to all of their data, your institution must be a subscriber. Take a look at the web site at:

http://www.ropercenter.uconn.edu

NOTES

1. As in the previous chapter, much of the data reported here is taken from the National Election Studies and General Social Surveys. The examination of social-welfare issues is complicated by the cross-time changes in question wording and format that occur in the NES series. In sum, before 1964 the usual question form used in the NES was a 5-point strongly agree–strongly disagree format. From 1964 to 1970, this was changed to a forced-choice alternative, which was expanded to a 7-point format in 1972. These variations in format were accompanied by changes in question wording, which make cross-year com-

parisons hazardous. We have strived to make these data as comparable as possible, while noting those instances where question wording makes trend comparisons impossible (Bishop, Oldendick, Tuchfarber, and Bennett, 1978; Bishop, Tuchfarber, and Oldendick, 1978; Sullivan, Piereson, and Marcus, 1978).

2. The issue of support of public schools is one where the change in question wording in the NES limits the extent of the time-series data on this question. The 1964 and 1968 NES included a question on whether "the government in Washington should help towns and cities provide education for grade and high school children" or whether this "should be handled by states and local communities." As Page and Shapiro (1992: 133) note, the public expresses skepticism about the role in education of "the government in Washington" as opposed to "states and local communities." As they point out, "local 'handling' does not preclude federal aid."

8

Americans' Views on Racial Issues

Questions to Consider:

Do Americans believe in equal rights for all Americans?

What should be the government's role in assuring equality?

How much integration of schools and neighborhoods do Americans prefer?

Will Americans elect a minority president?

On what issues do blacks and whites hold very different views?

The place of race in the history of the United States makes it almost inevitable that race and racism will be issues in American society. Race has been a continual source of social and political division from the origins of the Constitution and the "three-fifths" compromise through the Civil War and Reconstruction, significant Supreme Court cases such as *Dred Scott v. Sanford*, *Plessy v. Ferguson*, and *Brown v. Board of Education*, the Civil Rights Movement, Black Power, affirmative action, and the more recent backlash against policies that provide preferences to members of minority groups.

In examining public opinion on racial issues, we should recognize that the period for which we have reliable survey information is also one during which there have been a number of significant upheavals in race relations in the United States. As noted by Mayer (1992: 22), "[I]n little more than two decades, a racial caste system that had prevailed for more than three centuries was stripped of every vestige of legal and moral support." It is important, therefore, to consider the historical context within which public opinion has developed in describing the current state of the American mind on racial issues.

In their examination of racial attitudes in America, Schuman, Steeh, and Bobo (1985: 2–29), trace the history of such attitudes in this country, from the inconceivability of a harmonious biracial society expressed by Jefferson, through the development of "biological racism," the shift to racial equalitarianism in American ideas, and the civil rights movement. As part of this research, they identified six aspects of recent history that are important to an understanding of trends in racial attitudes: (1) a period of prelude to civil rights politics, that involved the discrediting of theories of biological racism; (2) the growing importance of "black ballots" in American politics; (3) the establishment of effective civil rights organizations; (4) crucial Supreme Court rulings; (5) the passage of landmark legislation, such as the 1964 Civil Rights Act; and (6) disputes over the unfinished civil rights agenda (1985: 8). Consideration of these factors is essential to understanding trends in public opinion on racial matters.

While considerable data on racial attitudes are available from recent years, there is little data on this topic from the early period of survey research. As Sheatsley has noted, the leading polling organizations had little interest in the study of racial attitudes during the 1930s. In his view, "the polls, for obvious reasons, tend to ask questions about issues that are hot, and it is clear that during the decade preceding World War II, race relations did not qualify on that basis, at least not for the elites who devised polls" (Sheatsley, 1966: 217).

Data on public attitudes on racial issues that are available indicate that "[T]he expressed attitudes of white Americans toward black Americans have undergone a great transformation over the last forty or fifty years, a change greater than on any other issue" (Page and Shapiro, 1992: 68). While most Americans today believe in desegregation and are in favor of government action to enforce legal equality, this was not the case fifty years ago. As Page and Shapiro (68–69) note, "[I]n the early and middle 1940s, then, large majorities of whites took for granted that blacks should be consigned to separate public accommodations, separate schools, and separate neighborhoods." Examining public opinion on racial issues provides a unique opportunity to track substantial changes in the American mind that correspond with a rather turbulent period in race relations in this country.

School Desegregation

The issue of racial desegregation is one that, in Carmines and Stimson's (1989: 14) terms, has had great long-term impact on the political system since the formation of the New Deal. In Schuman, Steeh, and Bobo's (1985: 77) discussion of the issue of school desegregation, they report that in 1942 the percentage of white respondents who felt that white students and black students should go to the same schools was 32%, which rose to 50% in 1956, 84% by 1972 and 90% in 1982. In Page and Shapiro's analysis (1992: 69), they found that the overall change on this issue "of more than sixty percentage points was the largest for any policy preference of any kind among the thousands we have examined." Data on this question from the General Social Survey [Table 8-1A]

Table 8.1 Opinions on School Desegregation

A. The government in Washington should stay out of the question of whether white and colored children go to the same school.

Response Category	1956	1958	1960
Strongly Agree	40%	40	38
Agree	9	9	7
Not Sure; Depends	7	6	8
Disagree	11	8	9
Strongly Disagree	33	38	38

SOURCE: American National Election Studies.

B. The government in Washington should see to it that white and colored children are allowed to go to the same schools.

Response Category	1962
Yes	56%
Yes; Qualified	3
Yes; but No Force	2
No; Qualified	1
No	38

SOURCE: American National Election Studies.

C. Do you think the government in Washington should see to it that white and Negro (colored) children are allowed to go to the same schools or do you think this is not the government's business?

Response Category	1964	1966	1968	1970	1972	1976
Government Should See to It	48%	53	43	56	42	33
Other; Depends	8	8	8	10	8	12
Not the Government's Business	44	39	50	34	50	55

Response Category	1978	1986	1990	1992	1994
Government Should See to It	35	44	49	45	41
Other; Depends	13	9	4	7	6
Not the Government's Business	52	48	47	47	53

SOURCE: American National Election Studies.

show (1) that by 1972, 88% of the public believed white and black students should go to the same schools; (2) that support for this position remained at an extremely high level between 1972 and 1985; and (3) that blacks are virtually

D. Do you think white students and (Negro/Black) students should go to the same schools or to separate schools?

Response Category	1972	1976	1977	1980	1982	1984	1985
Same Schools	88%	86	87	89	92	93	93
Separate Schools	12	14	13	11	8	7	7

SOURCE: General Social Surveys.

E. Is achieving racial integration an important enough goal to justify busing children out of their neighborhood schools or is having children attend their neighborhood schools important enough to justify opposing busing?

Response Category	1972	1974	1976	1980	1984
1. Bus to Achieve Integration	5%	4	5	4	4
2.	2	2	3	3	2
3.	2	3	2	3	3
4.	5	6	7	6	8
5.	4	5	5	6	10
6.	7	10	9	18	21
7. Keep in Neighborhood Schools	75	70	69	61	52

SOURCE: American National Election Studies.

F. In general, do you favor or oppose the busing of (Negro/Black/African-American) and white school children from one school district to another?

Response Category	1972	1974	1975	1976	1977	1978	1982	1983	1985
Favor	21%	22	18	16	16	21	20	24	23
Oppose	79	78	82	84	84	79	80	76	77

	1986	1988	1989	1990	1991	1993	1994	1996	
Favor	29	34	29	36	37	31	34	38	
Oppose	71	66	71	64	63	69	66	62	

SOURCE: General Social Surveys.

unanimous in their views on this issue [Table 8-2D]. Given the large change in attitudes that occurred on this issue between 1942 and 1985, responses to this item "can no longer show substantial overall change for the simple reason that part of the sample is already close to unanimity in choosing the positive response" (Schuman, Steeh and Bobo, 1985: 79). In sum, there is **consensus** among the American public that white and black students should go to the same schools.[1]

Table 8.2 Opinions on School Desegregation by Race

A. Percentage Disagreeing that the Government Should Stay Out of the Question

	1956	1958	1960
Whites	42	43	45
Blacks	64	70	70

B. Percentage Saying that the Government Should See to Same Schools

	1962
Whites	59
Blacks	83

C. Percentage Saying that the Government Should See to Same Schools

	1964	1966	1968	1970	1972	1976
Whites	43	49	37	48	37	28
Blacks	86	85	89	89	81	76

	1978	1986	1990	1992	1994
Whites	29	36	43	40	36
Blacks	78	83	79	76	76

D. Percentage Saying "Same Schools"

	1972	1976	1977	1980	1982	1984	1985
Whites	86	85	86	88	90	92	93
Blacks	96	97	93	97	96	97	97

E. Percentage Saying "Keep in Neighborhood Schools" (Categories 5, 6, and 7)

	1972	1974	1976	1980	1984
Whites	90	88	88	90	87
Blacks	52	54	38	43	56

F. Percentage Opposing Busing from One School District to Another

	1972	1974	1975	1976	1977	1978
Whites	86	85	86	87	87	83
Blacks	45	37	53	48	52	48

	1982	1983	1985	1986	1988	1989
Whites	84	79	81	75	71	74
Blacks	44	44	43	38	42	46

Percentage Opposing Busing from One School District to Another

	1990	1991	1993	1994	1996
Whites	69	68	73	71	66
Blacks	37	37	41	40	41

SOURCE: General Social Surveys.

This consensus is not apparent when the aspect of government's role in this issue is introduced into this question. The data presented in Tables 8-1A, 8-1B, and 8-1C show the responses to different versions of this question asked in the American National Election Studies between 1952 and 1994. While there are variations in responses over time, for the most part there is a fairly even division in opinion on this issue between those who believe that the government should see to it that white and black children are allowed to go to the same schools and those who think this is not the government's business. The major deviation in this pattern occurs between 1970 and 1978. In 1970, 56% felt that government should see to it that white and black children were allowed to go to the same schools. This percentage declined to 42% in 1972 and to about one-third in 1976 and 1978, before rising back to the mid-40% range in 1986 and after.

The decline between 1970 and 1978 in the number of people who felt that black and white children should go to the same school was particularly evident among whites [see Table 8-2C]. In 1970, 48% of whites thought that the government in Washington should see to it that children of different races should go to the same schools. This percentage dropped to 37% in 1972 and 28% in 1976 and remained at this level in 1978. While the percentage of blacks who felt that black and white children should go to the same schools also declined during this period, the change was not as great as that for whites.

This change is likely due, at least in part, to the fact that during this time "government seeing to it that white and black children are allowed to go to the same schools" became increasingly associated with **busing,** an issue that "the mass white public has been strongly opposed to ... ever since it has become a visible public issue" (Sears, Hensler, and Speer, 1979: 371). In 1971, the United States Supreme Court, in the case of *Swann v. Charlotte-Mecklenburg School District* (1971) held that lower federal courts could order busing as an appropriate remedy to end dual school systems. School busing plans were implemented in a number of American cities during the early 1970s, but Supreme Court rulings in more recent years have turned away from forced busing as a means of achieving school integration.

Table 8-1E shows the results from the NES question on busing asked between 1972 and 1984, while Table 8-1F presents those from the GSS item from 1972 to 1996. If responses 5, 6, and 7 to the NES question are treated as "anti-busing," the percentage of such responses during this period varies between 83% and 86%. While the proportion of respondents voicing the most extreme anti-busing position (point 7) declined steadily during this period, public sentiment on this issue is overwhelmingly opposed to busing as a means to achieve racial integration in schools. This conclusion is supported by the results from the GSS question, for which the percentage opposed to busing ranged from 84% (1976) to 62% (1996). Opposition to busing appears to be strongest during the period when the courts were ordering more school busing plans to be implemented (1972–1977), and to have declined somewhat as the courts have moved away from this position. Nonetheless, a solid majority of about two-thirds of the American public is opposed to busing.

As might be expected, there are significant differences in the opinions of blacks and whites on the question of busing. On the NES question (Table 8-2E), for example, close to 90% of whites took a "keep in neighborhood schools" position throughout this period. In each year, the percentage of whites who held this view was significantly higher than the percentage of blacks, although when the issue was posed in this form a majority of blacks held an anti-busing position in 1972, 1974, and 1984. The GSS data also show large racial differences, reaching as high as 48% (85% vs. 37%) in 1974, with a difference of 25% (66% vs. 41%) in the most recent survey (Table 8-2F). Moreover, these data indicate that during the height of the busing period a majority of blacks were opposed to busing black and white school children from one school district to another. In examining similar questions, Page and Shapiro (1992: 73) concluded that a substantial proportion of blacks have opposed busing, "presumably because the hassle and disruption (if only as a result of white opposition) are seen to outweigh the benefits."

In sum, there is a consensus among the American public on the general principle that black and white children should go to the same schools. There is less agreement, however, on how to achieve school integration. The public is roughly evenly divided on the question of whether or not it should be the role of the government in Washington to see to it that children of different races go to the same schools, and is opposed to busing as a specific remedy for achieving this goal. Opposition to busing is evident among blacks as well as whites.

Residential Integration

Closely related to the issue of school desegregation is the question of residential integration. Data from an NES and GSS item on this issue are presented in Table 8-3. As these data demonstrate, opinions on residential integration have moved in a liberal direction over the past 30 years. On the NES question, 32% of respondents in 1964 felt that white people had the right to keep black people out of their neighborhood if they wanted to. This percentage declined steadily during the period this question was asked as part of the NES, and by 1976 only 9% expressed this view.

A question asked by NORC covers a different time period but shows the same pattern. When NORC asked the question in 1963, 60% of white respondents agreed; in 1968, 56% agreed; and in 1970, 47% agreed. When asked in

Table 8.3 Opinions on Neighborhood Segregation

A. Which of these statements would you agree with: White people have a right to
   keep black people out of their neighborhood if they want to, or, black people have
   a right to live wherever they can afford to, just like anybody else?

Response Category	1964	1968	1970	1972	1976
Whites Have Right to Keep Out	32	25	19	17	9
Blacks Have Right to Live Wherever	68	75	81	83	91

SOURCE: American National Election Studies.

B. White people have a right to keep (Negroes/Blacks/African-Americans) out of their
   neighborhoods if they want to, and (Negroes/Blacks/African-Americans) should respect that right.*

Response Category	1980	1982	1984	1985	1987	1988
Agree Strongly	15	13	10	10	9	7
Agree Slightly	15	13	14	15	14	14
Disagree Slightly	28	30	26	29	26	24
Disagree Strongly	41	44	50	46	52	55
	1989	**1990**	**1991**	**1993**	**1994**	**1996**
Agree Strongly	8	8	7	4	5	5
Agree Slightly	14	13	10	10	10	6
Disagree Slightly	23	24	22	21	25	19
Disagree Strongly	55	55	60	65	60	69

*This question was included in the 1972, 1976, and 1977 GSS's, but in these years it was only asked of white
respondents.

SOURCE: General Social Surveys.

the GSS beginning in 1972 [Table 8–4B], close to 40% of white respondents
agreed that white people had a right to keep black people out of their neighborhoods. After 1977, this percentage slowly declined until by 1996 only 13%
agreed with this statement. In little more than 30 years, the percentage of
whites who believed that white people have a right to keep blacks out of their
neighborhood had declined by almost 50%.

As was the case for school desegregation, there were significant differences
in the opinions of blacks and whites on this issue (see Table 8–4). On the NES
question, blacks are virtually unanimous throughout the period in their view
that blacks have a right to live wherever they can afford, while among whites
the percentage expressing this sentiment increased from 65% in 1964 to 90%
in 1976. On the GSS question, a higher percentage of blacks than whites
in each year disagreed that whites have a right to keep blacks out of their

Table 8.4 Opinions on Neighborhood Segregation by Race

A. Percentage Saying Blacks Have a Right to Live Wherever They Can Afford

	1964	1968	1970	1972	1976
Whites	65	66	76	81	90
Blacks	98	95	98	99	99

SOURCE: American National Election Studies.

B. Percentage Disagreeing that Whites Have a Right to Keep Blacks Out of Neighborhood

	1972	1976	19˙77	1980	1982	1984	1985	1987
Whites	61	61	58	67	70	74	74	75
Blacks	—	—	—	86	90	86	82	90

	1988	1989	1990	1991	1993	1994	1996
Whites	76	77	76	80	85	84	87
Blacks	91	90	88	94	93	91	96

SOURCE: General Social Surveys.

neighborhood, with the trend showing the gap between the races tending to narrow over time. By 1996, 96% of blacks and 87% of whites disagreed with this statement. As was true in the case of school desegregation, by the end of the 20th century Americans have reached a consensus on the general principle that people should have the right to live wherever they can afford.

Fair Employment Practices

Another aspect of racial discrimination involves the treatment of minorities in terms of job opportunities. Unfortunately for comparison with the issues treated previously in this chapter, there is not a "pure" measure of this issue that asks simply "whether minorities should receive fair treatment in jobs"; instead the items that deal with this question all include some measure of whether assuring fair treatment should be "the government's business."

The NES item asked in strongly-agree/strongly-disagree format from 1956 to 1960 found that about 70% of the American public agreed that if minorities were not getting fair treatment in jobs and housing that the government should see to it that they do (see Table 8-5A). In the forced-choice version of this item asked beginning in 1964 (Table 8-5B), the public was more divided on this issue, with 45% saying that the government should see to it that blacks get fair treatment in jobs, 47% believing that this was not the government's business, and 8% giving a middle response. Opinion on this item remained relatively evenly divided when it was asked in 1968 and 1972. There is a gap be-

Table 8.5 Attitudes toward Minority Employment

A. If Negroes are not getting fair treatment in jobs and housing, the government should see to it that they do.

Response Category	1956	1958	1960
Strongly Agree	49	54	52
Agree	21	18	20
Not Sure; Depends	7	7	8
Disagree	7	6	5
Strongly Disagree	15	15	15

B. Should the government in Washington see to it that Negroes (colored people/black people) get fair treatment in jobs or leave these matters to the states and local communities?

Response Category	1964	1968	1972
Government Should See to It	45	44	50
Other; Depends	8	7	7
Not Government's Business	47	49	43

C. Should the government in Washington see to it that Negroes (colored people/black people) get fair treatment in jobs or is this not the federal government's business?

Response Category	1986	1988	1992	1996
Government Should See to It	56	54	55	48
Other; Depends	4	5	3	4
Not Government's Business	40	41	41	47

Source: American National Election Studies.

tween 1972 and 1986 in which a question like this was not asked, and during this period opinion moved slightly in the liberal direction, with roughly 55% of the public during the late 1980s and 1990s believing that the government should see to it minorities get fair treatment in jobs (Table 8-5C).

There is a stark contrast in the opinions of blacks and whites on this issue (see Table 8-6). From 1956 to 1960 blacks were virtually unanimous in their view that if minorities were not getting fair treatment in jobs and housing, the government should see to it that they do, while the percentage of whites who expressed this sentiment hovered around 70%. On the forced-choice versions of this item (1964–1972 and 1986–1996), the percentage of black respondents who said that the government in Washington should see to it that minorities get fair treatment in jobs was consistently around 90%, while the percentage of whites who shared this view ranged between 38% (1968) and 49% (1992). In 1996, 92% of blacks and 42% of whites felt the government in Washington should see to it that minorities get fair treatment in jobs.

Table 8.6 Attitudes toward Minority Employment by Race

A. Percentage Agreeing that Government Should See to Fair Treatment

	1956	1958	1960
Whites	68	70	69
Blacks	97	97	98

B. Percentage Saying that Government Should See to Fair Treatment

	1964	1968	1972
Whites	39	38	45
Blacks	94	89	91

C. Percentage Saying that Government Should See to Fair Treatment

	1986	1988	1992	1996
Whites	47	48	49	42
Blacks	90	90	89	92

SOURCE: American National Election Studies.

Affirmative Action

The earlier discussion of school desegregation described the sharp contrast between Americans' support of the general principle of integrated schools and their opposition to a specific approach to achieving this goal, school busing. A similar contrast exists in the public's views on the general principle of fair treatment in jobs for minorities and achieving this end through affirmative action.

In an attempt to put teeth into the 1964 Civil Rights Act, in 1965, President Johnson first applied the concept of **affirmative action**—which is a policy that gives special consideration or compensatory treatment to traditionally disadvantaged groups in an effort to overcome the effects of past discrimination. By the early 1970s, regulations imposing numerous employment goals and timetables had been applied to every company that did more than $10,000 worth of business of any sort with the national government (Schmidt, Shelley, and Bardes, 1997: 155).

Affirmative action programs have always been controversial, because they sometimes result in discriminatory acts against majority groups. An early Supreme Court case dealing with this issue was *Regents of the University of California v. Bakke* (1978), which involved a white student, Alan Bakke, who had been denied admission to medical school at the Davis campus of the University of California even though his academic record was better than those of some minority applicants who got into the program. In this case, the Supreme Court ruled that race could be one of many criteria for admission, but not the only one. In so doing, they held that affirmative action programs, but not specific quota systems, were constitutional. More recent Supreme Court rulings,

such as in the case of *Adarand Constructors, Inc. v. Pena* (1995) have further limited the principle of affirmative action. The Court's current position is that any
program that uses racial or ethnic classifications must be narrowly tailored to
meet a compelling government interest.

Other events have also sought to limit affirmative action programs. In November, 1996, for example, voters in California were asked to consider Proposition 209, also known as the California Civil Rights Initiative, which stated:

> The state shall not discriminate against, or grant preferential treatment
> to, any individual or group on the basis of race, sex, color, ethnicity, or
> national origin in the operation of public employment, public education,
> or public contracting.

This initiative passed by a margin of 55% to 45%. After a court challenge
that delayed its implementation, the U.S. Circuit Court held Proposition 209
to be constitutional. Similar laws are being considered in other states, including Oregon, Washington, Nevada, and Idaho.

The trend in recent court rulings and the passage of laws limiting affirmative
action programs reflect public opinion on this topic. While there is not a great
deal of time-series data on this issue, the information that is available reflects consistent public opposition. This issue was first addressed in the National Election
Studies in 1978 when respondents were asked whether "minorities and women
should be given preferential treatment in jobs and admissions" or if "only an individual's experience and ability should count." If we consider responses 1, 2, and
3 as representing the "preferential treatment" side of the issue and responses 5, 6,
and 7 as the "consider only ability" position, the balance in opposition to affirmative action is clearly evident: 11% supported preferential treatment, while 78%
believed only ability or experience should be considered (see Table 8-7A).

The NES next addressed this issue in 1986 with a question that asked
whether blacks should be given preference in hiring and promotion because
of past discrimination or whether such practices were wrong because they gave
blacks advantages they haven't earned. As the data in Table 8-7B indicate, public opinion as measured by this question was decidedly opposed to preferential
treatment, with between 75% and 86% of respondents during this period saying they opposed preferential treatment. Results from the GSS question asked
in 1994 and 1996 (Table 8-7C) reinforce this conclusion, with 83% of respondents in each year opposing preferences in the hiring and promotion of blacks.

The expected racial differences on this question are evident in Table 8-8.
On the 1978 NES question, 39% of blacks compared to 8% of whites fell on
the "give preferential treatment" side of the issue. A much higher percentage
of whites (52%) than blacks (28%) were found at the extreme "consider only
ability" position.

The NES question from 1986 to 1996 and the GSS question each indicate
that more than four-fifths of white respondents in each year opposed preferences in the hiring and promotion of blacks, with the greatest opposition
(91%) occurring in 1994. On the other hand, a majority of blacks in each year
favored preferential treatment. The opinion of blacks on this issue varies more
than that of whites, ranging from 74% in favor of preferences in the 1990 NES

Table 8.7 Opinions on Affirmative Action

A. Should minorities and women be given preferential treatment in jobs and admissions or should only an individual's ability or experience count in hiring and school admission?

Response Category	1978
1. Give Preferential Treatment	5
2.	2
3.	4
4.	11
5.	10
6.	18
7. Consider Only Ability	50

SOURCE: American National Election Studies

B. Should blacks be given preference in hiring and promotion because of past discrimination or is such preference in hiring and promotion of blacks wrong because it gives blacks advantages they haven't earned?

Response Category	1986	1988*	1990	1992	1994	1996
Strongly For	12	12	15	11	8	11
For—Not Strongly	12	8	9	8	6	6
Against—Not Strongly	20	17	20	18	22	17
Strongly Against	56	63	55	63	64	66

*In 1988, the second option read, ". . . wrong because it discriminates against whites?"

SOURCE: American National Election Studies.

C. Some people say that because of past discrimination, blacks should be given preference in hiring and promotion. Others say that such preference in hiring and promotion of blacks is wrong because it discriminates against whites. What is your opinion—are you for or against preferential hiring and promotion of blacks?

Response Category	1994	1996
Strongly Support Preferences	10	10
Support Preferences	7	7
Oppose Preferences	26	27
Strongly Oppose Preferences	57	56

SOURCE: General Social Surveys.

to 50% in favor in the 1994 NES and 1996 GSS. As Citrin (1996: 40) has noted, "[W]here specific policies are concerned, it is clear the 'soft' opportunity-enhancing approaches are accepted, while 'hard' preference-giving programs are widely unpopular."

Table 8.8 Opinions on Affirmative Action by Race

A. 1978 Preferential Treatment

	Whites	Blacks
1. Give Preferential Treatment	2	24
2.	2	6
3.	4	9
4.	11	17
5.	10	9
6.	19	7
7. Consider Only Ability	52	28

SOURCE: American National Election Studies.

B. Percentage Opposed to Preferences in Hiring and Promotion

	1986	1988	1990	1992	1994	1996
Whites	85	87	82	87	91	88
Blacks	31	35	26	44	50	38

SOURCE: American National Election Studies.

C. Percentage Opposed to Preferences in Hiring and Promotion

	1994	1996
Whites	89	89
Blacks	44	50

SOURCE: General Social Surveys.

Government Aid to Minority Groups

Another race-related item that has been asked of the American public in the National Election Studies since 1970 involves not a specific aspect of discrimination such as school integration or jobs, but rather the general question of government aid to minority groups. Beginning in 1970, and in every NES since, respondents have been asked, "should the government help blacks and other minority groups or should minority groups help themselves?" Responses to this 7-point scale item are provided in Table 8-9 and summarized in Figure 8-1.

If we again treat responses 1, 2, and 3 as representing the "liberal" side of this issue and 5, 6, and 7 as the conservative stance, these results indicate that more Americans consistently place themselves on the "minorities help themselves" end of the spectrum. Moreover, the proportion adopting this position has tended to increase during this period. In 1970, about one-third of the

Table 8.9 Government Help Blacks and Other Minority Groups, 1970–1996

Response Category	1970	1972	1974	1976	1978	1980	1982
1. Government Help Minorities	15	13	14	13	12	5	8
2.	8	7	7	9	6	5	6
3.	8	13	12	13	10	12	11
4.	25	24	24	22	25	30	30
5.	12	11	12	12	16	21	16
6.	11	12	9	10	12	13	17
7. Minorities Help Themselves	21	19	22	21	19	14	12

	1984	1986	1988	1990	1992	1994	1996
1. Government Help Minorities	9	9	8	8	6	5	4
2.	8	7	5	7	5	5	4
3.	15	13	9	11	11	10	10
4.	31	31	24	26	26	26	23
5.	18	19	16	15	16	17	20
6.	10	12	15	15	15	17	19
7. Minorities Help Themselves	9	9	22	17	21	20	20

SOURCE: American National Election Studies.

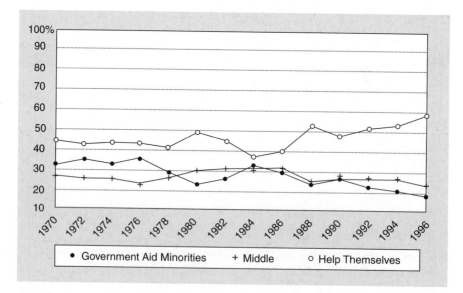

FIGURE 8.1 Government Help Blacks and Other Minority Groups, 1970–1996

SOURCE: American National Election Studies.

**Table 8.10 Government Help Blacks and
Other Minority Groups by Race**

Percentage Saying that Government Should Help Minorities (Categories 1, 2 and 3)

	1970	1972	1974	1976	1978	1980	1982
Whites	25	29	27	30	23	18	21
Blacks	84	78	79	72	65	51	58

	1984	1986	1988	1990	1992	1994	1996
Whites	28	26	18	22	19	17	16
Blacks	59	47	44	52	43	43	40

SOURCE: American National Election Studies.

public was on the "government help minority groups" side of this issue, while about 40% thought that minority groups should help themselves. With slight variations, this pattern was evident through the mid-1980s. In the late 1980s, there was a shift in the conservative direction, with a majority falling on the "minorities help themselves" side of the issue in 1988, 1992, 1994, and 1996. By 1996, 59% of the public were on the conservative side of this issue, compared to 18% who felt that government should aid minority groups.

In what should be becoming a familiar pattern by this point, there were significant differences in black and white opinion on this issue throughout this period (see Table 8-10). The views of blacks and whites on this question were substantially different when this question was first asked. In 1970, 84% of blacks fell on the government should aid minority groups side of this question compared to 25% of whites, and in 1972 78% of blacks and 29% of whites gave a liberal response. The gap between black and white opinion tended to narrow throughout this period, and by 1996 there was only a 24% difference (40% to 16%) in the percentage of blacks and whites who gave this response. Even though the percentage of whites who felt that government should aid minority groups declined between 1970 and 1996, the gap in opinion between the races narrowed due to a steeper decline in the percentage of blacks who thought that government should help minority groups. While the percentage of blacks who believed that government should aid minorities approached a consensus in 1970, by 1996 only 40% expressed this view. In 1996, blacks remain significantly more likely than whites to feel that government should aid minority groups, but over the past quarter century there has been an increasing sentiment among blacks that minority groups should be more responsible for helping themselves.

Spending on Racial Issues

In the GSS, opinions on the general question of race have been tapped by two items on spending. Between 1973 and 1996, the GSS has included an item on whether we are spending too much, too little, or about the right amount on

Table 8.11 Opinions about Spending on Racial Issues

A. Are we spending too much money, too little money, or about the right amount on improving the conditions of blacks?

Response Category	1973	1974	1975	1976	1977	1978	1980
Too Little	35	33	29	30	28	26	27
About the Right Amount	42	45	44	43	46	47	48
Too Much	23	22	26	28	26	27	25

	1982	1983	1984	1985	1986	1987	1988
Too Little	30	32	38	32	37	37	38
About the Right Amount	48	47	46	46	46	46	45
Too Much	22	21	16	22	16	16	17

	1989	1990	1991	1993	1994	1996
Too Little	37	41	39	39	34	35
About the Right Amount	46	43	45	44	44	43
Too Much	17	16	16	17	22	21

SOURCE: General Social Surveys.

B. Are we spending too much money, too little money, or about the right amount on assistance to blacks?

Response Category	1984	1985	1986	1987	1988	1989
Too Little	26	29	23	28	29	31
About the Right Amount	46	45	48	48	46	45
Too Much	28	26	29	24	25	24

	1990	1991	1993	1994	1996
Too Little	31	35	27	27	27
About the Right Amount	46	45	45	44	45
Too Much	23	20	28	29	28

SOURCE: General Social Surveys.

improving the condition of blacks, while from 1984 to 1996 these surveys have contained an item on spending for "assistance to blacks." The data for these items are presented in Table 8–11.

One of the most striking features of these results is the remarkable consistency in the percentage of people who said "about the right amount" to each of these items. On the question of "improving the condition of blacks," the percentage who gave the middle response only varied between 42% and 48% over the 20 times this item has been asked, while the "about the right amount" response to the assistance to blacks item varied only between 44% and 48% across 11 surveys.

There is slightly more variation in the percentage giving either the "too much" or "too little" responses. For the "improving the condition of blacks" item, 35% said that we were spending "too little" in 1973. This percentage declined slightly during the 1970s, then began to increase through the 1980s, reaching a peak of 41% in 1990, then declining again slightly during the 1990s. The distribution on this item in the most recent (1996) survey is virtually identical to that found at the beginning of this series in 1973.

There is even less variation evident during the shorter time span covered by the "assistance to blacks" item. Again, the distribution in 1996 is essentially unchanged from that observed in 1984. Throughout this period, about 45% of the American public believed that we are spending about the right amount of money on assistance to blacks, approximately 30% thought we were spending too little, and close to one-fourth said we were spending too much.

The data on racial differences in attitudes on these spending items, presented in Table 8-12, extend the pattern of substantial distinctions in the views of blacks and whites. Throughout this period the average percentage of black respondents who thought that "too little" was being spent on improving the condition of blacks was 81%, with the percentage ranging from a high of 89% in 1982 to 70% in 1985. Conversely, the percentage of whites who thought too little was being spent on this activity averaged 26% over this span, and ranged from 19% in 1978 to 34% in 1990.

The breakdowns by race of the data for spending on assistance to blacks show a similar pattern. The average percentage of blacks saying "too little" was 78% and varied between 72% and 82%, while the average percentage for whites was 21% and ranged between 17% and 27%. Throughout this period blacks were much more likely than whites to express the view that too little was being spent on programs designed to benefit minorities.

The Civil Rights Movement, Impact of Slavery, and Voting for a Black Candidate

The final three items examined in this chapter involve more general questions on the condition of blacks in American society: the speed of the civil rights movement, the impact of slavery, and support for a minority candidate for president. In 1964, the NES instituted a question on whether respondents thought that civil rights leaders were trying to push too fast, going too slowly, or moving at about the right speed. The data presented in Table 8-13 show that at the height of the civil rights movement in the mid-1960s, a significant majority of the public felt that civil rights leaders were trying to push too fast. This declined to about 50% in 1970 and 1972, with around 40% in these two years saying the speed of the civil rights movement was about right and the remaining 10% feeling that it was not moving fast enough. The percentage who felt that civil rights leaders were trying to move too fast continued to decline until 1986, when it reached about 25%, and it has remained at about this level.

Table 8.12 Opinions about Spending on Racial Issues by Race

A. Percentage Saying Spending "Too Little" on Improving the Conditions of Blacks

	1973	1974	1975	1976	1977	1978	1980
Whites	28	26	22	24	20	19	20
Blacks	83	82	84	83	80	83	80

	1982	1983	1984	1985	1986	1987	1988
Whites	23	27	32	28	29	32	30
Blacks	89	80	71	70	75	80	81

	1989	1990	1991	1993	1994	1996
Whites	30	34	29	32	25	26
Blacks	83	82	82	84	81	85

B. Percentage Saying Spending "Too Little" on Assistance to Blacks

	1984	1985	1986	1987	1988	1989
Whites	20	22	17	21	21	24
Blacks	77	81	78	82	79	79

	1990	1991	1993	1994	1996
Whites	22	27	20	18	19
Blacks	80	73	74	77	72

SOURCE: General Social Surveys.

Table 8.13 Opinions on Speed of the Civil Rights Movement

Do you think that civil rights leaders are trying to push too fast, are going too slowly, or are moving at about the right speed?

Response Category	1964	1966*	1968	1970	1972	1976
Too Fast	68	73	65	50	48	42
About Right	26	22	28	37	43	50
Too Slowly	6	5	7	13	9	8

Response Category	1980	1984	1986	1988	1990	1992
Too Fast	36	31	25	26	29	25
About Right	51	56	61	58	59	57
Too Slowly	13	12	14	16	12	18

*Variant response categories.

SOURCE: American National Election Studies.

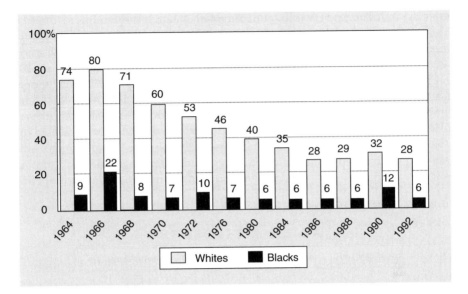

FIGURE 8.2 Opinions on the Speed of the Civil Rights Movement by Race, 1964–1992 (percentage saying "too fast")

SOURCE: American National Election Studies.

Since 1976 a majority of respondents have felt that civil rights leaders are moving at about the right speed, while about one-sixth of those surveyed feel the civil rights movement is going too slowly.

Opinions of blacks and whites on this issue show significant differences in outlook, with the decrease in the distinction over time resulting from changes in the opinions of whites (see Figure 8-2). Since 1964, about one in ten or fewer black respondents have held the view that civil rights leaders are pushing too fast.[2] On the other hand, the percentage of whites who hold this view has declined significantly over the past 30 years. Close to three-fourths of white respondents in 1964, 1966, and 1968 said that civil rights leaders were trying to push too fast. This proportion declined until 1986, when it reached about 30%, where it remained in succeeding years in which this question was posed. As was the case with the questions on spending to solve racial problems, blacks are more likely than whites to view the results of the civil rights movement as something that would benefit them. It is not surprising, therefore, to find that fewer black respondents feel that civil rights leaders are pushing too fast to achieve their goals.

The shape of the American mind on the question of the effect of slavery shows that the public generally feels that generations of slavery and discrimination have created conditions that make it difficult for blacks to work their way up (see Table 8-14). When this question was first asked in the NES in 1972, a clear majority of those surveyed agreed that previous discrimination

Table 8.14 Opinion on the Impact of Slavery

Generations of slavery and discrimination have created conditions that make it difficult for blacks to work their way up.

Response Category	1972	1986	1988	1990	1992	1994
Agree a Great Deal	30	21	16	19	19	14
Agree Somewhat	42	40	34	35	34	33
Neither Agree nor Disagree	—	9	12	12	10	11
Disagree Somewhat	16	18	24	22	23	24
Disagree a Great Deal	12	12	14	12	14	18

SOURCE: American National Election Studies.

made it difficult for blacks.[3] In 1986, 61% agreed with this statement, 30% disagreed, and 9% neither agreed nor disagreed. The percentage agreeing dropped
to about 50% in 1988 and has remained at about this level since.

Although the differences in opinion between blacks and whites on this issue are significant, they are not as large as those for many of the issues examined previously in this chapter. Since 1986, an average of 50% of whites and
71% of blacks have agreed that a history of slavery and discrimination have
made it difficult for blacks. While there have been some slight fluctuations in
this trend over time, the tendency is in the direction of fewer people agreeing
with this item, and the change in this direction is evident among both blacks
and whites (see Figure 8-3).

The final question that we examine in our discussion of racial issues involves
voting for a minority candidate for president. Since 1972 the GSS has included
the item, "If your party nominated a (Negro/Black/African-American) for
president, would you vote for him if he were qualified for the job?" and a similar question was asked in the Gallup Poll beginning in 1958. In the late 1950s,
approximately 40% of white respondents said that they would vote for a minority candidate for president, a percentage that rose to 60% by 1965, and to 75%
when the question was first asked in the GSS in 1972. Results for the GSS
question for the complete sample and by race are presented in Figure 8-4.[4] In
1974, 84% of those interviewed indicated that they would vote for a qualified
minority candidate for president. This already high percentage increased slightly
over time and has remained at about 90% throughout the 1990s.

In 1972, three-fourths of white respondents said they would be willing to
vote for their party's nominee if he were black. This percentage slowly increased, and by 1996 92% expressed this view. Not surprisingly, throughout
this period blacks have been almost unanimous in their willingness to support
a candidate of their race. While it appears that some remnants of racism remain
in the responses to this item, over the past 40 years public sentiment has
changed from a point at which less than a majority indicated a willingness to
vote for a black person for president to a virtual consensus on this issue.

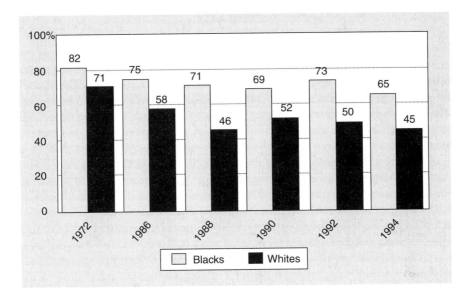

FIGURE 8.3 Opinions on the Impact of Slavery, by Race, 1972–1994
(percentage agreeing that "slavery has made it difficult")

SOURCE: American National Election Studies.

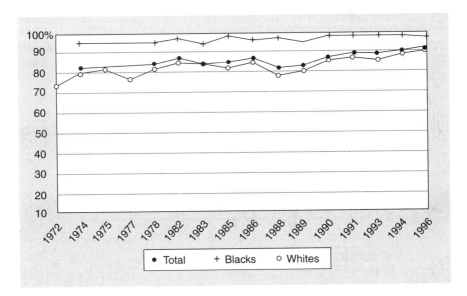

FIGURE 8.4 Opinions on Voting for a Black Candidate for President,
1972–1996

SOURCE: General Social Surveys.

SUMMARY

Overall, the data on race-related issues examined in this chapter demonstrate that there is a consensus in the American mind on the general idea of racial equality. Overwhelming majorities of the public believe that minorities have the right to live wherever they can afford, that white and black students should attend the same schools, and that minorities should receive fair treatment in jobs and housing. Similarly, there is a consensus on the question of willingness to vote for a qualified minority candidate for president.

The agreement on the general principle of racial equality in the American mind ebbs somewhat when the question of the government's role in ensuring equality is considered and diminishes even more when specific approaches for achieving this goal are evaluated. For example, the public is about evenly divided on the questions of whether the government in Washington should see to it that white and black children are allowed to go to the same school and whether government should see to it that black people get fair treatment in jobs. And the public has shown relatively strong opposition to specific solutions to these problems, such as busing of school children and affirmative action programs.

The findings discussed here are consistent with those of Lipset and Schneider (1978: 44) who reported that, [O]n every issue we have analyzed, the public opinion data show a 'positive' pro-civil rights consensus when only egalitarian considerations are at stake, but a 'negative' anti-civil rights consensus when the issue also pushes up against basic notions of individualism." Most Americans favor equal rights and equal opportunity, but this consensus breaks down "when *compulsory integration* is involved" (44).

Other analyses of trends in racial attitudes have examined data similar to those displayed here and reached the conclusion that there has been a great deal of change in a "pro-integrationist" direction in white racial attitudes in the past fifty years (for example, Mayer, 1992; Page and Shapiro, 1992; Schuman, Steeh, Bobo, and Krysan, 1997). As summarized by Schuman and his colleagues (1997: 288), there have been "fundamental changes in the values of white Americans. . . . The data indicate that there is no longer any attempt . . . to justify segregation in principle, and that this evolution has occurred steadily not only through the 1970s but indeed to the present day."

This does not mean, however, that analysts are agreed upon the interpretation of these data. Some researchers have looked at the difference between opinions on support for the general principles of equality and racial integration and for implementation of specific policies, such as busing or affirmative action, and concluded that this distinction represents a new form of racism. Their argument is that racism lies at the heart of whites' opposition to policies that would benefit minorities.

This "new racism" has been given a number of different labels, including symbolic racism, covert racism, modern racism, subtle racism, and racial resentment (Sears, Hensler, and Speer, 1979). Whatever its label, the core premise is that white attitudes "are based not on self-interest (for example, having one's own children involved in court-ordered busing), but rather on a more general sense that blacks are violating American values of individualism through their persistent demands for special treatment like affirmative action" (Schuman, Steeh, Bobo, and Krysan, 1997: 293). Individuals who dislike blacks and other minorities need only declare that they opposed government assistance to them not because of dislike, but because they believe in self-reliance (Sniderman, Piazza, Tetlock, and Kendrick, 1991: 424). Symbolic stances, therefore, are seen as "a way of expressing general anti-black attitudes in terms that seem culturally appropriate" (Link and Oldendick, 1996: 150).

While elements of racism remain in American society, there is little question that whites' racial attitudes have changed dramatically during the period in which they have been tracked by survey researchers. The "old-fashioned racism" that incorporated both a biologically-based theory of African racial inferiority and support for racial discrimination has been supplanted, and the principle of equal treatment now enjoys majority support (Sears, van Laar, Carillo, and Kosterman, 1997). It is the gap between support for this general principle and the specific application of this principle that has become the defining feature of contemporary research on racial attitudes.

The data presented here have also shown systematic and fairly substantial differences between the views of blacks and whites. There is a vast amount of additional data to which we could point to demonstrate the distinct views of the races (see, for example, Blendon, Benson, Brodie, Altman, and Brossard, 1998; Ladd, 1998A), such as the much higher percentage of blacks who believe that improving race relations is one of the most important things we need to do for the future of the country or the larger proportion who believe that racial minorities are routinely discriminated against in the United States.

We began this chapter with the assertion that it is inevitable that race will be an issue in our society. As evidence of the continuing presence of the race issue, in June 1997 President Clinton appointed a seven-member commission whose role was to lead the country in a national conversation on race. Given the differences in the opinions of blacks and whites on many issues and the fact that discussions of race-related issues are now dominated by specific policies that are more divisive, such as affirmative action, than by the general principles on which Americans agree, the commission faces "a daunting task" (Blendon, Benson, Brodie, Altman, and Brossard, 1998: 66). Race continues to be an important issue on the American political scene.

Polls, Polling, and the Internet

If you are interested in whether and how members of the public in one state might differ from citizens of another state on topics such as school integration and civil rights, you might want to look at a number of state polls that are archived at the Institute for Research in Social Science at the University of North Carolina. The data from the National Network of State Polls (NNSP) can be found at:

http://www.irss.unc.edu/nnsp

NOTES

1. By 1999, the distribution of opinion on school desegregation issues reached such a level of consensus that it might be considered a *valence issue* as discussed in Chapter 1.

2. The exception to the general pattern in 1966 is likely due to different response categories that were used for this question in this year.

3. Note that the 1972 distribution is not strictly comparable to those of later years, since the 1972 item did not include a "neither agree nor disagree" middle category.

4. This question was not asked of black respondents in 1972, 1975, and 1977. As a result, the data for "blacks" and for the "total sample" in these years are not presented in Figure 8-4.

9

Public Opinion
on Highly
Controversial Issues

Questions to Consider:

Is the American mind increasingly "tough on criminals?"

Why is the right to an abortion such a controversial issue?

Do Americans support the patient's "right-to-die?"

To what extent do Americans support gun control legislation?

Some issues simply seem to be more inflammatory than others when it comes to public policy. Whenever Congress or the president or, for that matter, politicians at any level, begin to discuss laws affecting certain issues such as abortion or the death penalty, emotions flare. Proponents and opponents use public opinion data to demonstrate their respective positions. Candidates for office often feel it necessary to state their own personal views on these issues early in a campaign to attract certain types of support and to get the issue out of the way for other voters. It is worth noting that in the late 1990s there seemed to be far more protests and acts of civil disobedience in regard to capital punishment and abortion issues than about civil rights or social welfare policies.

Is public opinion on these issues—crime, the death penalty, drug laws, abortion, euthanasia, and gun control—structured differently than on other domestic issues? As will be discussed in this chapter, the answer is both yes and no. For most of these issues, partisanship is a poor guide to public opinion. While the Republican Party has, since 1980, moved to espouse a tough position on capital punishment and an anti-abortion stance, these issues do not define that party for its identifiers. Political ideology is, on some issues, correlated to the distribution of opinion. In fact, Stimson (1991) examined these issues and others over time and found that the distribution of views within the public moved from liberal to conservative and then back toward the center, parallel to the movement of the American public away from liberal identification during the 1980s. However, some issues show very stable distributions of opinion over 20 or 30 years, demonstrating unusual consistency within the public. In these cases, especially, the roots of the opinion preferences may be in specific values or religious orientations and behaviors that are more deeply rooted than party or ideology.

Such highly controversial issues are particularly interesting to students of American politics because of the impact of public opinion on the policy process. These "hot topics" have the capacity to generate special interest groups that are dedicated to a single cause and to motivate supporters to give their personal time and resources to protect their viewpoint. Thus, politicians may be unwilling to vote against such a vocal minority for fear of being defeated by the group's efforts. Sometimes, the vehemence of the opinions expressed actually brings the political system to stalemate, as it has in the case of abortion policies since *Roe v. Wade.* On other issues, such as euthanasia and gun control, individual states have been able to adopt policies that cannot be considered on the national level and that will serve as social experiments for the public to observe.

In the sections that follow, we will look at the trends in public opinion on issues concerning crime and criminal justice, including the death penalty; issues of life and death including abortion and euthanasia; and the hotly contested issue of gun control.

THE POLITICS OF CRIME AND CRIMINAL JUSTICE

Public views on the causes of crime and the treatment of criminals have moved through several cycles since the end of World War II. The public moved toward more liberal views on the treatment of criminals, including a decline in support for the death penalty through the 1950s and early 1960s, but in the years since the mid-60s, the majority opinion has steadily moved to more conservative positions on the need for punishment, on the death penalty, and on the need for strict law enforcement. In the view of Stimson, the public's views on these societal issues are part of the long-term swing from liberalism to conservatism and back (Stimson, 1991). Page and Shapiro take a different approach to understanding the public's views on these issues, asserting that, "the public has exhibited rational opinions, differentiating clearly among alternative policies and reacting to changing realities" (1992: 90).

What were the changing realities that might have moved public opinion from a more liberal stance to more conservative opinions? Following a period of economic strength and relative domestic peace, the 1960s saw the beginning of the protests against the Vietnam conflict and, by the late 1960s, urban unrest and riots in many of America's major cities. Civil unrest continued until the end of the Vietnam conflict, which was followed by the Watergate scandal and the trials of the figures involved in it. During this period, the use of illicit drugs spread to new segments of the population and public awareness of the drug problem and the crimes it engendered rose to a new high. By the election of Ronald Reagan in 1980, the tide of public sentiment had turned on a number of issues, with the majority of the public seeking stricter enforcement of laws and stiffer penalties for criminals.

Perceptions of Crime

Fear of crime is a frequent topic in the media and public life in the United States, as is any increase or decrease in violent crime rates. However, it has been very difficult to measure public fear about crime because it is an issue that has both national and personal dimensions. If we look at the question that the Gallup organization has asked for several decades, "What is the most important problem facing the nation," crime and violence were only named most important in 1994 and 1995. In most of the years that the question was asked, economic issues—unemployment, inflation, or the budget deficit—gained the highest percentage of choices. In fact, from 1984 through 1993, only 5% of those surveyed said that crime was the most important problem (Roberts and Stalens, 1997: 54). However, the number increased to 9% in 1993, and in 1994, to 37% of those surveyed. At the same time, the rates of violent crime had actually begun to decline in many urban areas. It may be that the general public, when asked the above question, is reacting more to media coverage of crime or specific crimes than to information about the actual occurrence of crime in the nation. This is not to fault the American public, since it would be very unlikely for most Americans to have specific information about the general increase or decrease in crime rates.

However, crime is not only a national problem: it is also a neighborhood problem and, most importantly, a personal fear. The intensity of opinion about crime and criminal acts is much stronger when individuals answer questions about their personal perceptions of crime. If for example, the question is put in the following way, "Would you tell me which two or three [items] you personally are most concerned about today?" as it is by Roper Starch Worldwide, the percentage naming crime and lawlessness increases dramatically. Table 9-1 shows the percentage since 1974 indicating crime and lawlessness as concerns.

In attempting to measure the personal dimension of fear, for several decades polling organizations have been asking Americans about their feelings of personal safety and the crimes that they most fear. The results are intriguing. Although an overwhelming number of Americans would say that crime is increasing in the United States—and indeed, for several decades, crime rates did increase—the measurement of personal fear demonstrates amazing stability. Polls conducted since 1965 by the Gallup Organization and NORC have

Table 9.1 Crime as a Personal Concern

Question: Would you . . . tell me which two or three [items] you personally are
            most concerned about today?

	1974	1982	1988	1992	1992	1994	1996
Percentage naming "crime and lawlessness"	30%	37	33	35	42	54	47

SOURCE: Roper Starch Worldwide, 1996, published in *The Public Perspective*, June/July 1997, p. 10.

asked the question, "Is there any area around here—that is, within a mile—
where you would be afraid to walk alone at night?" In 1965, only 34% of
Americans answered yes to that question; by 1982, 48% answered in the affirmative. However, since that time, the proportion expressing fear of walking
near home declined to 42% in 1996 (*The Public Perspective*, 1997: 11). Viewed
over a thirty-year span, the total variation of 14% is not very large, considering
the amount of attention given to crime problems.

     The relatively modest variation in perceived neighborhood fear also ap-
pears in several other questions that have been asked for a long period of time.
When asked about the ethical standards and honesty of police officers, between 37% and 44% of Americans surveyed over a 15-year series said that such
standards were high or very high. Americans also have shown considerable stability in their views of government spending to halt the increase in crime: between 1973 and 1993, about two-thirds of those polled said that the government spends too little on crime. Finally, the question of whether courts deal
harshly enough with criminals has been asked for almost twenty years. Between 1972 and 1993, 70% to 85% of Americans polled responded that courts
do not deal harshly enough. After reviewing all of these trends in opinions toward crime, Timothy J. Flanagan concludes that American opinions have
demonstrated "remarkable temporal stability" (1996: 10).

     In looking further at the fear of crime expressed by individuals in society, a
number of studies have asked Americans about their fear of specific types of
crimes. Not surprisingly, the level of fear expressed does vary with the crime
described. For example, when asked if they fear their home being burglarized
when they are away, 45% of Americans admit that they are worried. While
only 19% of those polled say that they worry about getting murdered, 39% express fear of sexual assault. While there are few demographic differences between groups on the issues discussed above—fear of walking in the neighborhood, government spending, and the court's harshness—there are significant
demographic differences relative to these different types of crime.

     As shown in Table 9-2, as Americans age, they are less afraid of sexual as-
sault but much more fearful of being mugged. Given their physical frailty, this
fear makes considerable sense. As you might expect, women are far more afraid
of sexual assault and being mugged then are men. The differences in fear ex-

Table 9.2 Fear of Victimization

Question: Do you worry *very frequently, somewhat frequently, seldom or never* about (A) yourself or someone in your family getting sexually assaulted . . . (B) getting mugged . . . (C) getting murdered . . . (D) your home being burglarized while no one is at home?

	Percent saying very/somewhat frequently worry about:			
	Sexual Assault	Mugging	Murder	Burglary
National	39%	28	19	45
Age				
18–29	34	22	19	47
30–39	41	24	18	47
40–49	43	35	23	48
50–59	43	34	17	53
60–69	38	29	16	38
70+	26	31	14	33
Race/ethnicity				
White	39	27	17	45
Hispanic	53	43	27	51
Black	28	28	30	45
Gender				
Male	29	21	14	44
Female	47	34	23	47
Household Income				
Less than $15,000	37	31	25	42
$15,000–30,000	44	26	21	47
$30,001–60,000	37	28	16	47
More than $60,000	37	27	16	45

SOURCE: Adapted from *The Public Perspective*, June/July, 1997, p. 13. Data from a survey by the Public Policy Research Institute at Texas A&M University and the College of Criminal Justice, Sam Houston State University, June 6–26, 1995.

pressed by whites, African Americans, and Hispanics are very telling, both in terms of cultural differences and, possibly, in terms of the areas where people of different ethnic backgrounds live. On the question of sexual assault, black Americans express less fear than whites, but Hispanic Americans are twice as fearful as African Americans. Hispanic respondents also express the greatest fear of being mugged and of burglary. African Americans are more afraid of being murdered than are any other group. While Hispanics may be victimized at a higher rate for some crimes, that rate is not proportional with the fear expressed. In a more simple case, females in American society have a relatively low rate of victimization from sexual assault, but they express great fear about this possibility. Criminal justice experts have suggested that this "vulnerability" expressed by women reflects their awareness of the inability to defend themselves (Haghighi and Sorensen, 1996: 29). Another factor that speaks to cultural issues or, perhaps, community perceptions within an ethnic group, is that household income seems to have very little influence on fear of these crimes. People who live in poorer households are very slightly more fearful of being mugged or murdered than are others. Wealthier individuals have less fear of murder, no doubt because they live in neighborhoods where murder seems to rarely occur.

Perceptions of Punishment

As noted earlier in this chapter, an overwhelming majority of Americans believe that the government should spend more to halt increases in crime and that the courts are too lenient with criminals that come before them. While Americans have consistently expressed these views for at least twenty years, such stability does conceal variations in Americans' views about the causes for crime and the goal of incarceration.

Two decades ago, Americans expressed much more liberal views about the causes of crime and the goals of the criminal justice system than they do today. Surveys conducted by various groups, including the Gallup Organization, ABC News, and NBC News/ *Wall Street Journal* have asked questions about the reasons for increasing crime rates since 1981. In that year, 37% of those polled said that unemployment and social conditions accounted for the increase in crime rates, 33% blamed the rise on failures of the criminal justice system, and 13% said that drugs were a cause. By 1994, the survey asked which factor was most responsible for crime. The public answered social conditions/unemployment, 8%; failure of the criminal justice system, 20%; crisis of personal values, 30%, and drugs, 20% (*The Public Perspective*, 1997: 14). In other years, surveys have found as much as 56% of the public placing the blame on drugs.

Given these changes in the public's view of the causes of crime, it is not as surprising that the American public has also changed its understanding of the goals of the criminal justice system. This change is documented in Table 9-3. As you will note, in the earliest poll cited, conducted by Louis Harris in 1966, 77% of those polled believed that prisons should be mainly corrective. By 1981, belief in rehabilitation was expressed by only 49%, and by 1994, only 16% of those surveyed by ABC News believed that the main purpose of prisons was to rehabilitate prisoners. Fifty-three percent believed prisons were meant to keep criminals out of society and 29% felt that they were meant to punish criminals.

On the question of the purpose of prisons, the American public does begin to show some differences related to demographics and, in a small way, to political views. The study conducted by the Public Policy Institute at Texas

Table 9.3 The Perceived Goals of Prisons

	Percentage agreeing			
Question	1966	1970	1981	1994
Should prisons be*				
Mainly corrective	77%			
Mainly punitive	11			
Main emphasis of prison should be*				
Punishing		8		
Rehabilitating		73		
Protecting society		12		
Main emphasis of prison should be*				
Punishing			17	
Rehabilitating			49	
Protecting society			31	
Main purpose of prisons is†				
Punish criminals				29
Rehabilitate criminals				16
Keep criminals out of society				53

*Survey by Louis Harris and Associates: June, 1968; October, 1970; January, 1981.
†Survey by ABC News, November 17, 1994.

SOURCE: Table adapted from *The Public Perspective*, June/July, 1997, p. 20.

A&M and Sam Houston State University in 1995 asked respondents to indicate what *should* be the most important purpose in sentencing adults: deterrence (stopping others from committing crimes); incapacitation (keeping criminals away from society); rehabilitation; or retribution (punishing criminals). The national data are shown in Table 9-4 along with the breakdowns by demographic groups, party identification, and political ideology. As you will note, rehabilitation is more likely to be seen as the purpose of sentencing among younger Americans, Hispanic and black respondents, college graduates, and liberals. Conservatives are the most likely to see punishment or retribution as the main purpose, but so are Democrats. There are few, if any, differences between men and women in their views of the purpose of prison.

The data in Tables 9-3 and 9-4 suggest that the American people generally wish to see punishment emphasized in the treatment of criminals. However, in other studies, Americans have also supported early release for good behavior, more community-oriented programs for minor offenders, and a wide range of training and educational programs that might help prisoners become productive citizens. In light of the opinions expressed about retribution, how can support for more rehabilitative measures be explained? After

Table 9.4 Rehabilitation vs. Punishment

Question: Which of these four purposes do you think should be the most important in sentencing adults . . . to discourage others from committing crimes (deterrence), to separate offenders from society (incapacitation), to train, educate, and counsel offenders (rehabilitation), or to give offenders the punishment they deserve (retribution)?

	Percentage Agreeing			
	Deterrence	Incapacitation	Rehabilitation	Retribution
National	13%	13	21	53
Age				
18–29	11	9	29	51
30–39	14	12	18	56
40–49	16	19	21	44
50–59	10	13	13	65
60–69	13	15	20	53
70+	6	11	21	63
Race				
White	14	14	18	54
Hispanic	10	10	30	50
Black	8	7	30	55
Gender				
Male	14	11	21	53
Female	12	15	20	53
Education				
Less than high school	5	6	23	66
High school graduate	11	10	20	59
Some college	17	16	19	49
College graduate	9	19	33	39
Party Identification				
Republican	17	17	14	52
Democrat	9	11	26	56
Independent	13	13	23	51
Political Ideology				
Liberal	14	9	29	48
Middle of the road	11	15	22	53
Conservative	15	13	15	56

SOURCE: Survey by the Public Policy Research Institute at Texas A&M University and the College of Criminal Justice, Sam Houston State University, June 6-26, 1995.

considering all of these seemingly inconsistent points of view, some scholars have suggested that what the public wants are effective, well-run prisons that are also humane and can help offenders who are capable to better themselves (Flanagan, 1996: 92).

The Death Penalty

As we have seen, the public's views on the purposes of incarceration have changed over the last two decades, from correction and rehabilitation to punishment and the segregation of criminals from society. This shift in the views of the public is also found in the pattern of public opinion about the use of the death penalty. In the 1930s, when polling data were first available, the Gallup Poll found that 61% of Americans favored capital punishment for those convicted of murder. The level of support for this penalty remained stable until the mid-1950s (see Figure 9-1) when it began to decline, finally reaching 42% in favor of the death penalty in 1966. Page and Shapiro suggest that this trend reflects the general liberalization of societal attitudes during the 1960s; they further suggest that the subsequent rise in support for capital punishment was associated with fear of crime after the urban riots of the 1960s (1992: 94).

During the same period of time that the public reconsidered its views on capital punishment, the Supreme Court of the United States handed down several very important rulings on the issue. After ruling in 1958 (*Trop v. Dulles*) that the constitutional prohibition against "cruel and unusual punishment" could be interpreted according to "evolving standards of decency" in a society, the court moved, in 1972, to outlaw the death penalty altogether (*Furman v. Georgia,* 1972). This case provoked a national outcry among law enforcement officials and encouraged public debates in virtually every state because the court, while finding the Georgia death penalty statute arbitrary and capricious, suggested that states could write death penalty laws that would meet a constitutional standard. In the four years following the Furman decision, 35 states wrote new death penalty statutes that specified the crimes for which the penalty could be sought and established specific procedures for recommending such a punishment. (Roberts and Stalans, 1997: 226). The new Georgia statute was ruled constitutional by the Supreme Court in 1976 (*Gregg v. Georgia*).

By the time that the Supreme Court struck down the first Georgia law in 1972, more than 60% of the public supported capital punishment for certain crimes. Since that time, as Figure 9-1 shows, support for capital punishment for persons convicted of murder has stabilized at about 72% of the public.

There are some differences in the level of support by demographic groups that are not very surprising. Women are less supportive of the death penalty (67%) than men (74%) and Republicans are more supportive (82%) than Democrats (74%) or independent voters (78%). As you would expect, conservatives are more supportive (84%) than liberals (75%), but that difference is not as great as one might have anticipated. The strongest difference of opinion on the death penalty is found between the races, and it has, as seen in Figure 9-2, been a consistent trend for the last twenty years. Black Americans are far less likely to support the death penalty than are white Americans. Given the fact that a much higher proportion of those convicted persons who are on death row are black, this opposition among African Americans is understandable, as is the view that recommendations for capital punishment may involve some elements of racial bias by juries or communities.

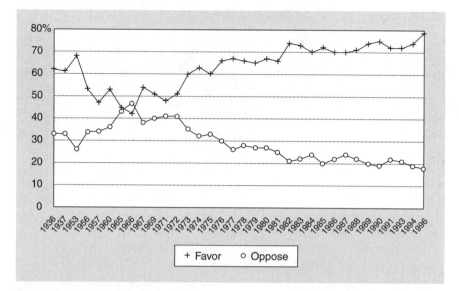

FIGURE 9.1   Public Opinion on the Death Penalty, 1936–1996

Question wording: in 1936–37, "Are you in favor of the death penalty for murder?";
from 1953 to the present, the wording has varied between "Are you in favor of the
death penalty for persons convicted of murder?" and "Do you favor or oppose the
death penalty for persons convicted of murder?"

SOURCE: The Gallup Organization, 1936–1972; Gallup and General Social Survey, 1973 through 1996, as published
in Stanley and Niemi, 5th edition, *Vital Statistics on American Politics*, p. 33 plus author's update.

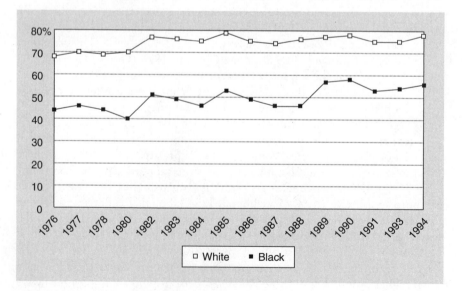

FIGURE 9.2   Support for Capital Punishment by Blacks and Whites, 1976–1994
Question: Do you favor or oppose the death penalty for persons convicted of murder?

SOURCE: General Social Survey.

As noted in Chapter 1, the public's views on capital punishment and the appropriate use of this penalty for convicted murderers may be considered one of those issues on which **public judgment** has occurred. Following Yankelovich's definition of public judgment, the data about the public's support for capital punishment show considerable change over time, a certain lengthy dialogue inspired by the Supreme Court's rulings, debates and legislation in most of the states, and, by the late 1990s, stability in the public's support for capital punishment as well as a fairly stable differentiation of opinion between black and white Americans.

THE POLITICS OF LIFE AND DEATH

Although the media frequently show the candlelight vigils held outside of prisons when a convicted criminal is about to be put to death, those protesting capital punishment are, for the most part, peaceful in their means and quite aware that they are expressing a minority view. In contrast, the opponents and proponents of two other issues of life and death—abortion and euthanasia— are much more intense in their views. The emotions and energy invested in debates about these issues reflect both the degree to which opinions are rooted in deeply-held values and the fact that the legal status of the abortion issue and that of the right-to-die issue are still in contention nationally and at the state level.

Public Opinion toward Abortion

Until the Supreme Court decision in 1973, the regulation of birth control information and devices and of abortion were matters for state law. Abortions were for the most part illegal across the United States, although the penalties and laws differed by state. As Page and Shapiro note (1992: 104–106), however, the debate over the regulation of private decisions about sexual activity and pregnancy first became public with the introduction of the birth control pill in the 1960s. Following the *Griswold v. Connecticut* case, decided by the Supreme Court in 1965, states could no longer bar physicians from distributing information about birth control or devices including the new pill. In fact, surveys about whether birth control information should be available showed wide public support from the mid-1930s; the Connecticut law and the Griswold decision were seen by many as anachronistic. That the debate would move on to the topic of abortion, which also deals with the ability of women to control their bodies, should not be surprising.

Although *Roe v. Wade* brought the topic of abortion to the forefront of public debate (and generated hundreds of poll questions), it is worth noting that the General Social Survey had been asking about whether abortion should be legal in specific circumstances since the early 1960s. In 1962, for example, 77% of the public felt that abortion should be legal if the mother's health was seriously endangered by the pregnancy; 55% supported abortion if the baby had a serious birth defect; but only 15% approved of an abortion if the family had a very low income and could not afford the child (Stanley and

Niemi, 1995: 36). Between 1962 and 1973, the proportion of Americans who believed that abortion should be legal in cases where the mother's health was endangered had risen to 91%. Support for an abortion in the case of rape was 81%; in case of a birth defect, 82%; and because of low income, 52%. Page and Shapiro assert that, in their view, the changes in American views on abortion and women's control of their own bodies actually occurred before the Roe decision in 1973.

Since that galvanizing decision, there have been hundreds of polls on the topic of abortion, the development of several different standard sets of items by the various survey research organizations, many books on the politics of abortion, and many state laws written that have re-regulated abortions within the limits of the Roe decision. The Supreme Court has, in fact, supported state laws that placed more barriers between women and abortion providers, including mandatory counseling; consent forms for the father of the baby or, in the case of minor women, their parents/guardians; and waiting periods. However, the essence of the Roe decision, which allows (1) abortions by physicians in the first trimester of pregnancy, (2) more state regulation of abortions in the second trimester, and (3) the banning of abortions in the third trimester by the states, still structures the debate.[1]

To begin to understand public opinion about the legality of abortions, survey organizations have, rightly, asked people about their support for abortion under different conditions. Generally, pollsters have asked respondents if they believe it should be legal or possible for a woman to obtain an abortion under the following six conditions:

—if the woman's health is seriously endangered by the pregnancy

—if she is pregnant as the result of rape

—if there is a chance of a serious birth defect in the infant

—if she is married and does not want any more children

—if the family is too poor to support any more children

—if the woman is single and will not be marrying the father of the baby.

To analyze how the individual respondent thinks about these different conditions, Cook, Jelen, and Wilcox (1992: 32–33) have suggested that we look at opinions toward *traumatic abortions* (mother's health, birth defect, rape) and *elective abortions* (poverty, lack of desire for children, single parenthood). Their research suggests that "there is a societal consensus that abortion should be legal in each of the traumatic circumstances" (35).

If we look at the data on these "conditional" questions since 1961, which are displayed in Table 9-5, we can see the evidence that brings Cook and her colleagues to this conclusion. The set of three conditions which they consider to be elective abortions do not, at any time, gather nearly the level of public support as the more traumatic conditions do. Support for making abortions available to women for the elective reasons reached a high in the decade following the Roe decision; since that time support for abortions in these situations has declined to more modest levels, as has support for abortion under any condition.

Table 9.5 Support for Legal Abortion under Different Conditions

Question: Please tell me whether or not you think it should be possible for a pregnant woman to obtain a legal abortion if there is a strong chance of serious defect in the baby? If she is married and does not want any more children? If the woman's own health is seriously endangered by the pregnancy? If the family has a very low income and cannot afford any more children? If she became pregnant as a result of rape? If she is not married and does not want to marry the man?

| | Abortion should be legal under these circumstances: | | | | | |
Year	Mother's Health	Rape	Birth Defect	Poor	Single Mother	No More Babies
1962	77		55	15		
1965	70	56	55	21	17	15
1969	80		63	23		
1972	83	75	75	46	41	38
1973	91	81	82	52	47	38
1974	90	83	83	52	47	46
1975	88	80	80	51	46	44
1976	89	81	82	51	48	45
1977	89	81	83	52	48	45
1978	88	81	80	46	40	39
1980	88	80	80	50	46	45
1982	90	83	81	50	47	46
1983	87	80	76	42	38	38
1984	88	77	78	46	43	41
1985	87	78	76	42	40	39
1987	86	78	77	44	40	38
1988	86	77	76	41	38	39
1989	88	80	79	46	43	43
1990	89	81	78	46	43	43
1993	86	79	79	48	46	45
1994	88	81	80	49	46	47
1996	89	81	79	45	43	45

SOURCE: General Social Surveys.

As with the conditions under which the public supports legal abortions, it is also possible to categorize individuals according to their position on these questions and others that ask about the degree of regulation of abortion. Cook, Jelen, and Wilcox (1992) suggest three categories of respondents: pro-life respondents who generally oppose abortion under any condition; pro-choice respondents who believe abortion should be legal under any condition; and *situationalists* who support abortions in some circumstances but not others. There are several ways to determine how many people or what proportion of Americans fall into each of these categories. Cook, Jelen, and Wilcox based their distinction on the number and type of conditions that a respondent finds acceptable for abortion, thus bringing the percentage of absolute pro-life

Americans to about 8% in the period 1987–1991 (140). Likewise, pure pro-choice Americans (who believe in no restrictions on the procedure) number less than 10% of Americans. Thus more than 80% of Americans might be judged to be situationalists, approving an abortion under some conditions but not others.

Although the categories suggested by Cook, Jelen, and Wilcox are very useful for their analysis, there are other series of poll questions that allow us to look at the broader contours of American opinion on the legality of abortion. A Gallup Poll question asks, "Do you think abortions should be legal under any circumstances, legal only under certain circumstances, or illegal in all circumstances?" A CBS/New York Times poll question asks, "Which comes closest to your view? (1) Abortion should be generally available to those who want it, (2) Abortion should be available but under stricter limits than it is now, or (3) Abortion should not be permitted." Looking at Table 9-6, the Gallup Poll, we see that the percentage of Americans who believe that abortion should always be illegal has fallen from 22% in 1975 to about 15%, while the percentage of those who believe that it depends on the circumstances remained about 55% through this period. The pro-choice proportion peaked at 33% in 1994, but has declined in recent years. The CBS News/New York Times poll question, presented in Table 9-7, finds that between 35 and 40% of Americans believe abortion should be generally available; about 40% prefer stricter limits; and 19% would not permit abortions at all. How do we account for the difference in proportions between these two polls? The proportion of Americans who truly oppose legal abortions is between 15 and 20 percent. At least 40% of Americans and probably, more likely 60 to 70% of Americans believe that it depends on the circumstances (or are "situationalists") and about 20 to 35% are pro-choice most of the time. The CBS/New York Times question allows the respondent to formulate his or her own definition of "generally available" and "stricter limits," while the Gallup question refers directly to circumstances. This question-wording difference prompts the respondents to answer differently, although the response patterns for both survey organizations have been surprisingly stable over the years.

Because the debate over abortion is often based on differing religious views, with the Catholic Church and some others taking official positions opposing abortion, it is not surprising to find that religious affiliation or belief is a major determinant of abortion opinion, although religion is not as dominant a predictor of individual attitudes as one might think. According to the work of Cook, Jelen, and Wilcox (1992: 104) the intensity and involvement of individuals with their church is the factor that differentiates pro-choice and pro-life members of the same denomination. They find, for example, that only 3% of Catholics who are involved at a low level with their church are pro-life in their attitudes, as compared to 25% of those who are highly involved. In the evangelical protestant denominations, the patterns are similar. Members of any Protestant denomination or the Catholic Church who believe that the Bible is inerrant are also more likely to be pro-life.

Groups that are likely to be pro-choice are younger people, especially those who identify with the Democratic party, and the most highly educated seg-

Table 9.6 Opinion on Abortions under What Circumstances

Question: Do you think abortions should be legal under any circumstances, legal only under certain circumstances, or illegal in all circumstances?

| Year | Percentage saying: | | |
	Legal under Any Circumstances	Legal Only under Certain Circumstances	Illegal in All Circumstances
1975	21	54	22
1977	22	55	19
1979	22	54	19
1981	23	52	22
1983	23	58	16
1988	24	57	17
1990	31	53	12
1992	31	53	14
1994	33	52	13
1996	25	58	15

SOURCE: The Gallup Organization.

Table 9.7 Opinions on Abortion Restrictions

Question: Which comes closest to your view? (1) Abortion should be generally available to those who want it; or (2)Abortion should be available but under stricter limits than it is now; or (3)Abortion should not be permitted.

| Year | Percentage Saying | | |
	Generally Permitted	Stricter Limits	Not Permitted
1989	41	42	15
1990	39	40	18
1991	37	38	22
1992	40	39	19
1993	42	36	20
1994	40	37	21
1995	40	37	21
1996	40	41	18
1997	32	45	22

SOURCE: CBS News/*New York Times* Poll.

ments of the society. In general, polls show women to be more supportive of legal abortions in all situations than men (about a 6% gap); Jewish respondents are much more supportive than are other religious groups; and black Americans are marginally more favorable than whites, although that distinction has varied over time.

Given the fact that the issue of abortion rights is central to the feminist political agenda, it seems natural that pro-feminist attitudes would predict opinions on abortion. The work of Cook, Wilcox, and Jelen (1992: 76–80) demonstrates that those who hold feminist views are more likely to be pro-choice in their views on abortion. They note that those respondents who can be classified as favoring "private feminism," namely, that are supportive of a woman's right to work full-time and have a family, are the most likely to be pro-choice. However, when Cook et al. compared holding feminist attitudes with conservative views on sexual morality and the belief that abortion is "a matter of life and death," they found that opinions on sexual morality are the strongest predictors of attitudes toward elective abortions (1992: 87).

The polls of the late 1990s have begun to show some decline in support for abortion in all situations across all demographic groups. In a 1998 article, Lydia K. Saad reported on a trend in the Gallup polls that found the proportion of Americans who said that abortion should be legal in all circumstances dropping from the stable one-third of prior years to 25% (Saad, 1998: 7). The *New York Times* also reported a similar decline in a January 15, 1998 article reporting on its most recent abortion poll. The CBS News/*New York Times* found that percentage of Americans who wanted stricter limits on abortion had increased from 40 to 45% (p. 1). It is possible that the change in opinion toward more limits on abortion was a result of the widespread debate over "partial-birth abortions" that was carried on in Congress during 1997. The bill outlawing this procedure was, in fact, vetoed by President Clinton because he said that the procedure was rarely used, and then only in cases of medical necessity. Pro-life forces promised to pursue legislation to outlaw the procedure.

When the data on public attitudes toward abortion are looked at from a larger point of view, it seems pretty clear that the majority of Americans support legal abortions under some circumstances, while small, intense minorities are totally pro-life or pro-choice. On this issue, the public has not come to a common view on the topic nor, given the minorities' strength of belief and their willingness to engage in political and legal action, is the debate likely to be solved in the near future.

Public Opinion toward the Right To Die

Another topic that involves deep religious and moral values is the right of a terminally ill person to commit suicide or to receive help in doing so from a physician or other health professional—the so-called "right to die." Dr. Jack Kevorkian, the Michigan pathologist who has helped a number of people to commit suicide, has greatly increased public attention to this question, although the basic issue has been a matter for public debate for many decades. The 1930s saw the founding of the Euthanasia Society of America, which first began advocating the right to die for patients (Clark, 1997: 7). In the 1970s the Karen Quinlan case brought public attention to the difficulties faced by families of comatose patients in their desire to end the patient's suffering. Since that time, a number of states have passed statutes that more carefully define when life support can be denied or withdrawn from a patient. Many Americans, cognizant of these issues, have executed legal documents that provide direction should they become terminally ill and unable to request an end to medical care. There are, in addition, publications and societies that are intended to assist patients in committing suicide in a painless way. Most of these efforts to improve the end of life for severely ill people are quietly proceeding through courts, medical associations, and legislatures.

What does the American public believe about these right-to-life initiatives? Like some of the other issues discussed in this chapter—capital punishment, the right to an abortion—euthanasia is a very controversial topic. In general, American opinions have become more liberal on right-to-die questions. In response to the question "Do you think a person has the right to end his or her own life if this person has an incurable disease?" 59% of Americans said "no" in 1977, compared to 38% who agreed with the statement. Although the trend has been less than linear, by 1996, opinion on this question showed a complete reversal: 61% of Americans support the right of a patient to end his or her own life in this situation while only 34% oppose it. The proportion of Americans who support allowing doctors to help patients end life if they request such help has increased from 60% to 68% over the same time period. Only 18% of Americans oppose such physician assistance. Gallup Poll data also provide evidence of this change in opinion: in 1947, only 37% of respondents agreed that doctors should be allowed to end a patient's life if he or she requests it, compared to 69% agreeing in 1996 that doctors should provide such assistance. In the 1996 poll, the Gallup Organization tested these opinions by splitting the sample and asking half the respondents if doctors should help a patient commit suicide if the patient requests such help. As noted in earlier chapters, question wording can have a strong impact on survey responses: when the Gallup question was changed to introduce the word "suicide," the percentage of respondents who approve physician assistance declined from 66% to 52%. Analysis of this data suggested that women and those respondents with the strongest religious attachment were most affected by the introduction of "suicide" into the question (Golay, 1997: 94). Although the debate over the right to die does go back more than 50 years, new medical advances continue to change the grounds of the debate, as do the various initiatives that have been put on the ballot in individual states and the court cases that follow. It is very likely that American minds will continue to change their opinions on this issue in the years to come.

AMERICAN VIEWS ON GUN CONTROL

Gun control is, without doubt, another one of the controversial issues that Americans debate in their local communities and in the halls of Congress. Like the issues of abortion and the right to die, legislative action is fairly constant. Gun control as an issue differs from abortion and other issues dealing with life and death in that there is only one intense minority at work: those Americans who oppose any increase in government restrictions on their right to purchase, keep, and use firearms. As we will see, those who oppose gun control do so on constitutional grounds and as a matter of libertarian philosophy, rather than for religious reasons. The proponents of gun control are usually arguing from the side of increased safety and the reduction of violent crime.

The Ownership of Guns

Surveys of the American people have indicated fairly consistently that about 40 to 50% of Americans own guns. About 70% of those who own guns have more than one in their possession. For the most part, polls have found that half of all gun owners say that the purpose of having a gun is for sport, while about 20% say that they own a gun for self protection (Adams, in Flanagan and Longmire, 1996, p. 110–111). When we look at the characteristics of gun ownership, the most important determinants are living in a rural area or small town, having a higher income, being male, and being white. Although gun ownership is often associated with being southern, higher proportions of people who live in the mountain states and in the midwest own guns than those who live in the south or on either coast.

Thinking about Weapons and Government Controls

To those who study public opinion on gun control, it seems quite clear that Americans are able to differentiate between the types of guns that they believe are appropriate for people to own. According to Page and Shapiro (1992: 94), Americans are quite able to distinguish "fairly sharply among types of weapons (long guns, handguns, cheap "Saturday night special" handguns, assault rifles, automatic weapons), among different types of policies, and among different types of possible gun owners." Polls have consistently shown levels of support for the banning of assault weapons and automatic weapons at 70% or higher, although the details of such weaponry are not well understood (Roberts and Stalans, 1997: 285). The majority of Americans support the banning of cheap, easily available handguns, but most do not approve banning guns used for sport or hunting. In terms of who should be prohibited from owning weapons, most polls show that strong majorities support banning the sale of guns to juveniles and to persons who would pose a risk to society, including convicted felons, mentally disturbed people, and convicted drug dealers.

   While Americans are certainly not ready to ban the ownership of guns, the majority of people do not see regulations that require the registration of gun ownership as a violation of the second amendment. As displayed in Table 9-8, more than two-thirds of those questioned in each survey between 1959 and 1996 approve of laws that require people to obtain police permits before they can buy a gun. In fact, the percentage supporting permits has almost stabilized

Table 9.8 Public Opinion on Gun Permits

Question: Would you favor or oppose a law which would require a person to obtain a police permit before he or she could buy a gun?

Year	Favor	Oppose
1959	75	21
1963	79	17
1965	73	23
1967	73	24
1971	72	24
1973	74	25
1975	71	28
1977	72	27
1980	69	29
1982	72	26
1984	70	27
1988	74	24
1990	79	20
1991	81	18
1993	81	17
1994	78	20
1996	81	18

SOURCE: Gallup Surveys (1959–1971); Survey Research Center, University of Michigan, and the General Social Survey.

at the 80 % level. With this high level of support for requiring police permits, it is no surprise that the Brady Bill, which also required a five-day waiting period to buy a gun, had strong support from the American public.

If there is such strong and stable support for government regulation of the purchase of guns, it is difficult to understand why such legislation is still so controversial. This is one of those issues in which the power of a national interest group that holds strong views on the subject and has enough vocal members to influence members of Congress makes a difference. A very interesting study by Adams (1996: 120–122) looked at the difference in activism and opinions between gun owners and non-owners. Adams found that gun owners were much more likely to promote their opinions on gun issues (25%) versus non-owners (12%). Of those who owned guns for sport and protection, 37% reported that they had voiced their opinions about gun control issues. As one might expect, gun owners were more likely to want less strict laws or to keep laws the same rather than to enact stricter laws. They were also much more likely to see guns as a defense against government abuse (22%) and for personal protection against criminals (50%). Although this study did not report whether gun owners were members of an interest group like the National

Rifle Association, their high level of activism is certainly one reason that gun control remains a controversial issue in the American mind.

SUMMARY

American opinions on these controversial issues show both stability and polarization. On the issues surrounding crime and criminal justice, it is clear that the American mind has moved from a more liberal approach to criminals in the 1950s, to a philosophy that supports punishment for the convicted criminal with support for rehabilitative services in prisons for those who benefit from them. The return to a more conservative view is most obvious on the death penalty: the Supreme Court opinion that effectively "outlawed" the death penalty in 1972 was, in part, an outgrowth of more liberal sentiments in the society, but it also forced states to redraw their death penalty statutes in a more rigorous fashion. Public opinion has supported the application of the death penalty in appropriate cases since that time.

Public opinion on the abortion issue, when observed over twenty-plus years, is quite stable. However, it differs from opinion on the death penalty because there remain intense and vocal minorities who contest the majority's view. As we have seen, most Americans believe that a woman has a right to an abortion under certain situations, although the American mind certainly has not reached consensus on exactly which situations. The strong minorities who hold extreme views rarely gain any more adherents, but continue to apply political pressure at all levels of government. The right-to-die issue is just beginning to evolve. Because it involves moral issues and the individual's right to choose, it is likely to escalate into as hot a debate as abortion in the years to come.

Another issue that remains controversial is that of gun control. With the increase in school shootings by children and gun accidents involving children, there is continued political pressure to regulate guns and gun owners. Although our examination of public opinion shows that most Americans support some regulation of guns and the banning of some types of weapons, the debate over who should be a legitimate gun owner and how the society makes that decision is likely to continue at all levels of government.

Polls, Polling, and the Internet

The commercial survey organization with the longest history of polling is, of course, The Gallup Organization. If you are interested in seeing the Gallup Reports (monthly) on current topics and on some of these "hot topics," point your browser to their very well organized web site at:

http://www.gallup.com

You may also write to the Gallup Organization with questions about the data available using the electronic mail feature on this web site.

NOTES

1. For an extensive discussion of the politics of the abortion issue and the impact of the various Supreme Court decisions, see Barbara Hinkson Craig and David M. O'Brien, *Abortion and American Politics*, New York: Chatham House, 1993.

10

How Americans View Foreign and Defense Policies

Questions to Consider:

Do Americans support an active role for the United States in world affairs?

To what extent does the public hold the same views about foreign policy as the elites in the United States?

Does the public support using American troops to intervene in crises overseas?

To what extent does the public pay attention to foreign issues?

The place of the United States in the world community has shifted so rapidly over the past two generations that it is hard to comprehend. On June 5, 1994, President Bill Clinton joined the leaders of our former European allies to commemorate the landing of Allied Forces on the beaches of Normandy in 1944, 50 years earlier. Joining him for that ceremony were many American GIs who were veterans of that epic invasion of Europe. The contrast between the experiences of the president and of those veterans could not be more stark.

The veterans who served in World War II for the United States were born in an era when their country was determined to avoid a role on the world stage. Their fathers may have served in World War I. But the United States became part of that struggle near its end. After the armistice, the United States Senate rejected the treaty that formed the League of Nations, even though the world organization was the creation of President Woodrow Wilson. The

United States retreated once again into its historical pose of isolationism. During the rise of fascism in Europe in the 1930s, most Americans believed that this nation should stay out of Europe's difficulties.

President Franklin Roosevelt extended various forms of aid from the United States to Great Britain in its fight against Hitler's Germany and persuaded the American people to support such forms of involvement. As documented by Page and Shapiro (1992: 184, 185), less than ten percent of the public thought that the U.S. should enter the war in late 1940, but by April, 1941, more than 70% thought that the U.S. should do everything to help England and 60% thought it important to defeat Germany. Not until the Japanese attack on Pearl Harbor did Americans support the entry of the United States into the war. By the end of World War II, the United States was the most powerful military nation in the world, with control of nuclear weapons and a strong industrial sector and workforce. It was the United States that reached out to rebuild allies and defeated enemies in Europe after the war and that founded the United Nations. Those GIs who entered the war to defend an isolated nation came home to be citizens of the nation with more global responsibilities than any other on earth.

Think about the upbringing and life experience of President Bill Clinton in contrast to those veterans. He was raised in a nation with multiple alliances and a global military force. The United States was embroiled in a cold war with the Soviet Union; both sides amassed weapons of mass destruction and the missiles to deliver them. He probably had no personal memories of the Korean War, but he certainly had memories of the Vietnam conflict. The President himself was one of millions of Americans who had made a personal decision about whether to fight in that war and, while a student in London, had protested against American involvement. By the time he became president, the Cold War had ended, the Berlin Wall had fallen, and the United States had no sworn enemies in the world. The experiences of these two generations—World War II veterans and Vietnam era Americans—provide the context within which most Americans think about foreign policy and defense issues.

The degree to which the United States will become involved or entangled with the affairs of other nations is a question which has challenged the nation since its founding. In his farewell address to the nation, President George Washington warned that it should be wary of forming ties to the nations of Europe. As he put it, "The great rule of conduct for us in regard to foreign nations is, in extending our commercial relations to have with them as little political connection as possible." This is probably the first articulation of the isolationist stance that the United States took as much for self protection as anything else. As James McCormick points out, the Monroe Doctrine, issued by President Monroe in 1823, carried this advice further by effectively separating the affairs of the Old World from those of the New World (1998: 14). The United States was to be interested only in affairs within its own hemisphere and, as the doctrine warned, European nations should stay out of that sphere.

The degree to which the United States adhered to a policy of nonattachment to European affairs is revealed in McCormick's analysis of international agreements (1998: 16). While the United States did enter more than six hundred agreements with other nations up to 1899, the vast majority were for commerce or the settlement of claims. Only one treaty of alliance was signed. In contrast, the period from 1947 to 1960 saw the United States enter almost five thousand international agreements, with more than a thousand being military or other alliances with other nations.

Given this strong history of isolationism, it is not surprising that the measurement of public opinion most often taken on foreign affairs issues is whether the United States should take an active role in the world or stay out of world affairs. The Gallup Poll began asking a variation of this question in its surveys in 1943 and the question has been repeated by Gallup, Roper, or NORC many times since then. As you will note from Table 10-1, more than two-thirds of those surveyed in 1943 said that the United States should take an active part in world affairs. Although many commentators felt that the disillusionment of the Vietnam era would influence Americans to become more isolationist, the table shows that the lowest proportion of respondents supporting an active role has been 61%, in 1975. The proportion stayed in the low 60s until 1985, when it rebounded to 70%. However, at no time in the postwar period has the majority of Americans endorsed a more isolationist stance.

Like some other "standard" questions in the development of survey research, this one has developed a "life of its own," and, if only one question is asked on foreign policy, this is likely to be the one chosen by survey organizations. In part because of the nation's isolationist years and because this question seemed to capture the postwar change so well, many scholars who study the American mind have suggested that all Americans could be divided into those who are isolationists and those who are internationalists. As we will see in this chapter, American opinions on foreign policy and national security issues are much more complex than that typology would suggest.

PUBLIC OPINION AND FOREIGN POLICY: WHICH OPINIONS?

Some analysts have been content to ask only whether Americans support an isolationist role, while others have cast doubt on whether Americans actually have attitudes toward more specific foreign policy issues and, if they do, whether those views have much political impact. The constitutional framework of the United States and the decisions of the Supreme Court clearly vest the power to conduct foreign affairs with the president; the Congress does retain the power to declare war and to pass the budget, and the Senate to approve ambassadors, and, of course, to approve any treaties. Historically, the Congress and the people have looked to the president and other agencies of the executive branch to define and conduct the nation's foreign policy. This historical fact, combined with the general isolationist history of the nation, led

Table 10.1 Support for an Active Role in the World, 1943–1996

Question: Do you think it will be best for the future of this country if we take an active part in world affairs, or if we stay out of world affairs (1947–1994)? (Other slight variations in wording in the rest of the years.)

	Percentage agreeing	
Year	Take an active part	Stay out
1943	76	14
1944	73	18
1945	71	19
1946	78	19
1947	66	26
1948	67	25
1950	66	25
1952	68	23
1953	71	21
1954	69	25
1955	72	21
1956	71	25
1965	79	16
1973	66	31
1975	61	36
1976	63	32
1978	64	32
1982	61	34
1983	65	31
1984	65	29
1985	70	27
1986	65	32
1988	65	32
1989	68	28
1990	69	27
1991	73	24
1994	65	32

SOURCE: *The Public Perspective*, March/April, 1993, p. 95 and August/September, 1997, p. 8.

to the idea of a bipartisan approach to foreign policy. Both political parties supported Roosevelt's leadership during World War II. At the end of that conflict, seeing the disarray of the global community, Republican and Democratic leaders of Congress called for bipartisan support for American foreign policy, particularly in the case of military force. As Senator Arthur H. Vandenberg often reminded his colleagues, "Partisanship ends at the water's edge."[1]

During the 1950s and 1960s, the Cold War reinforced the need for a united, bipartisan approach to foreign policy among America's leaders. Divisive elite opinions on foreign policy issues were not in evidence until the Vietnam conflict, when some members of both parties opposed the war while their colleagues supported it. The result of these years of bipartisanship is that few foreign policy issues have been or are defined in terms of ideological or partisan terms for the public. This, in turn, may make it more difficult for ordinary citizens to shape their own opinions on international issues, since there are few cues given by party leaders.

In addition, most members of the American public are not very interested in international affairs over the long term. Studies have shown Americans are not very knowledgeable about world geography or about the political systems of other nations. From time to time, polls ask questions about current international issues that demonstrate this low level of knowledge: for example, in a poll conducted by CBS News / New York Times in 1994, respondents were asked if Germany was a member of the Security Council: while 39% said yes, 48% said that they did not know. Thirty-two percent believed that Japan is a permanent member of the Security Council of the United Nations, while 49% admitted that they did not know the answer. However, 67% felt that Japan should become a member of that council and an equal amount supported Germany's membership in that body.[2] (Actually, neither is a member). There have been numerous other studies that found similar low levels of knowledge about specific foreign policy issues (Delli Carpini and Keeter, 1996: 82–83). Critics suggest that the opinions expressed by most Americans on foreign policy issues should be given little weight due to the low levels of information and interest they demonstrate on these questions.

This concern for the ability of average Americans to formulate opinions on international issues has its roots in an elitist view of foreign policy decision making. Perhaps the foremost proponent of that view was Walter Lippmann, who believed that Americans were too deeply involved in their own affairs and too easily swayed by emotional appeals to be able to make reasoned judgments on foreign policy questions. (Lippman, 1922). Lippmann and others such as Hans Morgenthau (1978) viewed foreign and defense policy as needing quick decisions based on information gathered by intelligence forces. Depending on the public to make judgments on such complicated issues would handicap the president in times of crises. Like Lippmann, Robert Dahl saw a need for the public to be educated by elites and policymakers on international issues so that they would support the decisions and actions taken by the nation. In Dahl's view, the media and local elites would act as a conduit to inform the public about international issues (1950). This "distrust" of the public's ability to formulate and express opinions on foreign and military issues has led to a considerable scholarly interest in the degree to which the opinions of the public match or differ from those held by elites. As we will see in our investigation of public views on specific issues, there are a number of datasets available that compare elite and mass opinions; there are almost no such comparable datasets available for examining opinions on domestic issues.

FOREIGN POLICY GOALS AND PRIORITIES

Another way to look at the public's views on foreign policy issues is to ask about the issues that confront the United States in the international arena. In a number of studies, this line of inquiry takes the form of asking respondents to indicate the importance of various goals for the United States. In this way, it is possible to rank the priority of foreign and defense policy goals for the American people. Looking at the priorities expressed by the American public lends considerably more detail to our understanding of public opinion than simply asking whether the United States should play an undefined internationalist role.

The longest ongoing study of public opinion on foreign policy has been conducted by the Chicago Council on Foreign Affairs,[3] which has sponsored seven national surveys of mass and elite opinion on foreign and defense policy. Many of the original questions about the foreign policy goals that should be pursued by the United States have been repeated throughout the series. Others have been dropped as they seemed less relevant, and new questions, addressing topics such as stopping drugs at the border and changing immigration policy, have been added in recent years.

The mass public's responses to the Chicago Council surveys from 1974 to the present on the foreign policy goals questions are displayed in Table 10-2. This presentation includes only those questions that have been asked at least five times over the course of the surveys. There appears to be considerable consistency within the public's responses over this 20-year period: The two items that have remained continuously at the top of the mass public's priorities are both concerned with protecting the well-being of the nation itself: Americans place a very high priority on maintaining adequate energy supplies and protecting the jobs of American workers. The next two goals suggest quite different perspectives on the nation's posture in the world. Americans have steadfastly expressed a desire to reduce hunger in the world, a sentiment that may account for public support for humanitarian efforts such as the sending of troops to Somalia in 1992. However, the goal of "containing communism" reminds us of the foreign policy priorities of the Cold War years.

In the middle of this list of goals are the responses to the goal of "strengthening the United Nations." Clearly this goal usually garners support from about half of the respondents, and the percentage is almost "flat" over the six surveys. Below the U.N. item are listed a series of questions that show generally low levels of support over the two decades, although there are some peaks in 1990. The levels of support for "protect weaker nations from aggression" and "bring democracy to other nations" suggest that the American people are not very interested in making intervention into the domestic affairs of other nations a high priority.

**Table 10.2 Most Important Goals for United States Foreign Policy,
1974–1994**

Goal Statement	Percent saying it should be a very important goal					
	1974	1978	1982	1986	1990	1994
Secure adequate energy supplies	80	82	73	71	61	62
Protect jobs of Am. workers	77	81	80	80	65	83
Worldwide arms control	64	64	64	69	53	—
Combat world hunger	62	62	61	64	—	56
Contain communism	58	64	62	60	56	—
Strengthen U.N.	50	52	52	48	44	51
Protect Am. business abroad	42	48	46	45	63	52
Defend human rights	—	42	46	43	58	34
Improve living standard in other nations	40	37	37	38	41	22
Defend allies' security	36	54	53	58	61	41
Protect weaker nations	31	37	37	34	57	24
Bring democracy to other nations	30	29	31	32	28	25

SOURCE: Data from the Chicago Council on Foreign Relations Surveys in the years indicated as presented in Barbara Bardes, "From the Cold War to the Clinton Years: The American Public Views a Changing World," presented at the American Political Science Association annual meeting, 1995.

Over the years, the priorities of the elites surveyed by the Chicago Council have often been different from those expressed by the general public. For example, the goal of improving the standard of living for other nations has generally ranked higher for the elites and the goal of protecting the jobs of American workers has ranked much lower than it does for the general public. If we look at the ranking of selected goals by elites and the general public in the 1994 study, we find that the public is highly supportive of two "new" goals: stopping the flow of drugs into the U.S. (85% said this was very important) and controlling and reducing illegal immigration (72%). As the data in Table 10-3 show, elites and the general public are in agreement on a number of issues, including the importance of preventing the spread of nuclear weapons and securing adequate energy supplies.

ISSUES OF WAR AND PEACE

Given the history of isolationism in America's foreign policy, it is not surprising that political leaders and commentators are intensely interested in the public's views on issues of peace and war. There is, in fact, a fair amount of controversy over the basic stance that Americans take toward any military involvement by American troops. If one sees the support and involvement of American citizens

Table 10.3 Comparing Elite and Public Views on American Goals, 1994

	Percent saying the goal is "very important"	
Goal	The Public	The Leaders
Stop the flow of illegal drugs into the U.S.	85	57
Protect the jobs of Am. workers	83	50
Prevent spread of nuclear weapons	82	90
Reduce illegal immigration	72	28
Secure adequate energy supplies	62	67
Reduce trade deficit	59	48
Combat world hunger	56	41
Protect Am. business abroad	52	38
Strengthen United Nations	51	33
Defend allies' security	41	60
Promote human rights	34	26
Promote democracy in other nations	25	21
Protect weaker nations	24	21
Improve standard of living in other nations	22	28

SOURCE: John E. Reilly, editor, *American Public Opinion and U.S. Foreign Policy 1995*, Chicago: Chicago Council on Foreign Relations, 1996, p. 15.

in World War II as an aberration in our history, then the public is regarded as basically suspicious of all military ventures overseas. This perception is heightened by the disillusionment suffered by the American public over the involvement in the Vietnam conflict. Alternatively, some commentators see the American public as dedicated to certain foreign policy goals and principles and, with appropriate leadership, willing to support the use of troops to achieve those goals. In some ways, this is a "Is the glass half empty or half full?" debate but, to policymakers who are trying to achieve foreign policy goals for the nation, the public's view is very important. They remember the degree to which public disapproval of Lyndon Johnson's leadership during the Vietnam era convinced a sitting president to leave office after one elected term.

The Vietnam Conflict

The Vietnam conflict tested the American public's resolve for military action overseas and, after many years of armed intervention, demonstrated that Americans have a limited tolerance for a war with no apparent strategy or likely outcome. If we look, however, at the early years of involvement in the Vietnam conflict, the American public strongly supported taking military action to defend American forces after the Gulf of Tonkin incident. In April, 1965, after President Johnson spoke to the public about the incident and his plans, 42% of the American public supported an increased escalation in the use of American

---

Vietnam: Opposition? Yes; Withdrawal? Maybe

The primary election campaign of 1968 provides an illustration of Americans' lack of awareness on foreign policy issues and the need for caution in interpreting survey results. In the campaign for the Democratic nomination, one of the challengers to President Johnson was Minnesota Senator Eugene McCarthy, who built his campaign around opposition to the war. While his stance was reported in the media, a survey conducted shortly before the New Hampshire primary found that 54% did not know his position on the war, 17% identified him as a "hawk," and only 29% identified him as in favor of de-escalation. His surprising success in the New Hampshire primary, in which he received 42% of the vote, was generally seen as an anti-war vote, but such may not have been the case. As Rosenberg, Verba, and Converse (1970: 49) note, "among the McCarthy voters, those who were dissatisfied with Johnson for not pursuing a *harder* line in Vietnam outnumbered those who wanted a withdrawal by a margin of three to two." Additionally, other studies of this election have shown that those voters who had favored McCarthy but later switched their support tended not to move toward candidates who favored an "anti-war" position, but toward the more "hawkish" George Wallace (Converse, Miller, Rusk, and Wolfe, 1969).

---

military force, with 19% of the public favoring the combination of military force and negotiation (Page and Shapiro, 1992: 229). The support for use of military force increased steadily throughout 1965, rising to a high of 75% by the end of that year, as reported by Gallup.

Americans continued to support the use of military force in Vietnam through 1966 and into 1967, although protests against the war had begun and some media were reporting dissension within the executive branch about the military action. But public opinion stayed supportive of the U.S. troops while simultaneously seeking a way out until after the Tet offensive in January, 1968. At first, Americans responded to the offensive by North Vietnam by becoming more aggressive in their outlooks, but within a few months, disillusionment with the war began to increase and support for American involvement declined.

After the secret bombings of Laos were revealed in early 1970, large majorities of Americans began to favor immediate withdrawal from the war. In May 1970, when President Nixon ordered American troops into Cambodia, the nation's campuses exploded with protests, resulting in the shooting of students by National Guard troops at Jackson State University in Mississippi and at Kent State University in Ohio. To quote Page and Shapiro (235), "the proportion of Americans that favored continuing U.S. withdrawal, even if the South Vietnamese government collapsed, rose 13% (to a full 67%) between October 1969 and April 1970, and continued rising to 70% by April 1971 and to 76% by July 1971."

The Vietnam conflict presents several very interesting issues for the study of American public opinion. First, it is important to remember that the public was extremely supportive of the military action in the beginning of the conflict and that the support for American troops stayed strong throughout. Additionally, a majority of Americans would *not* call the military action a mistake until six months after the Tet offensive. This long and extremely difficult military action became much more of a mistake for most American citizens and for their political leaders in hindsight rather during the war itself. The view of the Vietnam conflict as a mistake continues into the 1990s, with a 1992 survey taken by the Roper organization showing that 47% of Americans believed the war in Vietnam was the "wrong thing" for the U.S. to do and only 21% saying it was the right thing (*Public Perspective*, 1993: 101).

The retrospective disapproval of the United States role in the Vietnam conflict has shaped the way that scholars and policymakers view American opinion toward the use of force in the last two decades. It is thought that the American public turned isolationist or at least much more cautious about committing troops after the Vietnam experience. Holsti and Rosenau have investigated the degree to which a "post-Vietnam syndrome" has influenced the way that American elites evaluate American foreign policy goals and actions. They did find that while the post–World War II consensus about the role that the United States should play in the world had, in their terms, "shattered," it was not at all clear that a new consensus had emerged to replace it. They reported that there were clear disagreements within American elites about the future role of the United States in the world. To some extent these disagreements were rooted in the positions that individuals had taken toward the Vietnam conflict, but the views held by elites years after the war were not explained totally by their stance toward the Vietnam experience (Holsti and Rosenau, 1984: 78).

The change in American support for the U.S. involvement in the Vietnam conflict led to another very interesting insight into the public's mind. Mueller compared the trends in support for American involvement in the conflict with the reports of casualties in both the Vietnam conflict and the Korean conflict 15 years earlier and reported that disapproval for involvement in the war increased in a fairly regular pattern as the number of American casualties rose (1973). This particular finding, based on data from two different conflicts, has become an important factor in the calculations of political leaders when they send American troops overseas. President Reagan, for example, quickly withdrew troops and ships from Lebanon in 1984 after several hundred U.S. Marines were killed in an attack on their barracks in Beirut.

The studies of public opinion during the Vietnam conflict were among the first to highlight the importance of race and gender in influencing attitudes toward the use of military force. Although Shapiro and Mahajan reported gender differences toward the use of force in earlier decades (1986), the analysis of Verba et al. was among the first to note the differences between men and women in support of escalation of the military effort in 1967 (Verba, 1967: 325). In analyzing a fairly intensive national study of attitudes toward the war, Verba and his colleagues were somewhat surprised to find that while the mass public had fairly structured attitudes toward the involvement of the United

States, the division between those who supported escalation and those who favored de-escalation was not related to standard demographic factors such as economic status, education, or region, nor were the divisions strongly related to political party identification or other political positions. However, in the case of gender, women were less informed about the war than were male respondents and were considerably less likely to support escalation of the effort. Race was an even stronger predictor of views on escalation, with African Americans significantly differing from white Americans in their preference for increased de-escalation of the war effort. This study, which was based on a survey completed in 1967, was the first to identify these gender and race differences on foreign policy issues.

The Persian Gulf War

Public support for the American-led military attack on Iraq after that nation's invasion of Kuwait provides a direct contrast to the pattern of public support in the Vietnam era. Iraq's army invaded Kuwait on August 2, 1990. That action was condemned by the United Nations the following day. In the weeks that followed the invasion, American troops were sent to bases in Saudi Arabia by the tens of thousands and the United Nations imposed an economic and financial boycott on Iraq. By November of 1990, the Pentagon called up thousands of reserves and the Bush administration announced that it would send another hundred thousand troops to the region. By mid-November, the coalition military forces in the region totaled half a million. In early January of 1991, after talks with Iraq stalled, President George Bush asked the Congress for a resolution approving the use of military force if Iraq did not withdraw from Kuwait by January 15. After heated debate, Congress approved the resolution on January 13. On January 17, during the evening news broadcast, American jets attacked Baghdad and the event was televised on CNN. Following intensive bombing and missile attacks by the United States and other coalition allies, the ground attack began on February 21 and ended on February 28 with the liberation of Kuwait and the defeat of the Iraqi army. Although there was talk of trying to capture Saddam Hussein, the Bush administration ended the war without toppling the Iraqi government. The Bush administration also decided not to intervene in the Iraqi attacks on Kurdish people within Iraq's border who had revolted against Hussein during the postwar period.

In contrast to the "retrospective" view of the Vietnam situation in which Americans now voice suspicion of foreign involvements, about two-thirds of the public agreed that the United States should take all action necessary, including the use of military force, to ensure the withdrawal of Iraq from Kuwait within one week of Iraq's incursion into Kuwait. Support for such a strategy stayed above 60 percent all the way up to the passage of the Congressional resolution. The only real decline in support for the administration's position occurred in the late fall, when the Bush administration faced a budget crisis and opinions became quite partisan, even on the Iraqi situation. The morning after the bombing began, support for the attack rose among the public and stayed high throughout the military campaign.

There were differences within the public over support for the Persian Gulf campaign, especially between men and women. In almost every survey from August through the campaign itself, women were less supportive than were men by 10 to 15 percentage points. However, since the overall level of support was so high, even the female respondents expressed support at levels of 50 to 70 percent.

Public opinion during the Persian Gulf War was remarkable for the strength of support given to the American military, both before and during the actual use of force. It was also remarkable as a demonstration of the **rally-round-the-flag effect.** First noted by John Mueller in his studies of public support for the president during the Korean and Vietnam conflicts (Mueller, 1973), this phenomenon is best described as a rapid improvement of presidential approval rating that occurs when the United States faces a foreign policy crisis or sends U.S. troops into military action. It has been suggested that the **rally effect** is caused by the public's identification of the good of the nation with that of the president and with the public's desire for cohesion in the face of an enemy. The **rally effect** is another manifestation of the bipartisanship that has characterized political debate on foreign policy for most of the nation's history.

The Persian Gulf War provided astounding evidence of the rally effect. Parker, who defines the rally effect as "invok[ing] feelings of allegiance toward national political institutions and policies," tracked public opinion toward President Bush, toward the other institutions of government, toward family finances, and toward trust in government before, during, and after the military action in the Persian Gulf (Parker, 1995). She found that the rally effect, while spectacular in the case of Bush's approval ratings (which increased as much as 30% during the crisis), carried over to the public's attitudes toward other politicians, toward their view of economic conditions, and toward other institutions of government. The rally effect even increased the proportions of people who trust the government. Even more interesting are the data collected after the crisis ended. Parker showed clearly that the rally effect is temporary, since, in the case of every survey question, responses dropped to the levels reported before the Gulf War. The public went from 57% saying Bush's job rating was good or excellent to 78% saying so during the crisis. The rating then returned to 59% after the Gulf War ended. Given these swings in public perceptions within one year, Parker concluded that "Rally forces appear to be prototypical period forces—they arise in response to particular events and have the potential of moving large segments of the population in the same direction during the same time period. For most attitudes, such boosts are relatively short-lived" (1995: 541).

Peacekeeping, Rescue, and Other Uses of Military Force

Since World War II, American presidents have used military force for many types of missions: peacekeeping, rescue of American hostages or soldiers, humanitarian delivery of food supplies, and quick military strikes. Although the Congress passed the War Powers Resolution[4] presumably to require presidents to consult with the Congress before using sending U.S. troops into military sit-uations, no president has abided by the letter of that law and most have simply announced that they believe the act is unconstitutional in light of their powers as commander-in-chief. Presidents who contemplate the use of force often consult with a few key leaders of the Congress about the possibility of using the troops or inform them after the troops have been ordered into action. To date, Congress has not attempted to force any president to meet the actual terms of the law by ordering troop withdrawals or cutting funding for the troops.

What do Americans think about these various uses of force? The lessons of Vietnam and the Persian Gulf War seem to hold for the most part: if the use of force is quick and successful, incurring few or no American casualties, most members of the public tend to approve of that use. However, if there is any possibility of Americans becoming mired in a complicated situation that will threaten their safety and require a long-term commitment, Americans are less anxious to support involvement. If we look at the survey results in Table 10-4, we can see that the American public was generally supportive of the use of force in some instances, such as the air attack on Libya in 1986, the invasion of Grenada in 1983, and the use of force in the Persian Gulf War.[5] Generally, the American people also supported the use of troops in Somalia in 1992 to assist in a humanitarian effort. However, after American Rangers were attacked by Somalian clans, support for the use of troops there dropped precipitously. Fi-nally, the use of troops in what might be called "peacekeeping" or "democra-tizing situations" is rarely supported by a majority of the American public. The survey results in Table 10-4 regarding the use of troops in Haiti and Bosnia show the divisive nature of such policies. Less than a majority of Americans supported the use of troops in Haiti up until the day that an agreement with the government there was struck. Support increased to barely over 50% on that day and then declined to less than majority levels immediately thereafter.

Generally speaking, the group differences discussed above hold in most of the situations. Women are likely to be less supportive than men in almost any hypothetical situation requiring the use of troops. African Americans are also likely to be less supportive than white Americans. The use of troops in Somalia produced a different type of public response, in that women were not less sup-portive than men nor were African Americans less supportive than whites. One might hypothesize that since the mission was cast as humanitarian rather than military, and since it targeted an African nation, the usual divisions within mass opinion did not develop. Neither women nor African Americans saw the usual dangers of military force associated with this use of American troops.

FOREIGN AID AND OTHER
INTERNATIONAL ISSUES

In the years since the end of World War II, the United States became the leader of the free world in terms of alliance-building, economic stability, and the for-mation of an international organization. In contrast to its refusal to join the

Table 10.4 American Opinions on Military Intervention, 1983–1994

Grenada, 1983	Approve	Disapprove
Would you say you approve or disapprove of the invasion of Grenada by U.S. troops?	71	22

ABC/Washington Post

Libya, 1986	Approve	Disapprove
Do you approve or disapprove of United States jets bombing Libya last night?	77	23

CBS News/New York Times

Persian Gulf, 1991	Worth it	Not
Given the loss of life and other costs of war in the Persian Gulf, do you think the war to defeat Iraq is likely to be worth the cost?	59	29

CBS/New York Times

Somalia, 1993	Approve	Disapprove
Do you approve or disapprove of the presence of U.S. troops in Somalia?	79	21

CNN/Time

Bosnia, 1993	Favor	Oppose
Do you favor or oppose the United States sending troops to the former Yugoslavia to help stop the civil war there?	54	34

NBC/Wall Street Journal

Haiti, 1994	Favor	Oppose
To remove the military and restore the elected president of Haiti, Jean-Bertrand Aristide, would you favor or oppose the United States sending in ground troops?	29	66

CBS/New York Times

	Approve	Disapprove
Do you approve or disapprove of the presence of U.S. troops in Haiti? (After President Clinton's speech and troop deployment.)	54	45

CNN/USA Today

League of Nations after World War I, the United States provided the leadership to create and, through its support, to sustain the United Nations. As part of the postwar leadership role, President Harry Truman put forth the Marshall Plan, which provided massive economic assistance to rebuild the shattered economies of Western Europe. The major goal of that assistance was to prevent some of those nations from moving toward the Communist bloc but, in fact, the Marshall Plan was foreign economic aid delivered at a scale never to be seen again. Responding to the leadership of President Truman and the bipartisan support in the Congress, the American public gave strong approval of the Marshall Plan, with 57% supporting this initiative in 1947 and 72% approving of the sending of economic aid to Western Europe in 1948 (*Public Perspective:* March/April 1993, p. 97).

Another legacy of World War II was the development of military and peacekeeping alliances led by the United States. As mentioned above, the United States helped create the United Nations and the Security Council system as a way to keep peace in the world. Then, as enmity developed between the United States and the Soviet Union, particularly in regard to the Eastern European states that became part of the Soviet bloc, the United States created NATO, the North Atlantic Treaty Organization, as a mutual defense pact with the European nations. American public opinion supported that alliance as well as many others created by the United States in the years of the Cold War. However, much has changed in the world situation since the late 1940s, and even though Americans still support a global role for the United States, there have been important changes in the public's support for some of the nation's postwar initiatives.

Foreign Aid

When asked what government programs should be cut to balance the budget, "foreign aid" is often high on the priority savings list for many citizens. When asked how much the United States spends on foreign aid in comparison to other nations, few citizens know that other nations outspend the United States as a proportion of their GNP. This is quite a change from the climate of opinion in the postwar years, when the Marshall Plan to rebuild European economies was proposed. In 1947, 57% of Americans approved the Marshall Plan; in 1948 72% favored "continuing to send economic aid to Western Europe under the Marshall Plan." That level of support stayed above 60% for the next four years (*Public Perspective,* March/April 1993: 97).

American support for foreign assistance efforts has declined precipitously since the postwar period among the mass public, although elites generally favor foreign assistance, particularly to specific regions of the world. If we look at the historic series of data from the Chicago Council on Foreign Affairs, shown in Table 10-5, the contrast between mass and elite support for the general policy of sending economic assistance is very clear, with elites' support at more than 85% for the 20-year period and mass support averaging less than 50%.

Table 10.5 Elite and Public Support for Economic Aid, 1974–1994

	Percentage in favor of giving economic aid	
Year	The Public	The Leaders
1974	52	—
1978	46	90
1982	50	94
1986	53	91
1990	45	90
1994	45	86

SOURCE: John E. Reilly, editor, *American Public Opinion and U.S. Foreign Policy 1995*, Chicago: Chicago Council on Foreign Relations, 1996, p. 31.

Looking at opinions on whether aid should be increased or decreased to specific nations or regions, the contrast between elite and mass opinion is, perhaps, even stronger. For example, the 1994 Chicago Council study found that elites favored increased aid to Eastern European nations, while the general public believed that such aid should be decreased. A similar contrast is found on the question of sending economic assistance to Russia: 40% of elite respondents favored increasing aid to Russia, as compared to 20% of the general public; 39% of the public preferred a decrease in aid to the former adversary, compared to only 14% of elite respondents.

Why is there such disparity among elites and masses on the question of foreign economic assistance? More detailed survey questions have been asked at various points about the implications of foreign assistance for the United States. To some, American foreign economic assistance is simply a waste of public funds, especially compared to the use of such funds to solve domestic problems. To others, foreign economic assistance and its cousin, foreign military assistance, are the forerunners of involvement in another nation's problems, including the use of American troops. Elites are much more conscious of the degree to which the American and world economy rests on the stability of individual nations and they support foreign economic assistance as a way to bring stable conditions to other nations.

The United Nations

From time to time Americans have been less than enthusiastic about the United Nations as an organization. Although the United States led the world's nations in the formation of the U.N., many Americans have questioned the U.N.'s efficacy over the years and, indeed, the economic support that the United States has given to the U.N. However, the data from the Chicago Council shows that there is a consistent pattern of support for the United Nations: when asked whether "strengthening the United Nations" was a very important goal, 46% of the respondents agreed in 1974. That percentage varied no more than two percentage points until 1994, when it increased to 51%. Compared to other foreign policy goals embraced by Americans, strengthening the United Nations is in the second tier of preferences but, nevertheless, has very consistent support.

American opinions about the United Nations are complicated by the changes in the world situation. During the Cold War, civil wars in less-developed nations such as Somalia or Vietnam frequently became surrogate conflicts between the United States and the Soviet Union, with each of the major powers backing one party to the conflict. The U.S. and the Soviet Union avoided direct confrontation but, through their rivalry, policed many of the lesser conflicts in the world. Neither of the powers nor their allies would allow the United Nations to become involved in these disputes. Since the end of the Cold War, this role has been given to the United Nations, with an ever-expanding peacekeeping function. By 1996, United Nations had peacekeeping forces stationed in 18 nations, with an annual budget of more than $3 billion for these activities.

As the United Nations role has become greater in the peacekeeping arena, Americans have raised questions over the degree to which U.S. troops should take part in these efforts. Numerous surveys have asked whether Americans approve U.S. troops participating in United Nations peacekeeping efforts around the world. An ABC News/*Washington Post* poll conducted in November 1993 found that 60% of Americans approved of sending U.S. troops, while 35% disapproved. The 1994 Chicago Council survey found 51% of their respondents agreeing that "the U.S. be part of a U.N. peacekeeping force in a troubled part of the world when asked" with 19% disagreeing and 23% saying that it depends on the circumstances.

The issue of sending U.S. troops to be part of a United Nations peacekeeping force is further complicated by the question of command structure. While it appears that a majority of Americans support U.S. involvement in these efforts, there is considerable disagreement over who should command those troops. A 1993 survey sponsored by the Los Angeles Times Mirror Corp. found that 69% of those questioned believed that U.S. troops should always remain under the command of an American officer, while 25% approved of placing troops under U.N. command. The 1994 Chicago Council surveyed showed a more evenly divided public, with 44% saying the U.S. should insist on American command for U.S. troops and an equal number (44%) agreeing to the idea of U.N. command. These 1993 and 1994 surveys were conducted during the debate over whether to send U.S. troops to the former Yugoslavia to enforce peacekeeping in the Balkan states. The problem of command was resolved by having NATO, the U.S.-European military alliance, conduct the peacekeeping efforts with commanders from the nations involved and a careful division of duties for the troops. For the most part, U.S. troops in Bosnia have not been stationed anywhere near the high-conflict areas, nor have they been asked to perform duties that might cause armed resistance.

The Soviet Union

As noted above, the American public has often been characterized as being fairly uninterested in foreign policy issues and uninformed about these topics. However, in a number of instances it is clear that Americans are aware of changes in the world situation and react to them in understandable ways. The pattern of American opinion toward the former Soviet Union illustrates this point.

After World War II, support for a firm stand against the spreading of communism was very high, with 48% of Americans supporting being "even firmer with Russia" in 1948. By 1950, 83% of Americans believed that it was "very important to try to stop the spread of communism in the world" (*Public Perspective,* November/December, 1991 p. 30). By the beginning of the Chicago Council surveys in 1974, support for "containing communism" as a foreign policy goal stood at 54% and held near that level through 1990. However, Americans were aware that the Soviet Union was undergoing change. By November 1989, an Associated Press poll found that 54% of Americans believed that communism around the world was on the decline. A series of polls taken by NBC News/*Wall Street Journal* in 1991 tracks the degree to which Americans were aware of changes in the communist bloc. As shown in Table 10-6, the percentage of Americans who believed that the Cold War was over increased from 46% in November 1989 to 60% in August 1991.

Similarly, the feeling thermometer question (respondents indicate their feelings toward the Soviet Union on a 0–100-degree scale) asked by the Chicago Council survey showed an average "thermometer rating" of 34 in 1974, which increased to 59 points in 1990 and fell back to 54 in 1994. Clearly, Americans were aware of the changes within the Soviet Union and appeared to revise their views of that nation as the changes occurred.

HOW DO AMERICANS THINK ABOUT FOREIGN POLICY?

Times have changed since Walter Lippman expressed his doubts in the wisdom of having the American people express opinions about foreign policy. With the advent of widespread media coverage of events worldwide and the ability of the president to reach all Americans using that same media, the opinions that American express about foreign policy decisions have become much more important in the political process. It appears, given the research cited earlier in this chapter, that the American mass public is not, on the whole, well-informed about international affairs, nor do most Americans follow international news on a frequent basis. This is not to say, however, that the mass public does not have opinions about the role played by the U.S. in world affairs or about specific policy questions. The longitudinal data on the role to be played by the U.S. in world affairs and the goals that the public thinks are most important

Table 10.6 Public Views on the End of the Cold War, 1989–1991

Question: Do you think the Cold War between the United States and the Soviet Union is still going on, or is it mostly over?

| | Percentage saying: | |
	Still going on	Mostly over
November 1989	46	46
March 1990	41	51
May 1990	44	49
August 1991	34	60

SOURCE: NBC News/*Wall Street Journal* in *The Public Perspective*, November/December 1991, p. 32.

show consistency and stability over more than twenty years. In the case of the global role questions, the responses are stable for more than forty years.

Americans are not only capable of holding stable opinions about these "big picture" questions but are also quite capable of formulating opinions about crises and foreign policy decisions when the information is made available to them. While the elites may see issues such as the use of troops in Bosnia or support for foreign aid in more global strategic terms, the mass public, when asked, expresses opinions quite clearly on these matters. Not only does the public formulate opinions about questions like using troops overseas for peace-keeping or in an emergency, but members of the general public follow the news enough to change their views over time. Tracking opinion about the So-viet Union clearly shows that the public was quite aware of the changes going on in Eastern Europe and the Soviet Union. Their opinions about that part of the world shifted dramatically as the Cold War ended.

Given this evidence of stability and change, students of public opinion continue to investigate the mechanisms by which members of the public come to hold either stable or changing opinions. We do know that political partisan-ship and ideology have limited influence on these views; generational experi-ence, gender, and race seem to have special effects; and educational achieve-ment is associated with a more internationalist perspective. What forces, then, in the absence of partisanship and ideology, lead people to adopt opinions and attitudes in the international arena?

The Prudent Use of Force

Perhaps there has been more attention to the public's views on the use of mili-tary force than on any other aspect of foreign and security policy. Since the Vietnam War and its political effects on President Johnson, politicians have been highly sensitive to the need to have public support for any use of troops that might risk the lives of Americans. One view of how Americans arrive at opinions about the proposed use of force is put forward by Jentleson (1992), who characterizes the citizenry as "the pretty prudent public." Jentleson hypothesizes that Americans view the use of force in the post–Vietnam period as falling into one of two general categories depending on the policy objective of the administration. One of the categories is "foreign policy restraint," meaning, in Jentleson's view, using force to restrain an adversary that is an active threat to the United States, to American citizens, or to our clear interests. He categorizes the American airstrike against Libya in 1986 and, of course, Operation Desert Storm, as these kinds of actions. In each case, it appears that public support for the use of force was strong both before and after the military effort.

The other category of policy objective cited by Jentleson is "internal political change," meaning the use of force to change the political structure within another nation. To some extent, the Vietnam conflict fit this objective. In addition, American use of force in Nicaragua, Panama, El Salvador, and, in a more recent case, Somalia, would fit this category. Americans are much less likely, according to this view, to support the use of troops in a situation where the U.S. is attempting to change the balance of power within another nation.

To summarize the view of Americans as a "prudent public," Jentleson believes that "the post post–Vietnam American public agrees that the world is a dangerous place . . . the American public is prepared to support the use of force to restrain [an] aggressor" (1992: 72). However, any administration that considers using force to get involved in the internal affairs of another nation must be quite cautious, because the public will be quite skeptical of such policy objectives.

Working from Types

Another way to understand how Americans come to hold specific opinions about international issues and decisions is to identify certain basic types or positions that may anchor individual opinions. A number of scholars have analyzed surveys of foreign policy issues and suggested that Americans hold opinions that can be aligned along two dimensions. Many of the opinions that Americans have expressed in the Chicago Council surveys, for example, can be grouped along a dimension that measures their propensity to use force, that is, a militarism dimension. Americans at one end of this dimensions eschew the use of force, while Americans at the other end would always choose to use force to achieve foreign policy goals. Another dimension expresses Americans willingness to participate in the international arena, with opinions ranging from "go it alone" views to multilateralist positions. By categorizing Americans according to their views on these two dimensions, scholars have suggested that there may be four basic "core positions" or types which then influence the actual opinions that people give to pollsters (Wittkopf, 1990; Hinckley, 1988; Holsti, 1996; Schneider, 1997).

The four basic "anchor" or "pure" types have been defined as follows: Isolationists, who prefer no involvement with global affairs for the nation; Hardliners, who prefer unilateral, military solutions to most international situations; Cooperative Internationalists, who believe in multilateral policy solutions but are less supportive of the use of force; and Militaristic Internationalists, who also support multination alliances but who also support the use of force. The interpretation of the dimensions and resulting core types varies somewhat from scholar to scholar but the basic premise is the same: individual Americans have basic predispositions on these issues of use of military force and cooperation with other nations and, when queried about their opinions on a specific policy or crisis situation, are likely to respond from this basic set of dispositions. Generally, scholars find that the majority of Americans fall into either the cooperative internationalist or militarist internationalist sectors with many fewer being identified as hardliners or true isolationists.

Using Cues or Schemas

The use of types or core predispositions is quite a strong predictor of opinions toward certain types of foreign policy issues such as the use of force or support for NATO. However, as the work by Jentleson suggests, many foreign policy issues are much more complicated politically: the decision to send American troops to Haiti to support the return of President Aristide is one such foreign policy decision that involved no real threat to the U.S. but, due to the constant immigration of Haitians to the United States, had serious domestic implications for the president and the Congress. The typology discussed above is quite limited in its ability to predict American views on issues like Haiti or the more strictly economic issues like joining NAFTA. Still other questions of foreign and national security policy such as extending aid to Russia or membership in NATO to Poland are quite tangential to the four-fold system outlined above.

Opinions and attitudes toward specific policies or actions may be rooted in cognitive structures known as schemas. Each individual carries with him or her certain sets of information and prior opinion that are sorted into mental files called schemas. The schema provides information that has been learned in the past, past attitudes or preferences expressed by the individual, and emotions or affective positions toward the topic. For example, a 70-year old American may carry a schema about Japan that includes not only what we know about Japanese technology and the economy today but memories of Japan as an enemy in World War II. If this citizen is a veteran of that conflict, he may have strong emotions about the Japanese that date back five decades. When confronted by a foreign policy issue that involves U.S. relations with Japan, the individual responds to the cue (Japan) and then utilizes the information and emotional attachments in that schema to respond to the issue. A number of scholars have investigated this view of how Americans respond and attempted to outline the structure of such schemas (Hurwitz and Peffley, 1987).

Because of the range of issues in the international field, and the complexity of these issues, it is unlikely that there is a definite outside limit on the number of dimensions or schemas that may structure attitudes and opinions (Bardes and Oldendick, 1978, 1981). Most scholars who have analyzed the Chicago Council datasets and other such surveys agree that clearly attitudes toward militarism form a specific dimension or position for most Americans. Attitudes toward international activity in general are also likely to be widespread across the general population. Other dimensions that may be found include: international organizations, foreign assistance, economic relations, terrorism, and American domestic interests. As the world situation changes and the United States faces quite different challenges to its interests and sovereignty, we would expect the dimensions of foreign policy to change within the American public. New information and new international contacts will shape both the informational content and the emotional content of schemas and, as generations succeed each other, new points of view will be generated.

SUMMARY

Not only is the world a "dangerous place" as pointed out by Jentleson, but it is a messy place as well for the ordinary American to think about. For the most part, the data reviewed in this chapter suggest that Americans are more consistent and more responsive to world affairs than was believed by scholars, commentators, and elites before 1950. Of course, there are many more sources of information for the ordinary citizen today and international contacts are much greater for many than in previous eras. And, given the global role played by the United States since World War II, many more Americans have had experience with the military and peaceful initiatives taken by the nation in recent decades. All of this leads us to view the American public as aware of international affairs, if not always attentive to the details; as competent to make judgements about foreign and military policies if given the information; and as showing remarkably consistent support for the role played by the United States in world affairs.

Polls, Polling, and the Internet

As news stories break on foreign policy issues, you might look for polling data on the web sites maintained by the major media, including:

ABC News:	http://www.abcnews.com
CNN:	http://www.cnn.com
Los Angeles Times:	http://www.latimes.com/HOME/NEWS/POLLS
USA Today:	http://www.usatoday.com
New York Times:	http://www.nytimes.com
Washington Post:	http://www.washingtonpost.com

NOTES

1. Quoted in Jay M. Shafritz, *The Dorsey Dictionary of American Government and Politics*, New York: The Dorsey Press, 1988, p. 56.

2. Under the terms of the United Nations Charter, there are five permanent members of the Security Council: the United States, the United Kingdom, France, the former Soviet Union (seat now held by Russia), and China. The other members are elected by the General Assembly for rotating terms.

3. The Chicago Council on Foreign Affairs has now sponsored seven national surveys (1974, 1978, 1982, 1986, 1990, 1994, and 1998) interviewing both mass and elite samples. Each survey has been comprehensive in regard to foreign and defense policy questions. Virtually no domestic policy issues are addressed. The surveys have received support at various times from the Ford Foundation and the MacArthur Foundation. Data are available for analysis through the Inter-University Consortium for Political and Social Research (ICPSR) at the University of Michigan.

4. The War Powers Resolution was passed in 1973 by the Democratically-controlled Congress to provide a way for Congress to check the actions of the president. Passage of the resolution was spurred by President Nixon's incursion of Cambodia.

5. In 1983, President Ronald Reagan ordered United States troops to the Caribbean island of Grenada to forestall a potential communist rebel take-over and to rescue American students there. In 1986, President Reagan ordered an American airstrike on Libya to dissuade that nation from supporting terrorist attacks against Americans and others. The Persian Gulf War took place in 1991, when the United States-led coalition of nations defeated Iraq after that nation had invaded Kuwait.

Part IV

Public Opinion: A Critical Perspective

11

Challenges Facing Public Opinion Research: Issues of Reliability and Trust

In the six preceding chapters, we have used the results of survey research to describe the origins of opinions on political issues, to discuss the public's orientation toward the political system, and to examine public opinion on social-welfare, racial, cultural, and foreign policy issues in an attempt to describe "the American mind." This chapter explores some of the challenges that face survey researchers and identifies a number of factors that should be considered in deciding how much confidence to place in the findings reported in a public opinion survey.

As part of its special 50th issue, the editors of *The Public Perspective* (1998B: 86–94), asked nine senior survey practitioners to write about "the greatest challenges, or problems, now confronting public opinion research in the U.S." Although each of these researchers cited a different aspect of the survey profession, the theme running throughout these articles concerned the reliability and trustworthiness of polls. While the specific challenges identified included the quality of data collection, response rates, interpreting results appropriately, and reporting them better, they all touched on the need to produce valid data. As Newport (1998: 87) noted, "the reliance on survey results to guide the ship of state necessitates that polls be trustworthy and reliable when they are first published." In order for public opinion data to be trustworthy, they must be **reliable,** producing consistent results, and **valid,** measuring what they intend to measure.

While it is somewhat ironic to attempt to measure the public's opinion about polls using data from a public opinion poll, previous research has shown that while Americans have some reservations about poll results, they generally view surveys in a positive light (Goyder, 1986; Kohut, 1986; Roper, 1986; Dran and Hildreth, 1995).

Previous research on this topic has shown that the public generally believes that polls interview typical, representative people; are honest and accurate; work for the interests of the general public; and are an enjoyable and satisfactory experience (Roper, 1986: 10–13). More recent research, such as that of Dran and Hildreth (1995; 1997) has shown a more mixed view of public opinion on the polls, with less than half of the public expressing confidence in their accuracy. A 1996 survey by the Gallup Organization found an increase in the number of people who pay attention to poll results. It also found that two-thirds of the public have faith in the accuracy of surveys. In addition, almost three-fourths of their respondents said that the country would be better off if the nation's leaders followed public opinion polls more closely, 87% felt polls are a "good thing" for the country, and 68% believed that polls work for the best interests of the general public (Gallup and Moore, 1996: 51–52).

A 1995 study for the Council for Marketing and Opinion Research also found a mix of positives and negatives in the public's view of surveys. On the positive side, for example, the public felt that the survey research industry serves a useful purpose (86%), believed that responding to surveys is in their best interest (64%), and recognized the usefulness of polls and surveys in providing government officials with an understanding of how the public feels about important issues. On the negative, the public felt that there are too many polls and surveys on subjects of little value (69%), was skeptical of the results reported in surveys (63%), and did not understand how the small number of people interviewed in the typical survey can represent an entire population (47%).

While the public's overall impression of polls is generally favorable, there is some skepticism in the American mind about how survey data are collected and how such information is used and reported. Despite the general confidence that the public has in polls, a number of factors can lead to errors in the way survey data are collected, interpreted, or reported that might cause the public to lose faith in the polling process. In the remainder of the chapter we examine several of these elements, including pseudo-polls, respondent factors, and technological developments.

PSEUDO-POLLS

Pseudo-polls involve contacts with individuals that have some elements of a legitimate survey but are not attempts to collect information from a representative sample of the public. Chapter 3 described one type of pseudo-poll, the "call-in" poll to an 800- or 900- telephone number, and we reiterate the point that such "polls" do not legitimately represent the views of any population. Such polls can be especially troubling, or cause confusion among the American public, when they are used by major news organizations, which also conduct scientific surveys and report results based on representative samples. In describing the results of one of the first such polls that was done in conjunction with an on-air broadcast, in which the distinction between the results of a call-in poll and a companion survey with a representative sample were not always clear, Kathy Frankovic, Director of Surveys for CBS News, noted "[W]e never wanted to say the 'poll' in referring to the callers. There were slipups in the course of the live broadcast, where the conclusion was drawn that the call-ins represented change" (Frankovic, 1992: 19). In commenting on this poll, Albert Cantril declared, "[T]he credibility of all public polls was set back when CBS News conducted its call-in "poll" . . . The broadcast was especially hazardous to polling credibility because of the stature of CBS as a source of news."[1] Whether reported by a major media source or your local radio station[2], the results of a call-in poll cannot be treated as representing the views of some larger population.

Another type of pseudo-poll, previously described in Chapter 3, is the push poll. There is no research component to a push poll; this is telemarketing under the guise of survey research. An example of a push poll that occurred during the 1996 Republican presidential campaign involved a call received by a supporter of Lamar Alexander who, after telling the interviewer that he would vote for Alexander in the primary, was asked "Well, if you knew he had raised taxes in Tennessee, would you still vote for him?" (Singhania, 1996). Such polls damage the electoral process in that "they injure candidates, often without revealing the source of the information" and "represent the worst kind of imposition on respondents" (Gawiser, 1995: 1). Push polling is condemned by survey research professional associations such as the American Association for Public Opinion Research and Council for Marketing and Opinion Research. As AAPOR's statement on push polling notes, "Push polls violate the AAPOR Code of Ethics by intentionally lying to or misleading respondents. They corrupt the electoral process by disseminating false and misleading attacks on candidates. And because so-called 'push polls' can easily be confused with real polls, they damage the reputation of legitimate polling, thereby discouraging the public from participating in legitimate survey research" (AAPOR, 1998).

Other types of pseudo-polls that can cause the public to lose faith in surveys include **sugging**—selling under the guise of research, **frugging**—fundraising under the guise of research, and **cugging**—campaigning under the guise of research. In sugging, telemarketers attempt to gain acceptance in order to make a sales pitch by initially defining their contact as being for the purpose of research. Similarly, frugging uses the facade of a research study to make fundraising attempts, and cuggers disguise their attempts at campaigning as a research effort. Each of these practices "trades on the prestige of science and . . . exploits the willingness of people to reveal information about themselves in the public interest" (Research Industry Coalition, 1996). These practices were made illegal by the Telemarketing Consumer Fraud and Abuse Prevention Act (1994), which requires telemarketers to disclose promptly their name and that the purpose of the call is sales related, including the nature and price of the product the caller is attempting to sell. While part of the intent of this law was to differentiate legitimate survey research calls from sales calls, it has not eliminated sugging, frugging, and cugging, especially by political campaigns, which are not, in fact, sales organizations. Such practices erode the public's willingness to participate in legitimate surveys and make the task of conducting reliable and valid survey research more difficult.

Mail "surveys" of constituents conducted by elected officials, typically members of Congress, represent another type of pseudo-poll. Such devices often contain questions that are worded in a way that the results will support the office holder's position, or are designed to provide information about the candidate (for example, "During the last session of Congress, Senator X voted for a bill that brought over $800 million in new federal highway funds to this state. Do you support this position?"). When the results of such totally nonscientific mail surveys are reported, they can lead to confusion among the public as to "what the public thinks."

RESPONDENT FACTORS

Abuse of survey research is one factor that can affect the public's confidence in its results. Another set of factors involves characteristics of the population; that is, aspects of the public that can affect the reliability and validity of poll findings. These characteristics, which we have labeled "respondent factors," include locating respondents, gaining their cooperation and getting them to provide candid answers to the questions asked of them.

Increasing public participation in the polls has been labeled "the greatest and most frustrating challenge" facing public opinion researchers (O'Neill, 1996: 54). In Chapter 4, we described the importance of selecting a sample appropriately to produce results that are representative of the population in which you are interested. But the results of the most carefully drawn sample can be called into question if the people selected do not participate in the survey.

Response rates involve both locating the individuals selected and convincing them to participate. During the time when most surveys of the general population were done by face-to-face interviewing, response rates were generally high. Individuals selected to be interviewed were relatively easy to contact and usually agreed to cooperate.

While certain studies, such as the Current Population Survey, have been able to maintain a relatively high response rate (Smith, 1995), "the prevailing view, both based on these trend data and from practitioners' knowledge of the situation, is that response rates are declining and have been doing so for some time" (Groves and Couper, 1998: 159). As noted by Brehm (1994: 45), "[R]esponse rates for all surveys—academic, government, business, media— have been falling since the 1950s." In the NES, for example, refusal rates have risen from 6% in 1952 to 21% in 1992. Overall nonresponse[3] to the NES was 23% in 1952 and 26% in 1992, but has reached more than 30% several times during this period (Luevano, 1994). Factors such as fear of crime, increased cynicism, and concerns over privacy issues have contributed to the increase in refusal rates, and societal changes, such as the increasing participation of women in the workforce and the reduction of the number of adults per household, means that households are occupied a smaller percent of the time than before, making contact more difficult. Moreover, as survey data collection has moved increasingly toward telephone interviewing, there has generally been a decrease in response rates, since response rates in telephone surveys are typically about ten percent less than those for face-to-face surveys (Brehm, 1993: 24–25). There can be little doubt that the increased use of telephone telemarketing campaigns for every type of product has had an impact on telephone survey research.

The implication of increases in refusal rates and overall nonresponse should be clear. As the number of individuals from whom data are collected becomes a smaller percentage of those initially selected, their opinions and characteristics tend to be become less representative of the overall population. The "public's view" as reported in the results of surveys may not be an accurate reflection of "the American mind." Survey research organizations must spend additional resources to locate respondents and increase cooperation in order to maintain the public's confidence in poll results.

Another "respondent characteristic" affecting the reliability and validity of polls involves the information that individuals provide as part of the interview. In Chapter 4 we detailed many of the factors to be considered in designing survey questions properly. Even with the most well-designed questions, however, we find that many respondents exhibit **nonattitudes;** that is, there is a significant proportion of the public who, for lack of information about a particular issue, offer meaningless opinions that vary randomly in direction during repeated trials over time (Converse, 1964; 1970). Similarly, about one-third of the public will give opinions on fictitious or largely obscure items (Bishop, Oldendick, Tuchfarber, and Bennett, 1980; Schuman and Presser, 1981).

Such "errors" in surveys, we believe, are not the product of people deliberately lying to pollsters, as at least one noted columnist has encouraged them to do (Royko, 1992). Instead, these responses reflect the interview situation, for a survey interview is a social interaction between the interviewer and respondent. In this situation the interviewer asks questions and the expectation is that the person being interviewed will respond. Faced with an issue with which they are unfamiliar, respondents can either answer "don't know" or quickly develop a response based on the information available to them in the question and the context in which the question is asked. The respondents' desire to present themselves in a favorable light (for example, as knowledgeable or agreeable) leads them to honor the interviewer's request for an answer (Martin, 1984). The interview, as a social interaction, represents more than a respondent providing answers to questions.

In Waller's (1992: 26) discussion of the 1992 British pre-election polls—in which every poll showed the election to be extremely close, with a slight tilt in favor of the Labour Party, when in fact, the Conservative Party won handily—he argues that large numbers of people did not lie to interviewers, and that respondents "may well have thought seriously of voting Labour in the circumstance of the interview." However, the act of deciding who will rule Britain for the next five years "is a different type of act than responding to a survey questionnaire." Waller concludes that, "[V]oters seem to have caught on to the fact that they can use the preelection polls to 'send them a message,' and then express their deepest underlying interests in the only poll that counts—the balloting on election day" (1992: 26).

Similarly, research has shown that respondents will provide different answers to interviewers of their own race than to an interviewer of a different race. Such results are particularly evident when the question has racial overtones. Over the past decade, some of the largest discrepancies between the results of election polls and electoral outcomes have involved contests in which one of the candidates was a racial minority (Oldendick and Link, 1998). In these situations respondents are more likely to give answers that "defer" to the race of the interviewer (for example, whites are more likely to voice support for a black candidate to black interviewers than to white; conversely, black respondents are more likely to indicate support for a white candidate to white interviewers). In cases where race is salient, respondents have a tendency to give "socially desirable" answers and are reluctant to be interpreted as racist (Davis, 1997; Finkel, Guterbock, and Borg, 1991; Hatchett and Schuman, 1975). Such race-of-interviewer effects again do not represent widespread "lying" on the part of respondents, but rather a recognition of the social nature of the interview and a desire to maintain "a polite conversation between the respondent and the interviewer" (Anderson, Silver, and Abramson, 1988: 319). Failure to account for such effects, however, can lead to inaccurate reporting of public attitudes and, over time, erode public trust and confidence in survey research.

TECHNOLOGICAL DEVELOPMENTS

Over the past twenty-five years, there have been a number of technological developments that have had an impact on the polling profession. Some of these, such as the development of computer-assisted telephone interviewing, audio-assisted computer-aided self-interviewing, and voice recognition technology, have improved the quality and efficiency of survey data collection. Other developments, however, have made the business of collecting information from a representative sample of the population more difficult. These include the increased use of telephone answering machines and caller-ID services.

As noted by Tuckel and O'Neill (1996: 34), the problem that these technologies pose for survey researchers is that "they may make it more difficult for telephone surveyors to establish contact with respondents and therefore compromise the representativeness of the samples selected for interviewing." Households with telephone answering machines can use the device to screen unwanted calls and, if a message is left by a survey organization, choose not to return the call. Similarly, users of caller ID are unlikely to recognize the phone numbers of most survey research organizations when these numbers are displayed on their units. If they are unwilling to answer calls from an unrecognized number, then the opportunity for public opinion researchers to contact them and determine their views on "issues of relevance to government" is diminished. As potential survey respondents systematically exclude themselves from participation through the use of these devices, the threat increases that the results of the survey will not accurately represent "what the public thinks."

When RDD (random-digit dialing) was being developed (Cooper, 1964) telephone answering machines for residential households were virtually non-existent. By 1990, an estimated 43% of U.S. households were equipped with such devices (Electronic Industries Association, 1991), and by 1995 two-thirds of households reported answering machine ownership (Council for Marketing and Opinion Research, 1995). Caller-ID services became available later than answering machines, but seem to be making the same rapid penetration into the U.S. market. In 1993, only 3% of households subscribed to caller-ID services, a percentage that increased to 10% in 1995. Moreover, as noted by Tuckel and O'Neill (1996: 35), "an additional 13% report they are either 'almost certain,' 'very likely,' or 'somewhat likely' to obtain this service within the next year."

As these devices have become more pervasive, they have made it more difficult for survey researchers to reach those selected to be interviewed (Link and Oldendick, 1998). To this point, however, it seems that substantial proportions of households continue to be accessible to survey researchers and that only about 5% of households may be using telephone answering machines to screen calls on a consistent basis (Oldendick and Link, 1994: 266; Tuckel and Feinberg, 1991: 206–207). Similarly, research on caller-ID to this point "can be thought of as heartening to telephone surveyors concerned with the impact of this technology on gaining access to potential respondents" (Tuckel and O'Neill, 1996: 40). While caller-ID subscribers do screen their calls frequently, they do so not to isolate themselves completely, but rather to filter out calls based on personal or family considerations. They are generally willing to pick up the phone when their unit displays an unrecognized number.

Although telephone answering machines and caller-ID do not yet appear to have had a major impact on the representativeness of samples in telephone surveys, there is a group of potential respondents using these devices to avoid "unwanted" calls, including those of survey researchers. As the percentage of households with such devices grows and the public becomes more inundated with the ubiquitous telemarketing call, sugging, frugging, and other attempts to access the household through the telephone, the use of devices to screen calls is likely to increase. Public opinion researchers will have to monitor these trends closely and commit increasing resources to maintain the representativeness of telephone samples on which many survey researchers have come to rely.

A very different type of technological development that is likely to have an impact on the future of survey research is the Internet. As more of the population gains access to the Internet—in 1998, it was estimated that 32% of U.S. households had access—survey researchers are developing ways to utilize this technology to collect information (Zogby, 1998: 94). In some ways, the role of the Internet in survey research in the late 1990s is analogous to that of the telephone in the 1950s, in that the proportion of the general population that has Internet access is too small and their characteristics too different from those of the general population to use this medium to collect information that is representative of the population at large. Those with Internet access tend to be younger, better educated, wealthier, and more likely to be white than their counterparts without access.

Even if Internet access becomes as universal as the telephone is today, its use to collect survey information will face some unique challenges, such as how to assure that the designated respondent is the person actually answering the survey, how to guarantee only one response per household, and issues of privacy and confidentiality. Some of these issues "ought to be resolved by more technology—for example, identification numbers, blocks to ensure that only one person per household can respond, barriers to further access to responses by outside groups" (Zogby, 1998: 94). While the Internet has been used successfully to conduct surveys of special populations who have access to and are familiar with the technology, and such use is likely to increase as more survey researchers turn their attention to the Internet, there are many hurdles to be overcome before this method can be used to gather data that are representative of the American mind. In Zogby's discussion of surveys and the Internet, he contends that the Internet will increasingly be a part of the future and that the challenge is to harness it for accurate, credible survey research. As he asks, "Will it be the boon to the industry that the telephone and the personal computer has been? Or will it actually create more headaches than it is worth?"

If you would like to be a respondent in an Internet survey, go to the web site for this book at: http://www.politicalscience.wadsworth.com. Are you representative of "the American mind" or will the results of this Web survey resemble those of the *Literary Digest* or a 900-number call-in poll in reflecting "what the public thinks?"

SUMMARY

Public opinion researchers face a number of challenges in providing reliable and valid information about the electorate's views on issues of interest to government. For the most part, the public seems to display a fair degree of confidence in the results of survey research. Large majorities of the public agree that surveys provide a chance for citizens to voice their opinions regarding public policies and political activities, and the industry is generally seen as serving a useful purpose. The public does, however, have some complaints about surveys. Almost half, for example, feel that surveys are often too personal. More importantly, it is widely believed that surveys are used to disguise a sales pitch (O'Neill, 1996: 54). Practices such as sugging, frugging, and cugging are threats to the public's continuing trust in survey research.

Similarly, when the results of pseudo-polls, based on unrepresentative samples, are reported as reflecting what the public thinks, they can mislead the citizenry and erode public confidence in the results of scientific surveys. Gaining cooperation from respondents in order to produce results that accurately represent those of the population is, in the view of many, the greatest challenge facing public opinion research. Societal factors, such as increased population density, the larger proportion of women in the workforce, the smaller number of adults per household, fear of crime, and privacy concerns have made it more difficult to locate respondents and have led to an increase in the refusal rate for many surveys. Moreover, the increasing use of telephone answering devices and caller-ID services make it increasingly difficult for survey researchers to assure that the information from those individuals surveyed represents the views of the larger population in which we are interested. As users of poll data, you should recognize and appreciate "the deep 'validity problems' that can inhere to even the best research" and be aware that assuring quality survey data is difficult and requires continuing effort (Ladd, 1998b: 86).

NOTES

1. Other media outlets have had similar experiences and have been subject to similar criticisms. During the 1980 election campaign, ABC News conducted a call-in poll following a televised debate between Ronald Reagan and Jimmy Carter. In addition to the self-selection and unrepresentativeness that attend to all call-ins, there were several additional sources of potential bias in this case. As noted by Moore (1992: 288)

> The debate ended late in the evening on the East Coast, thus favoring respondents from the Western parts of the country, which were more heavily for Reagan than Carter. The cost of 50 cents would deter some of the less affluent from participating, yet they were proportionately more likely to support Carter. And an electronic glitch made it more difficult for urban areas than rural areas to complete their calls, again a bias against Carter's political support.

In reporting the results of call-in polls, ABC would include a disclaimer that the results were "unscientific," but during programs the results "would be discussed as though they reflected the general opinion of the American public" (288).

2. While preparing this chapter, one of the authors heard the results of a radio station call-in poll in which all 57 callers thought the management of the Cincinnati Reds was "on the wrong track." Only later in the broadcast did the host find out that the telephone number to call to register an "on the right track" opinion was not in working order. Such are the perils of the call-in poll.

3. While refusals are the largest contributor to nonresponse in surveys, overall nonresponse includes other factors, such as being unable to locate respondents or to collect information from them during the study's fielding period, or failures to complete the interview due to illness or a language barrier. Telephone surveys also suffer from nonresponse due to consistent non-answered telephone numbers or repeated attempts to contact a household which reach an answering machine.

12

Measuring the American Mind: The Sum of Its Parts

G iven all of the polling that has been done since surveying began and all of the scientific research on the data generated by those surveys, what can be said about the state of the American mind? At least one scholar, John Geer, has proposed a new theory of democratic leadership (1996) that rests on the proposition that today's politicians and national leaders operate on the basis of new information about what the public believes, information derived from survey research. Other commentators on the national political scene note the important role that public opinion plays, if not in shaping legislators' own views, then in the presentation of those views to their constituents (Jacobs and Shapiro, 1997). As Michael Barone puts it, "Polls are part of the air politicians breathe" (1997: 1). However political leaders use the information gained from polling—to defend their own decisions or to build support for a specific policy initiative—there is, as we have seen, a body of knowledge about what Americans believe that can be considered by elected officials, civil servants, and those who report and interpret our political system. In this final chapter, we will consider this body of knowledge and propose a characterization of the American mind.

THE POLITICAL CONTEXT

A recent commentary on the state of American politics in 1998 asked the question, "Is All Politics Local?" and answered it, "Yes, except when it's not" (Cook, 1998: 2). By that, the author meant that most elections are fought and won on the basis of local constituency politics, except for some strong national forces that may defeat a party's candidates unexpectedly. In the same way, one might ask, are Americans very political? Given the research on political partisanship and ideological identification, the answer might well be: most Americans are not very political except when they are, and they've been this way for a long time.

Party Identification

As discussed in Chapter 6, about two-thirds of Americans are willing to identify themselves as partisans of one of the two major political parties. About one-third or more of Americans choose to see themselves as independent voters. Although the percentage of party identifiers is less than it was at the end of World War II, the variation in the proportion of Americans declaring themselves Democrats and Republicans has been relatively slight. Furthermore, research on political socialization tells us that partisan identity is linked to the family and community of origin for many of these party identifiers. For others, the effects of coming of age in a specific political era are a strong determinant of party identification. Furthermore, the polling research over time indicates that these patterns of partisanship transmission are quite robust.

The importance and stability of partisan identification are bolstered by two additional factors: the demographics of party identifiers and the public's appraisal of party strengths. Since the beginning of the National Election Studies, polling data (from that series and all others) show that Americans of higher incomes and those in the older age brackets were much more likely to be Republicans. Additionally, those who consider themselves conservatives are also likely to be Republicans. The groups that are most like to identify themselves as Democrats are liberals, black Americans, younger Americans, poorer Americans and those with less education. This pattern of attachment reflects quite clearly the differing philosophic and political appeals of the two major American parties.

When we turn to the views of the general public about the political parties, a similar consistent pattern of perception is found. Public opinion has generally seen the Republican Party as better than the Democratic Party at handling foreign affairs, reducing the deficit, cutting crime, and avoiding tax increases. Depending on the year, either party may be seen as best able to keep the economy going. The Democratic Party is viewed more favorably in terms of health care, Social Security, solving the problems of the poor, and improving race relations.

Other polling data have identified the Republicans as the party of business, suburbanites, higher income people, farmers, and the financial sector, while Democrats are seen as the party of blue-collar voters, Jewish voters, minorities, the poor, and urban dwellers. These patterns of perception have also been stable for long periods of time. What this suggests is that the parties and their platforms are understood by their adherents and by the general public.

The Ideological Spectrum

With regard to ideology, Americans are more willing to identify themselves as conservatives, liberals, or moderates than one might think. However, they are not as evenly divided as they are in terms of partisan identification. The percentage of Americans who will identify themselves as liberals has declined over the last twenty years to about 25% of those polled. The percentage of Americans who consider themselves conservatives is closer to 45%. It is worth noting, however, that Americans are most likely to avoid the extremes of these categories with the majority of Americans saying that they are closer to the "middle of the road": they say they are "slightly liberal" (14%), "slightly conservative" (20%), or "moderate" (30%). This preference for the middle of the ideological spectrum suggests that Americans are not very ideological in the sense of perceiving all issues through a consistent world view. Moreover, Americans do not exhibit the depth of political thinking or consistency among their policy preferences reflective of "ideological thinking." Given the general pragmatism of American politics, including the tendency of American parties and candidates to appeal to the middle of the political spectrum, it is not surprising that Americans are not as polarized on this spectrum as are citizens of some other Western democracies.

Political Attachment

At the beginning of this chapter, the question was raised, "are Americans very political?" The answer to that question becomes much more complicated when we consider the evidence about Americans' attachment to the political system. When asked to appraise the nation's future, the vast majority (83%) of Americans say that the United States is still the very best place in the world to live (Roper Center Poll, 1994), and 54% believe that the nation's best times are still ahead. Other polls have shown that new immigrants to the United States may have even more optimism than those citizens born here. Yet, other indicators suggest that while the nation retains the public's loyalty, the government does not.

Public confidence in the nation's major institutions and their leadership has shown a major decline since the 1970s. Most dramatically, confidence in the presidency and the Congress is so low that further decline seems impossible. Similarly, Americans' sense of trust in the government to do what is right has declined steeply, as has their confidence in the competence of government. While Americans express less efficacy or sense of being able to influence government, this indicator has not fallen as sharply as the trust measure.

The American mind seems to have a paradoxical approach to these political orientations. People are willing to become attached to the political parties, work in campaigns, register and vote, but regard the government and the parties with great distrust and, some would say, cynicism. One might expect that, given the level of cynicism, fewer and fewer Americans would identify with parties or articulate a political philosophy, but that has not been case. What is the explanation for this paradox? It may be that Americans feel efficacious in their own communities and states; trust the political leaders that they know and vote for (especially for their own member of Congress), and understand very well the basic divisions between the political parties and, indeed, the ends of the political spectrum. Yet, the American mind remains suspicious of the responsiveness of government and the political system as a whole, so suspicious and cynical that 81% of Americans agree with the statement that, "political events these days seem more like theater or entertainment than like something to be taken seriously" (Hunter and Johnson, 1997: 36). Based on these data and the long decline in confidence and trust, Hunter and Johnson (1997: 38) characterize the American mind this way: "high-mindedness and cynicism co-exist; idealism and exasperation abide side by side."

THE ISSUES AGENDA

Although Americans are expressing more cynicism about their government, they continue to hold and be willing to express ideas about the political and social issues facing the nation. Increasing levels of distrust or, perhaps, alienation have not kept most members of the public from paying some level of attention to the nation's problems and, as we shall see, moderating their opinions in response to a changing society.

Providing for the General Welfare

Looking at the views of the public on issues such as increasing government services, the provision of jobs for people, Social Security, education, and health care provides further examples of the tension within the American mind over the role of government. For the most part, Americans do hold the government accountable for the general welfare and domestic tranquility of the nation. They believe that there are issues that the government ought to be handling because there is no other entity to do so. Some programs, like Social Security, have become so popular that politicians refer to any attempt to change them as "the third rail of politics" (to touch them is political suicide). However, on almost every other social welfare issue, Americans express some ambivalence about government action. In some cases, the culture of rugged individualism still seems pervasive.

In looking at the overall provision of government services to the people, the balance of opinion has been through a number of cycles. At some periods in time, the public supports more government programs and at others, particularly when the economy is strong, the proportion of the public that wants fewer services may increase. When we turn to more specific social issues, opinions are more stable. For example, the public has consistently expressed the view that the government should spend more money on education, with the proportion supporting this position growing from 51% in 1973 to 70% in 1996. Health care is also a major concern for the American public, with large majorities saying that the government should spend more on improving the

nation's health. Here, the proportion supporting increased government spending is fairly stable, at 63 to 70%. However, in the case of health care, there is a
substantial minority of Americans who believe that paying for hospital bills is a
matter of individual responsibility or a joint individual/government responsibility. As discussed in Chapter 7, the Clinton administration proposal to completely reform the health care industry was defeated early in the first term
largely because it became identified with big government bureaucracies.

The issue of providing jobs and supporting a standard of living for everyone is more controversial. Depending on how the question is asked, there is
strong support for the individual "getting ahead on his own." If we look at several series of questions about the role of the government in providing jobs, it
appears that the American mind supports government's role in creating jobs
and a strong economy, but believes that the individual is still responsible for his
or her own job.

When we turn from jobs to helping poor people or welfare, it is clear that
question wording taps certain aspects of the American political culture. While
there is strong support for the government aiding those who are poor or who
cannot help themselves, asking about "welfare" brings a new dimension into
the American mind. Support for government spending on welfare programs is
considerably less than support for spending to assist "the poor." This lack of
support for the concept of welfare undergirded the welfare reform efforts of
the 1990s. Those reforms placed an emphasis on employment for all Americans and administration of welfare programs by the states.

Like dealing with foreign nations, protecting the environment is a policy
issue that seems to require national government action. Indeed, public support
for government regulation in the environmental sphere is very high, with more
than 80% of Americans supporting the need for government regulation, and
more than 60% saying that the government is not spending enough money for
environmental protection. On this particular issue, the people support government regulation of business and of individual decisions. However, there is little
connection in the American mind between regulation and the cost of improving the environment: while 50% say they would pay higher prices to protect
the environment, only about one-third of Americans are willing to pay higher
taxes or reduce their standard of living to achieve environmental protection.

In general, support for increased governmental services in these social programs is found among the demographic groups that need these services. For
example, poorer, less educated Americans support government creation of jobs
and support for health care, while higher income Americans generally want
fewer government programs. Support among liberals across these issues (and
opposition from conservatives) is consistent and stable, again validating the
public's perception of ideological positions.

Equality and Racism

The American mind has demonstrated a tremendous capacity for change on issues involving race, one of the most contentious issue arenas in American society. Although the end of racism and the attainment of full equality by minori-

ties remain far in the future, Americans have come to a common understanding on some of the issues that divided the races at the end of World War II.

Among the issues that have seen significant shifts in American opinion are the racial integration of the schools, integration of housing and other accommodations, and the willingness of whites to elect black Americans to office. Acceptance of the fairness of integrated schools is the most extreme change in the American mind documented by survey research to date. However, the acceptance of integrated schools as a goal did not include some of the methods that were chosen to meet this goal: most white Americans opposed busing of schoolchildren, although there has been some lessening of that opposition. About 40% of blacks also opposed busing as a remedy. Similarly, another remedy for segregated schools, integrating neighborhoods, has faced opposition. While both blacks and whites show strong support for the proposition that blacks should be able to live anywhere they can afford to, white support for the right to keep blacks out of their neighborhood has declined slowly, finally reaching 13% in 1996.

Perhaps one of the most divisive issues over the years since the beginning of the modern civil rights era is the policy of affirmative action. While there has been consistent approval (about 40 to 50 %) of the amount of government spending to assist minorities and blacks, black and white Americans have quite different perceptions of affirmative action programs. Generally, black Americans approve special efforts to help minorities get ahead, including preferential treatment, while white Americans maintain strong opposition to this policy. As the 1990s draw to a close, the concept of affirmative action is under fire both through state referenda and in the federal courts. By 1996, various surveys found that between 38% and 50% of black Americans were also opposed to preferential treatment.

Issues of Life and Death

Issues and controversies that are rooted in moral and religious values are not new to American society. Temperance societies and the abolition movement raised the stakes in political debates of the early nineteenth century. In the contemporary period, the results of four decades of polling help us to see how the American mind considers such issues and, in some instances, comes to a resolution of the issue. Other issues, on which public divisions are long-standing and very stable, show no signs of resolution because of the depth of feeling they arouse.

Among the issues that have come "full circle" in the post–World War II era is the question of the death penalty. During the 1950s and 1960s, the public held out considerable hope that prisons could perform a rehabilitative function in society and, in a similar liberal vein, the public's approval of the death penalty declined. With the increase in urban violence in the 1960s and a growing increase in violent crime in the 1970s, Americans changed their views of incarceration, choosing the protection of society and the punishment of convicted criminals as primary goals, rather than rehabilitation. At the same time, support for the death penalty increased, stabilizing at about 70% of the American public. Support for the death penalty is not nearly as high among black

Americans, who are over-represented in prison and on death row. Although there are still many Americans who oppose the death penalty for moral reasons, the level of opposition has declined and the society seems to have accepted this form of punishment.

The debate over abortion stands in direct contrast to that over the death penalty. Since the *Roe v. Wade* decision in 1973, Americans have made little progress toward a societal resolution of the debate. The percentage of Americans who oppose abortion for any reason and the percentage who approve abortion for any reason has varied little since the *Roe* decision. The vast majority of Americans support the right of a woman to have an abortion under certain situations, such as becoming pregnant by rape or incest or in the case of severe birth defects. However, there are so many ways to legislate regulation of abortions and to specify the situations under which an abortion is available, that the legislative battles in the halls of Congress and state legislatures seem to be endless. This is one instance in which it is fairly easy to explain the state of the American mind, but almost impossible to reach a legislative solution to the debate.

Gun control is not usually considered to be a moral or religious issue but, instead, one that has constitutional and cultural roots. The debate over government regulation of gun sales and gun ownership is rooted in the American culture of individualism and distrust of the government. However, as with the issue of abortion, zealots on both sides—those in favor of gun control and those opposed to any type of control—fight on in local, state, and national legislative arenas. And as with the abortion issue, it is not difficult to understand the American mind on gun control. For many decades, the majority of Americans have supported registration of firearms and the regulation of gun sales. They differ on exactly how this goal is to be achieved and the exact types of weapons to be regulated. Strong vocal minorities argue for everything from the outlawing of gun ownership to freedom from any regulation. As for the abortion issue, there are so many arenas for debate and so many ways to write legislation that the battle is likely to continue indefinitely. The American mind, however, has a moderate position on this issue, as it has on many others.

The United States and the World

Most polls conducted in the United States face inward, seeking to measure public opinion on domestic issues, domestic politics, and domestic political campaigns. However, there is a body of knowledge about how the American mind perceives the rest of the world and, more specifically, what role the United States should play in the world. Since World War II, the American mind has accepted and supported the leadership role played by the United States in world politics. Although there have been slight variations in the level of support for playing an active role, most obviously during the Vietnam era, the majority of Americans support a global role for their country. When it comes to the exact part to be played by the United States, there is much more variation in American opinion. The use of military force is, of course, the most controversial international action that can be taken. While Americans support the use of force to defend our allies, sending American troops to foreign soil requires considerable leadership by the president and members of the elite. Americans have been divided over the use of force, notably by the end of the Vietnam conflict and the Korean War. Other divisions are related to gender and race: neither women nor African Americans are as likely to support the use of force overseas as are their white, male counterparts.

Under the general umbrella of world leadership, other issues have arisen that challenge the American mind. While Americans are generally supportive of humanitarian efforts overseas, such as the sending of troops to Somalia in 1992, they are almost uniformly distrustful of foreign aid and wish to see the amount of aid decreased. Foreign aid, unlike humanitarian help, connotes corruption and welfare. Americans also view the United Nations with mixed feelings: while general support for the United Nations is high as an organization, Americans also feel that the United States spends too much money on the organization and they resist having American troops under United Nations commanders. Other issues including trade policy, NATO, and immigration provide further opportunities for Americans to disagree about the precise nature of American involvement in world affairs.

THE AMERICAN MIND: COMMON PRINCIPLES OR COMMON SENSE

As noted in the beginning of Chapter 6, one of the longest running debates in American political science concerns the way that ordinary Americans think about politics and political issues. The science of survey research has provided a great deal of information that feeds into this debate, some of which has been discussed in this book. One of the most surprising findings of the early survey researchers (Lazarsfeld, for example) was that Americans do not think about political parties and candidates in nearly as sophisticated a way as do citizens of nations with more ideological parties. Using the National Election Studies, Converse and others documented the relatively informal way that Americans come to make voting decisions and the relative lack of connections between that vote choice and their preferences on issues. Additionally, it became clear through these studies and many subsequent ones that most Americans do not find it important to maintain consistency in their political beliefs, that is, they do not necessarily respond to survey questions about issues and candidates in a way that would indicate a clear philosophical or ideological viewpoint.

Further undermining the portrait of an "ideal citizen" were data gathered by polls about the lack of knowledge held by Americans. Not only could survey researchers ask about totally fictitious policy issues and legislation and get answers from respondents, but other surveys found that dismal proportions of Americans could answer such "easy" questions as the name of their representative or senator, or give basic information about the Constitution or Bill of Rights. In their analysis of Americans' political information, Delli Carpini and Keeter (1996) conclude that there are many reasons for the relative lack of political knowledge displayed by Americans, including low economic and social status, lack of education, and less than adequate sources of information. They also believe that most Americans are information "generalists" who have broad knowledge about the system and preferences about issues and politics, but are not likely to have detailed knowledge about an issue unless it is very relevant to their own lives.

While individual-level opinions may be volatile, the aggregate of the American mind is generally quite stable, and changes slowly in predictable ways. As Page and Shapiro (1982: 39–40) note, "Our examination of the data indicates that there has been considerable stability in Americans' policy preferences . . . when changes did occur, they were not random or inexplicable; they were usually related to important changes in citizens' lives and in their social and economic environments." On many issues, ranging from gun control to the impact of slavery, the American mind has expressed stable and sensible preferences about what the government should or should not do.

Moreover, public opinion has been shown to have an impact on policy. Researchers such as Monroe (1979) have shown that not only does the public follow politics and express opinions but that, over time, government policy often follows public preferences. In examining the relationship between public opinion and policy change, Page and Shapiro (1983: 189) conclude that, "opinion changes are important causes of policy change. When Americans' policy preferences shift, it is likely that congruent changes in policy will follow."

Monroe (1979, 1998) has also studied the relationship between public opinion on individual policy issues and the changes that may occur in response to those opinions in later years. His original study looked at policy change and public preferences between 1960 and 1979: he found that policy changes or maintenance of the status quo corresponded to the public's expressed opinions in 63% of the cases. His most recent work (1998: 12) reported a decline in the percentage of times that policy was consistent with opinion to 55%. Furthermore, the most consistency was found on foreign policy and defense issues, presumably due to the ability of the president to take decisive action in this area. The policies that were most likely to be inconsistent with public views were in the areas of political reform, including campaign finance and other electoral reforms. Monroe notes that resistance to policy change has been higher since 1980 and suggests that strongly divided government (with a president of one party and Congress controlled by the other) might contribute to stalemate in making policy changes. He also suggests, however, that the increasing complexity of issues, combined with increased partisanship in the Congress, may have prevented policy changes consistent with public views.

The work of Monroe, Page and Shapiro, and many others, on the linkages between policy and public opinion is extremely interesting because it suggests that the public does have the power to direct the outcomes of the government. However, this research only hints at the complexity of the forces at work in a democracy: the media, interest groups, political manipulation of the public agenda, campaign strategies, presidential initiatives, Congressional needs, and the public, to name only a few. Understanding that dynamic is work for scholars and researchers in the future.

Faced with this interplay of political forces is the American public which, as we have seen, has a modest attachment to political ideologies and a rather broad, pragmatic approach to partisanship. Yet, it is quite clear that Americans understand their political environment: conservatives and liberals, as well as Republicans and Democrats, hold issue preferences that make sense in relation to their philosophic positions or party platforms. Even more striking is the congruity between group interests especially for blacks, for blue collar workers, for the wealthy, and for members of religious groups, and their perceptions of parties and issue positions.

The American mind—loyal to the nation, aware of national issues, involved in the varied and on-going concerns of contemporary life in the United States—generally shows stability in its outlook on the policy issues facing the country. It does not shy away, though, from tough decisions or from adapting to a new viewpoint if the needs of the nation require it.

Appendix A

-·❋·-

Programs or Projects of the Federal Government

Following are the major programs or projects of the federal government for which the Bureau of the Census accumulates, prepares, processes, and provides information.

Access to Care Survey

Adults on Probation

Agriculture Census

Automated Inventory Control System

Alternative Questionnaire Experiment

American Indian Reservation Test

American Travel Survey

Annexation Population Count

Annual Capital Investments Survey

Annual Housing Survey—Metropolitan Sample

Annual Housing Survey—National

Annual Jail Survey

Annual Retail Trade Survey

Annual Survey of Communication Services

Annual Survey of Government Finance

Annual Survey of Manufacturing

Annual Trade Survey

Bureau of Labor Statistics—Rent

Boundary and Annexation Survey

Building Permits

Congressional Budget Office

Census of Probation and Parole Agencies

Census of Jails

Children in Custody

Commodity Flow Survey

Company Organization Survey

Construction Progress Reporting Survey

Consumer Expenditure

Current Industrial Report

Current Point of Purchase Computer-Assisted Telephone Interviews

Current Population Survey

Customer Satisfaction Survey

Disability Follow-Back Survey

Economic Census

Ethnographic Evaluation

Exports

Fishing, Hunting and Wildlife Recreation Survey

Housing Sales

Housing Starts

Imports

Improvement Coverage Measurement Test

Industrial Research and Development

Integrated Post-Secondary Education Data System

Investment Plan Survey

Law Enforcement Survey

Long-Term Care

Manufacturers Energy and Consumption Survey

Manufacturing Energy Consumption Survey

Market Absorption

Medical Expenditure Survey

MPO (Metropolitan Planning Organization) Map Shot

Mobile Homes Survey

Monthly Advanced Retail Trade Survey

Monthly Wholesale Trade

National Content Survey

National Correction Reporting Program

National Crime Victimization Survey

National Health Interview Survey

National Health Provider Inventory

National Home and Hospice Care

National Hospital Ambulatory Medical Care Survey

National Institute of Standards and Technology/Manufacturing Extension Partnership Survey

National Judicial Reporting Program

National Longitudinal Alcohol Epidemiologic Survey

National Longitudinal Survey

National Mortality Follow-Back Survey

National Nursing Home Survey

National Prisoners Survey—Inmates in State Corrections

National Prosecutors Survey Program

National Survey of Ambulatory Surgery

National Survey of Homeless Assistance Providers and Clients

New York City Housing and Vacancy Survey

Outreach Evaluation

Plant Capacity Utilization Survey

Preliminary Housing Starts

Prisoners Census

Private School Survey

Property Owners and Managers Survey

Public Employee Survey

Quality Control Studies

Quarterly Births Survey

Quarterly Survey of Property Tax Collection

Retail Sales and Inventory Reports

School and Staff Survey

School and Staff Survey Pre-List

School and Staff Survey Research

Service Annual Survey

Special Census

Special Census 2000

State and Federal Adult Correction Facility Census

Survey of Local Inmates

Survey of College Graduates

Survey of Construction/Housing Sales, Starts/Completions

Survey of Income and Program Participation

Survey of Inmates in Local Jails

Survey of Manufacturer Technology

Survey of Plant Capacity

Survey of Program Dynamics

Survey of Residential Alterations and Repairs

Survey Research and Development

Teacher Follow-Up Survey

Telephone Point of Purchase

The American Community Survey

Transportation Annual Survey

Women-Owned Business

Appendix B

~·❋·~

Sources of Public Opinion Data

Throughout this text we have described how to collect and evaluate public opinion data and have presented a wide range of results from surveys of the American public. While you may never have the need to conduct your own survey, this material has, hopefully, sparked your interest in "what the public thinks." If so, there are a number of available sources of public opinion data to which you can turn.

One of the largest collections of data—not just on public opinion, but for a variety of studies—is maintained by the Inter-university Consortium for Political and Social Research (ICPSR). The ICPSR is a membership-based organization of colleges and universities that provides access to the world's largest archive of computer-based research and instructional data for the social sciences. Information about the data available through the ICPSR is described in its *Guide to Resources and Services,* which can be obtained by contacting:

ICPSR
P. O. Box 1248
Ann Arbor, MI 48106
(734) 764-2570

Much of this data is also available through the ICPSR web site, located at: http://www. icpsr.umich.edu.

This web site also contains information on the two series from which much of the data in this book come, the American National Election Studies and the General Social Survey. The address for the NES is: http://www.

icpsr.umich.edu/~nes, while that for the GSS is: http://www.icpsr.umich.edu/ ~gss. Each of these series has available content indexes of the questions that are asked in different years, which makes it easier to conduct cross-time analysis.

Also available at the ICPSR site are data from the series of surveys on American foreign policy opinion conducted in 1975, 1979, 1982, 1986, 1990, and 1994 for the Chicago Council on Foreign Relations. To locate these data, go to the site http://icpsr.umich.edu/ archive1.html, then point to "Mass Political Behavior, Attitudes," then to "Public Opinion on Political Matters— United States."

Other examples of the type of data archived at the ICPSR site are the polls conducted by news organizations, such as ABC News, CBS News, the *New York Times* and the *Washington Post*. To locate data from these sources, follow the same path as for the Chicago Council on Foreign Relations data.

Another valuable archive that contains a wealth of information on public opinion is maintained by the Institute for Research in Social Science (IRSS) at the University of North Carolina. The IRSS maintains a computer-searchable catalog of the more than 2,800 studies and series in its data collection. Two unique aspects of the IRSS archive are (1) that it is the exclusive national repository for Louis Harris public opinion data—containing information on over 1,000 surveys going back to 1958—and (2) that it administers the data for the National Network of State Polls (NNSP). The NNSP data provide researchers with access to over 350 state-level studies consisting of more than 31,000 questions from 22 survey organizations in 19 states. You can contact the IRSS for more information at

Institute for Research in Social Science
Manning Hall CB #3355
University of North Carolina
Chapel Hill, NC 27514
(919) 966-3348

Access to data from the Louis Harris Polls is available on the Internet at http://www.unc.edu/depts/irss/lharris.htm. NNSP data can be found at http://www.irss.unc.edu/nnsp.

A similar extensive collection of data is archived at the Roper Center for Public Opinion Research, which can be contacted at

Roper Center for Public Opinion Research
Box 440
University of Connecticut
Storrs, Connecticut 06268
(860) 486-4440

The Roper Center's online database, POLL, is "the most complete, updated online source of public opinion data in the U.S.," and contains over a quarter-million questions covering the period from 1935 to the present. While a subscription is required to gain access to much of the data, some information, such as cross-time trends on presidential approval as measured by a number of organizations or opinions on selected current topics, is freely available. This site is located at http://www.ropercenter.uconn.edu.

If you are concerned about issues related to the press and public policy, then information available from the Pew Research Center may be of particular interest. This center describes itself as "an independent research group that studies attitudes toward press, politics and public policy issues . . . best known for regular national surveys that measure public attentiveness to major news stories, and for our polling that charts trends in values and fundamental political and social attitudes." Their web site is http://www.people-press.org. Those interested in the media will also find some useful information at the Public Agenda Online (http://www.publicagenda.org), which is described as "the journalist's inside source for public opinion and policy analysis."

While media polls from previous years are accessible through various archives, news releases and information on surveys conducted more recently are often available on the web sites of these news organizations. To locate polling data, access the organization's web site, then do a search of the site using the word "poll." Following are the web site locations for some of the major news organizations:

ABC News:	http://www.abcnews.com
CNN:	http://cnn.com
CBS News:	http://www.cbsnews.com
Los Angeles Times:	http://www.latimes.com/HOME/NEWS/POLLS
NBC News:	http://www.nbc.com
New York Times:	http://www.nytimes.com
USA Today:	http://www.usatoday.com
Washington Post:	http://www.washingtonpost.com

A number of academic survey research organizations have established web sites that provide information on polls that they conduct, many of which are statewide or local polls. Among these are:

Arizona Poll (Northern Arizona University)
http://www.nau.edu/~srl/azsurv.html

Eagleton Poll (Rutgers University)
http://www.rci.rutgers.edu/~eaglepol/

Keystone Poll (Millersville University)
http://millersv.edu/~politics/results.htm

Quinnipiac College Polling Institute
http://www.quinnipiac.edu/pollmain.html

Marist Institute for Public Opinion
http://www.mipo.marist.edu

Ohio Poll (University of Cincinnati)
http://www.ipr.uc.edu/survey/ohiopoll/opfront.htm

Commercial polling firms, such as the Gallup Organization, Louis Harris and Associates, and the Roper Organization conduct both proprietary studies, the results of which are generally not available to other users, as well as studies for which you can access the data. As noted earlier, data from many of the publicly released studies of these organizations are available through different data archives. Information from more recent Harris Polls is available through the IRSS web site, and results from current surveys of the Roper Organization are available at the Roper Center site. Access to findings and press releases from recent Gallup polls is available at http://www.gallup.com.

Data from recent public opinion surveys as well as historical trends are also available through published sources. *The Polling Report,* for example, is "an independent survey of trends affecting elections, government, and business" that provides data on a variety of issues, with a particular emphasis on campaigns and elections. *The Public Perspective* also provides public opinion data on an array of political, social, and cultural issues, together with analysis and discussion. More information on these publications is available from

The Polling Report, Inc.
P.O. Box 42580
Washington, DC 20015-2580
(202) 237-2000

The Public Perspective
University of Connecticut
Roper Center for Public Opinion Research
341 Mansfield Road—U164
Storrs, Connecticut 06269-1169
(860) 486-4440

Some information from *The Polling Report* is also available on its web site at http://www.PollingReport.com, while selected data from *The Public Perspective* can be found at the Roper Center's site.

An extensive compilation of survey items and responses is available in the annual publication *American Public Opinion Index.* This volume contains polling information from a wide range of sources. It is also available on CD-ROM, which facilitates locating data on specific topics.

The increasing use of the Internet for providing information about and access to survey data has reduced to some extent the need for extensive published collections of such information. Following are several historical sources that may be useful for identifying and analyzing trend data:

Converse, Philip E. 1980. *American Social Attitudes Data Sourcebook, 1947–1978.* Cambridge, MA: Harvard University Press.

Miller, Warren E., and Santa Traugott. 1989. *American National Election Studies Data Sourcebook, 1952–1986.* Cambridge, MA: Harvard University Press.

Southwick, Jessie C., ed. 1975. *Survey Data for Trend Analysis: An Index of Repeated Questions in U.S. National Surveys Held by the Roper Public Research Center.* Williamstown, MA: Roper Public Opinion Research Center.

For a more extensive review of sources of poll data as well as strategies for locating data, see Tom W. Smith and Frederick D. Weil, "The Polls—A Report. Finding Public Opinion Data: A Guide to Sources," *Public Opinion Quarterly* 54 (Winter, 1990): 609–626. For more information on sources of data of all types available on the Internet, visit the web site of the University of California, San Diego at http://odwin.ucsd.edu/idata.

Appendix C

⚜

Questions from the American National Election Studies and General Social Surveys

Much of the data presented in this text comes from two extensive series of surveys of the American public, the American National Election Studies (NES) and the General Social Survey (GSS). The following provides the question wording for the items from these two data series.

AMERICAN NATIONAL ELECTION STUDIES

Political Orientations

Political Ideology

We hear a lot of talk these days about liberals and conservatives. Here is a 7-point scale (extremely liberal; liberal; slightly liberal; moderate, middle-of-the-road; slightly conservative; conservative; extremely conservative) on which the political views that people hold are arranged from extremely liberal to extremely conservative. Where would you place yourself on this scale, or haven't you thought much about this?

Party Identification

Generally speaking, do you think of yourself as a Republican, a Democrat, an Independent, or what?

(If Republican): Would you call yourself a strong Republican or a not very strong Republican?

(If Democrat): Would you call yourself a strong Democrat or a not very strong Democrat?

(If Independent, Minor Party, or other): Do you think of yourself as closer to the Republican or Democratic Party?

Trust in Government

How much of the time do you think you can trust the government in Washington to do what is right—just about always, most of the time, or only some of the time?

Would you say the government is pretty much run by a few big interests looking out for themselves or that it is run for the benefit of all the people?

Do you think that people in the government waste a lot of the money we pay in taxes, waste some of it, or don't waste very much of it?

Do you feel that almost all of the people running the government are smart people who usually know what they are doing, or do you think that quite a few of them don't seem to know what they are doing?

Do you think that quite a few of the people running the government are a little crooked, not very many are, or do you think hardly any of them are crooked at all?

Political Efficacy

Do you agree or disagree with the following statements:

People like me don't have any say about what the government does.

Voting is the only way that people like me can have any say about how the government runs things.

Sometimes politics and government seem so complicated that a person like me can't really understand what's going on.

I don't think public officials care much about what people like me think.

Generally speaking, those we elect to Congress in Washington lose touch with the people pretty quickly.

Parties are only interested in people's votes, but not in their opinions.

Power of the Federal Government

Some people are afraid the government in Washington is getting too powerful for the good of the country and the individual person. Others feel the government has not gotten too strong for the good of the country. Have you been interested enough in this to favor one side over the other? [If yes]: What is your feeling, do you think the government is getting too strong or the government has not gotten too strong?

Social-Welfare Issues

Government Services

Some people think the government should provide fewer services, even in areas such as health and education in order to reduce spending. Other people feel it is important for the government to provide many more services even if it means an increase in spending. Where would you place yourself on this scale or haven't you thought much about this issue? (Seven-point scale shown to respondents, with point 1 labeled "government should provide fewer services, reduce spending a lot"; point 7 labeled "government should provide many more services, increase government spending a lot"; and points 2 through 6 not labeled.)

Education

(1956, 1958, 1960; 1962—slight variation in wording)
If cities and towns around the country need help to build more schools, the government in Washington ought to give them the money they need. Do you have an opinion on this or not? (If yes): Do you think the government should do this? (Five response categories: agree strongly; agree, but not very strongly; not sure, it depends; disagree, but not very strongly; disagree strongly.)

(1984, 1988, 1990, 1992, 1996)
Should federal spending on public schools be increased, decreased, or kept about the same?

Medical Care

(1956, 1960)
The government in Washington ought to help people get doctors and hospital care at low cost. Do you have an opinion on this or not? (If yes): Do you think the government should do this? (Five response categories: agree strongly; agree, but not very strongly; not sure, it depends; disagree, but not very strongly; disagree strongly).

(1964, 1968)
Some people say the government in Washington ought to help people get doctors and hospital care at low cost; others say the government should not get into this. Have you been interested enough in this to favor one side over the other? (If yes): What is your position? Should the government in Washington help people get doctors and hospital care at low cost or stay out of this? (Forced-choice item, with an "other, depends" middle category.)

(1970, 1972, 1976, 1978, 1984, 1988, 1992, 1994, 1996)
There is much concern about the rapid rise in medical and hospital costs. Some people feel there should be a government insurance plan which would cover all medical and hospital expenses. Others feel that medical expenses should be paid by individuals and through private insurance like Blue Cross. Where would you place yourself on this scale or haven't you thought much about this? (Seven-point scale shown to respondents, with point 1 labeled "government insurance plan;" point 7 labeled "individuals/private insurance;" and points 2 through 6 not labeled.)

Jobs and Living Standards

(1956, 1958, 1960)
The government in Washington ought to see to it that everybody who wants to work can find a job. Do you have an opinion on this or not? (If yes): Do you think the government should do this? (Five response categories: agree strongly; agree, but not very strongly; not sure, it depends; disagree, but not very strongly; disagree strongly.)

(1964, 1968)
In general, some people feel that the government in Washington should see to it that every person has a job and a good standard of living. Others think the government should just let each person get ahead on his own. Have you been interested enough in this to favor one side over the other? (If yes): Do you think that the government should see to it that every person has a job and a good standard of living or should it let each person get ahead on his own? (Forced-choice item, with an "other, depends" middle category.)

(1972, 1974, 1976, 1978, 1980, 1982, 1984, 1986, 1988, 1990, 1992, 1994, 1996)
Some people feel that the government is Washington should see to it that every person has a job and a good standard of living. Others think the government should just let each person get ahead on his (their) own. (1972–78: And, of course, other people have opinions somewhere in between.) Where would you place yourself on this scale, or haven't you thought much about this? (Seven-point scale shown to respondents, with point 1 labeled "government see to jobs;" point 7 labeled "let each person get ahead on own;" and points 2 through 6 not labeled.)

School Integration

(1956, 1958, 1960)
The government in Washington should stay out of the question of whether white and colored children go to the same school. Do you have an opinion on this or not? (If yes): Do you think the government should stay out of this question? (Five response categories: agree strongly; agree, but not very strongly; not sure, it depends; disagree, but not very strongly; disagree strongly).

(1962)

The government in Washington should see to it that white and colored children are allowed to go to the same schools. Do you have an opinion on this or not? (If yes): Do you agree that the government should do this or do you think the government should not do it? (Five response choices: (1) yes; (2) yes, qualified; (3) yes, but no force; (4) no, qualified; (5) no.)

(1964, 1966, 1968, 1970, 1972, 1976, 1978, 1986, 1990, 1992, 1994)

Some people say that the government in Washington should see to it that white and Negro (colored/black) children are allowed to go to the same schools. Others claim that this is not the government's business. Have you been concerned enough about this to favor one side over the other? (If yes): Do you think the government in Washington should see to it that white and Negro (colored/black) children go to the same schools or stay out of this area as it is none of its business? (Forced-choice item, with an "other, depends" middle category.)

Busing

(1972, 1974, 1976, 1980, 1984)

There is much discussion about the best way to deal with racial problems. Some people think that achieving integration of public schools is so important that it justifies busing children to schools out of their own neighborhood. Others think letting children go to their neighborhood schools is so important that they oppose busing. Where would you place yourself on this scale, or haven't you thought much this? (Seven-point scale shown to respondents, with point 1 labeled "bus to achieve integration"; point 7 labeled "keep in neighborhood schools"; and points 2 through 6 not labeled.)

Neighborhood Integration

(1964, 1968, 1970, 1972, 1976)

Which of these statements would you agree with: White people have a right to keep black people out of their neighborhood if they want to; or, black people have a right to live wherever they can afford to, just like anybody else? (Forced-choice item.)

Minority Employment

(1956, 1958, 1960)

If Negroes are not getting fair treatment in jobs and housing, the government should see to it that they do. Do you have an opinion on this or not? (If yes): Do you think the government should do this? (Five response categories: agree strongly; agree, but not very strongly; not sure, it depends; disagree, but not very strongly; disagree strongly.)

(1964, 1968, 1972)

Some people think that if Negroes (colored people/black people) are not getting fair treatment in jobs the government in Washington ought to see to it that they do. Others feel that this is not the federal government's business. Have you had enough interest in this question to favor one side over the other? (If yes): How do you feel? Should the government in Washington see to it that Negroes (colored people/black people) get fair treatment in jobs or leave these matters to the states and local communities? (Forced-choice item, with an "other, depends" middle category.)

(1986, 1988, 1992, 1996)
Some people think that if black people are not getting fair treatment in jobs, the government in Washington ought to see to it that they do. Others feel that this is not the federal government's business. Have you had enough interest in this question to favor one side over the other? (If yes): How do you feel? Should the government in Washington see to it that black people get fair treatment in jobs or is this not the government's business? (Forced-choice item, with an "other, depends" middle category.)

Affirmative Action

(1978)
Some people say that women and minority group members should be given preferential treatment in getting jobs or being admitted to colleges or professional schools. Other people say that the individual's ability or experience should be the only consideration in hiring people or admitting them to school. Where would you place yourself on this scale or haven't you thought much about this question? (Seven-point scale shown to respondents, with point 1 labeled "give preferential treatment to a woman or minority member;" point 7 labeled "the individual's ability or experience should be the only consideration;" and points 2 through 6 not labeled.)

(1986, 1988 (alternate wording), 1990, 1992, 1994, 1996)
Some people say that because of past discrimination blacks should be given preference in hiring and promotion. Others say that such preference in hiring and promotion of blacks is wrong because it gives blacks advantages they haven't earned. What about your opinion—are you for or against preferential hiring and promotion of blacks? (Respondents answer "for" or "against" and are then asked whether they "favor preference in hiring and promotion strongly or not strongly" or "oppose preference in hiring and promotion strongly or not strongly.")

Aid Minority Groups

(1970, 1972, 1974, 1976, 1978, 1980, 1982, 1984, 1986, 1988, 1990, 1992, 1994, 1996)
Some people feel that the government in Washington should make every possible effort to improve the social and economic position of Negroes (blacks) and other minority groups. Others feel that the government should not make any special effort to help minority peoples but they

should be expected to help themselves. Where would you place yourself on this scale, or haven't you thought much about this? (Seven-point scale shown to respondents, with point 1 labeled "government help minority groups"; point 7 labeled "minority groups help themselves"; and points 2 through 6 not labeled.)

Speed of the Civil Rights Movement

(1964, 1966 (variation in response categories), 1968, 1970, 1972, 1976, 1980, 1984, 1986, 1988, 1990, 1992)
Do you think that civil rights leaders are trying to push too fast, are going too slowly, or are moving at about the right speed? (Forced-choice item.)

Impact of Slavery

(1972, 1986, 1988, 1990, 1992, 1994)
Please tell me whether you agree or disagree with each reason as to why white people seem to get more of the good things in life. Generations of slavery and discrimination have created conditions that make it difficult for blacks to work their way up. Do you strongly agree, agree somewhat, neither agree nor disagree, disagree somewhat, or disagree strongly?

GENERAL SOCIAL SURVEY

Confidence in Institutions

I'm going to name institutions in this country. As far as the people running these institutions are concerned, would you say you have a great deal of confidence, only some confidence, or hardly any confidence at all in them?

Military
Major companies
Organized religion
Education
Executive branch of government
Banks and financial institutions
Supreme Court
Organized labor
Congress
Medicine
Press
Scientific community
Television

Government Spending

We are faced with many problems in this country, none of which can be solved easily or inexpensively. I'm going to name some of these problems, and for each one I'd like you to tell me whether you think we're spending too much money on it, too little money, or about the right amount. Are we spending too much money, too little money, or about the right amount on . . .

Social security

Improving the nation's education system

Improving and protecting the nation's health

Improving and protecting the environment

The environment

Improving the conditions of blacks

Assistance to blacks

Medical Care

In general, some people think that it is the responsibility of the government in Washington to see to it that people have help in paying for doctors and hospital bills. Others think that these matters are not the responsibility of the federal government and that people should take care of these things themselves. Where do you put yourself on this scale or haven't you made up your mind on this? (Five-point response scale with point 1 labeled "government responsibility"; point 3 labeled "agree with both"; point 5 labeled "people care for themselves"; and points 2 and 4 not labeled.)

Jobs and Living Standards

(1975, 1983, 1984, 1986, 1987, 1988, 1989, 1990, 1991, 1993, 1994, 1996)
Some people think that the government in Washington should do everything possible to improve the standard of living of all poor Americans; they are at Point 1 on this card. Other people think it is not the government's responsibility, and that each person should take care of himself; they are at Point 5. Where would you place yourself on this scale, or haven't you made up your mind on this? (Five-point response scale with point 1 labeled "government responsibility"; point 3 labeled "agree with both"; point 5 labeled "people help themselves"; and points 2 and 4 not labeled.)

(1985, 1989, 1990, 1991)
On the whole, do you think it should or should not be the government's responsibility to provide a job for everyone who wants one? (Four-point response scale: (1) definitely should be; (2) probably should be; (3) probably should not be; (4) definitely should not be.)

Environment

(1993, 1994)
If you had to choose, which one of the following comes closest to your views? Government should let businesses decide for themselves how to protect the environment, even if it means they don't always do the right thing, or government should pass laws to make businesses protect the environment, even if it interferes with business' right to make their own decisions. (Forced-choice item.)

(1993, 1994)
If you had to choose, which one of the following comes closest to your views? Government should let ordinary people decide for themselves how to protect the environment, even if it means they don't always do the right thing, or government should pass laws to make ordinary people protect the environment, even if it interferes with people's right to make their own decisions. (Forced-choice item.)

(1993, 1994)
How much do you agree or disagree with the following statement. In order to protect the environment, America needs economic growth. (Five-point scale: (1) strongly agree; (2) agree; (3) neither agree nor disagree; (4) disagree; (5) strongly disagree.)

(1993, 1994)
How much do you agree or disagree with the following statement. Economic growth always harms the environment. (Five-point scale: (1) strongly agree; (2) agree; (3) neither agree nor disagree; (4) disagree; (5) strongly disagree.)

(1993, 1994)
How much do you agree or disagree with the following statement. People worry too much about human progress harming the environment. (Five-point scale: (1) strongly agree; (2) agree; (3) neither agree nor disagree; (4) disagree; (5) strongly disagree.)

(1993, 1994)
How much do you agree or disagree with the following statement. We worry too much about the future of the environment, and not enough about prices and jobs today. (Five-point scale: (1) strongly agree; (2) agree; (3) neither agree nor disagree; (4) disagree; (5) strongly disagree.)

(1993, 1994)
How willing would you be to pay much higher prices in order to protect the environment? (Five response choices: (1) very willing; (2) fairly willing; (3) neither willing nor unwilling; (4) not very willing; or (5) not at all willing.)

(1993, 1994)
How willing would you be to pay much higher taxes in order to protect the environment? (Five response choices: (1) very willing; (2) fairly willing; (3) neither willing nor unwilling; (4) not very willing; or (5) not at all willing.)

(1993, 1994)
How willing would you be to accept cuts in your standard of living in order to protect the environment? (Five response choices: (1) very willing; (2) fairly willing; (3) neither willing nor unwilling; (4) not very willing; or (5) not at all willing.)

School Integration

(1972, 1976, 1977, 1980, 1982, 1984, 1985)
Do you think white students and (Negro/Black) students should go to the same schools or to separate schools? (Forced-choice item.)

Busing

(1972, 1974, 1975, 1976, 1977, 1978, 1982, 1983, 1985, 1986, 1988, 1989, 1990, 1991, 1993, 1994, 1996)
In general, do you favor or oppose the busing of (Negro/Black/African-American) and white schoolchildren from one school district to another? (Forced-choice item.)

Neighborhood Integration

White people have a right to keep (Negroes/Blacks/African-Americans) out of their neighborhoods if they want to, and (Negroes/Blacks/African-Americans) should respect that right. (Four response choices: (1) agree strongly; (2) agree slightly; (3) disagree slightly; (4) disagree strongly.)

Affirmative Action

Some people say that because of past discrimination, blacks should be given preference in hiring and promotion. Others say that such preference in hiring and promotion of blacks is wrong because it discriminates against whites. What is your opinion—are you for or against preferential hiring and promotion of blacks? (Four response categories: (1) strongly support preferences; (2) support preferences; (3) oppose preferences; (4) strongly oppose preferences.)

Voting for a Black Candidate for President

(1972, 1974, 1975, 1977, 1978, 1982, 1983, 1985, 1986, 1988, 1989, 1990, 1991, 1992, 1994, 1996)
If your party nominated a (Negro/Black/African-American) for president, would you vote for him if he were qualified for the job?

Glossary

acquiescence response set: The tendency of some respondents to agree with a statement regardless of its content.

affirmative action: A policy that gives special consideration or compensatory treatment to traditionally disadvantaged groups in an effort to overcome the effect of past discrimination.

agenda-setting: The media's role in identifying the most important issues and concerns facing the electorate.

agree-disagree format: A way of presenting questions in which respondents are read a statement and asked whether they agree or disagree with its content.

archive: A collection of documents, reports, statistics, data, and other material that are accessible to researchers and other interested individuals.

attitude: A relatively enduring orientation toward objects that provides individuals with a mental framework for making economical sense of the world.

audio-CASI: See *computer-assisted self interview.*

belief: The inclination to accept something as true.

benchmark poll: A poll taken before a political campaign that begins to identify the candidate's image and issue positions with the electorate.

biased sample: A sample that systematically produces results that are different from those in the population of interest.

bivariate analysis: Examining the relationship between two variables, generally by constructing some type of table or correlation.

busing: The transportation of public school students from areas where they live to schools in other areas to eliminate school segregation based on residential patterns.

census block: The smallest entity for which the Census Bureau collects and tabulates decennial census information; bounded on all sides by visible and non-visible features.

census tract: A small, relatively permanent statistical subdivision of a county in a metropolitan area or a selected nonmetropolitan county used for presenting decennial census data. Census tract boundaries normally follow visible features, but may follow governmental unit boundaries and other nonvisible features in some instances; they always rest within counties. Census tracts usually contain between 2,500 and 8,000 inhabitants.

closed-ended question: A question in which respondents select their answer from a list of choices provided for them.

cluster sample: A sample in which the population is divided into groups (clusters), often on the basis of geography. Cluster samples generally involve several stages of sampling after the initial groups have been selected.

computer-assisted personal interviewing (CAPI): The use of portable laptop computers to assist interviewers in data collection for field surveys involving face-to-face interviews.

computer-assisted self interview (CASI): Use of a laptop computer by respondents to complete a self-administered questionnaire. In **audio-CASI**, an audio component is added, in which respondents can listen to the questions through a headset at the same time they appear on the screen.

computer-assisted telephone interviewing (CATI): The use of interactive computing systems to assist interviewers and their supervisors in performing the basic data collection tasks of telephone surveys.

confidence level: The estimated probability that a characteristic of a population lies within a given range of values based on the value of the characteristic in a sample.

consensus: General agreement among the population on an issue.

constraint: Consistency among idea elements.

context effect: A condition in which responses to a survey question are influenced by the items preceding it in a questionnaire.

convenience sample: The collection of data from individuals who are easy to locate and gather information from; a convenience sample is a nonprobability sample and the information cannot be use to generalize about the characteristics of some larger population.

cross-time analysis: Comparing results on the same survey question asked at different points in time.

cugging: Campaigning under the guise of research.

element: The units of which the population is composed, such as adult residents of a state, members of a labor union, or clients of a program.

errors in forecasting: Errors in predicting some event, frequently an election outcome. When based on survey information, such errors can result from factors such as a biased sample, poor questionnaire design, non-response, poor data collection, or flawed analysis of the data.

establishment bias: A theory which sees the media as exhibiting bias toward the government and other established institutions of society.

exit poll: A poll taken outside the election polling place which asks a random sample of voters to answer questions about the election immediately after they have voted.

external efficacy: The belief that the authorities or the regime is responsive to influence attempts.

feeling thermometer: A type of question based on the concept of a thermometer, generally ranging from zero degrees to 100 degrees, that is often used to measure reactions to political figures, countries, or groups.

filter question: A question that is frequently included as part of opinion items in order to limit responses to some subset of the sample, such as those who have an interest in an issue.

forced–choice format: Presenting respondents with two sides of an issue and asking them which comes closer to their point of view.

framing: Defining how a story should be understood by the citizens through the way the media attributes responsibility for the problem or issue.

frugging: Fundraising under the guise of research.

gender gap: Differences in the political views of men and women.

generational effects: Political beliefs or attitudes that are attributable to events which impact a particular generation.

horse–race journalism: A view of the coverage of campaigns and elections by the various news media which sees that coverage as overly concerned with the polls and considerations of which candidate is leading.

hostilization: The process by which some children learn and internalize attitudes of hostility toward politics and political authority.

idealization: Children's view of political figures or institutions as benevolent and trustworthy.

institutionalization: Children's development of the concept of political institutions as apart from the individuals who hold public positions.

intensity of opinion: The strength of an individual's views on an issue.

internal efficacy: An individual's belief that the means to influence the government are available to him or her.

issue publics: A group of people who are knowledgeable and have meaningful beliefs about an issue and who are more likely to write letters to the editor, contact public officials, or change their vote on the basis of this issue.

liberal–conservative continuum: The primary dimension underlying political thinking in the United States.

life cycle effects: Changes in political opinions and attitudes that are attributable to aging or other changes in the life cycle.

Likert–type item: A type of question that uses responses such as strongly agree, agree, disagree, and strongly disagree—often with a neutral or middle alternative—to measure an individual's attitude.

middle alternative: A logical position between two extremes that some respondents might prefer to either of the contrasting alternatives in a survey question.

modified area sample: A form of sampling in which geographical areas such as census tracts or blocks serve as sampling units.

multiple publics: The variety of groups or sets of individuals that a policymaker considers in deciding how to act on some issue. The general population, interest groups, members of a particular union, or clients of a program are examples of potential "publics."

multivariate analysis: Examining relationships among three or more variables.

nonattitudes: Meaningless opinions that vary randomly in direction in repeated trials over time.

nonprobability sample: A sample that is based on human judgment or self-selection. The characteristics of a nonprobability sample do not represent those of some larger population.

non–response bias: The difference between the characteristics of the population and the estimates of these characteristics in a sample resulting from the fact that individuals from whom data are not collected (because they are not in the sampling frame, cannot be located, refuse to participate, etc.) may differ in a significant ways from those who do participate.

open–ended question: A question to which respondents supply their own answer in their own words and are not limited to a set of choices provided for them by the researcher.

opinion: The verbal expression of an attitude.

panel: A study in which data are collected from individuals at several points in time.

paper-and-pencil interviewing (PAPI): Survey data collection in which interviewers ask respondents questions and record their answers on a paper questionnaire.

party identification: A "standing decision" to support one party or the other. It is generally a psychological identification, which can persist without legal recognition or evidence of formal membership and even without a consistent record of party support.

personalization: The view of a young child which sees individuals such as a policeman or the mayor as being the government.

pilot investigation: A small-scale trial of a study for the purpose of checking all aspects of the study design.

political authority: The concept of the government, its institutions and officials as having power over the individuals and the society.

political cynicism: The belief that the government is not producing results in accord with individual expectations.

political efficacy: The belief that individual political action does have, or can have, an impact on the political process.

political ideology: A closely linked set of beliefs about the goal of politics and the most desirable political order.

political socialization: The process by which children and adults learn political attitudes, beliefs, and behaviors that are accepted by their culture.

politicization: The process by which children become aware of political authorities beyond their families and immediate experience.

population coverage: The extent to which the group that a researcher is interested in can be reached by the mode of data collection.

population of interest: An identifiable group of individuals whose opinion on some issue or set of issues is important to a policymaker.

prepared data entry (PDE): Data collection in which the survey organization provides respondents with a questionnaire that they can complete using their computer.

presidential approval: A measure included in many polls which asks whether the respondent approves or disapproves of the job being done by the president.

primacy effect: A condition in which the alternative that is given to the respondent first is selected more often, simply because it is presented first.

priming: How the media's choice of issues and stories prepare citizens to form opinions about political issues.

probability sample: A sample in which each individual or combination of individuals in the population has some known chance of being selected.

pseudo–polls: Contacts with individuals that have some elements of a legitimate survey but are not true attempts to collect information from a representative sample of some population.

public judgment: A state of highly developed public opinion that exists once people have engaged an issue, considered it from all sides, understood the choices it leads to, and accepted the consequences of the choices they make (Yankelovich, 1991).

public opinion: The combined personal opinions of adults toward issues of relevance to government.

purposive study: A study in which elements are selected based on the researcher's judgment as to their usefulness. Purposive studies use nonprobability samples and the results are not representative of some larger population.

push poll: A poll which includes negative information about an opposing candidate in its questions. The intent of these polls is to manipulate the opinions of the respondent rather than measure their attitudes.

quota sampling: A type of non-probability sample in which units are selected into the sample on the basis of pre-specified characteristics.

rally-round-the-flag effect: The tendency for public support for the president to increase when American troops are sent into conflict or harm's way.

random-digit dialing (RDD): Telephone interviewing coupled with the use of a sample of telephone numbers generated completely at random.

ranking scale: A type of question in which respondents are presented with a list of items and asked to order them along some dimension, such as importance, desirability, or preference.

rating scale: A type of question in which respondents are asked to make judgments along a continuum varying between two extremes, such as from excellent to poor or from extremely satisfied to extremely dissatisfied.

recency effect: A condition in which the alternative that is given to the respondent last is selected more often, simply because it is presented last.

reliability: The extent to which measurements are repeatable by different researchers or by the same researcher at different points in time.

representative sample: A subset of a population selected in a way that its characteristics represent those of the larger population from which it is drawn.

response format: The way in which choices in survey questions are presented to respondents. Examples of response formats include agree-disagree format, forced-choice format, Likert-type scales, rating scales, ranking scales, and feeling thermometers.

response rate: The extent to which those selected for a sample actual participate. The response rate is calculated by dividing the number of complete interviews with reporting units by the number of eligible reporting units in the sample.

sample: A subset of the population which, when selected using probability methods, is designed to represent the characteristics of the population.

sample size: The number of elements for which data are collected.

sampling error: The potential difference between the results from a sample and the actual value in the population, resulting from the fact that data are not obtained from all members of the population.

sampling frame: The list of units composing a population from which a sample is selected.

secondary analysis: Analysis of data by researchers other than those who originally collected the data.

seven-point forced choice scale: A form of a forced-choice format in which the alternatives are placed at points "1" and "7" of the scale and the remaining points are left for respondents who have opinions that fall between the two extremes.

simple random sample (SRS): In a simple random sample each element in a population has a known and equal probability of being selected in the sample. In the typical

simple random sample each element in the population is listed and assigned a number, and a sample drawn using a computer program or a random number table to generate the selected elements.

stratified sample: A sample in which the elements of the population are divided into groups (strata) and independent samples (either random or systematic) are selected within each stratum.

straw poll: A form of gathering public opinion information, particularly about voting intentions, that has been used in the United States since the early 1800s.

sugging: Selling under the guise of research.

systematic random sample: A sample typically drawn from a list of elements that involves randomly selecting a single number, then taking every kth number in the list until the desired number of elements have been selected.

tone of wording: The language used in framing survey questions.

touchtone data entry (TDE): Data collection in which the respondent calls a computer and responds to questions using the telephone keypad.

tracking poll: Daily polls using a very small sample, usually less than 200 respondents, which are aggregated to give an indication of changing voter opinions.

trial heats: Polls that attempt to determine which candidate is leading in an election campaign.

trust in government: Evaluation of the government in which citizens are either satisfied with the procedures and products of government (trust) or believe that it is not producing policies according to expectations (cynicism).

univariate analysis: The analysis of a single variable for purpose of description.

valence issue: Those issues on which there is uniform agreement or disagreement.

validity: The extent to which measurement taps what it intends to measure.

voice recognition entry (VRE): Data collection in which the respondent calls a computer and responds to questions by speaking the appropriate digits.

References

Abramowitz, Alan I., and Kyle L. Saunders. 1998. "Ideological Realignment in the U.S. Electorate." *Journal of Politics* 60 (August): 634–652.

Achen, Christopher H. 1975. "Mass Political Attitudes and the Survey Response." *American Political Science Review* 69 (December): 1218–1231.

Adams, Kenneth. 1996. "Guns and Gun Control." *Americans View Crime and Justice: A National Public Opinion Survey.* Ed. Timothy J. Flanagan and Dennis R. Longmire. Thousand Oaks, CA: Sage.

Adams, William C., and Paul H. Ferber. 1980. "Measuring Legislator-Constituency Congruence: Liquor, Legislators and Linkage." *Journal of Politics* 42 (February): 202–208.

Adarand Constructors, Inc. v. Pena, 115 S.Ct. 2097 (1995).

Allport, Gordon W. 1935. "Attitudes." *Handbook of Social Psychology.* Ed. Carl Murchison. Worcester, MA: Clark University Press.

Almond, Gabriel. 1950. *American People and Foreign Policy.* New York: Harcourt Brace.

American Association of Public Opinion Research. "Statement Condemning Push Polls." http://www.aapor.org/ethics/pushpoll.html.

Anderson, Barbara A., Brian D. Silver, and Paul R. Abramson. 1988. "The Effects of the Race of the Interviewer on Race-related Attitudes of Black Respondents in SRC/CPS National Election Studies." *Public Opinion Quarterly* 52 (Fall): 289–324.

Anderson, Lee, Lynn B. Jenkins, James Leming, Walter B. MacDonald, Ina V. S. Mullis, Mary Jane Turner, and Judith S. Wooster. 1990. *The Civics Report Card.* Princeton, NJ: Educational Testing Service.

Arterton, F. Christopher. 1974. "The Impact of Watergate on Children's Attitudes toward Political Authority." *Political Science Quarterly* 89 (June): 269–288.

Austin, Erica Weintraub, and C. Leigh Nelson. 1993. "Influences of Ethnicity, Family Communication, and Media on Adolescents' Socialization to U.S. Politics." *Journal of Broadcasting and Electronic Media* (Fall): 419–435.

Babbie, Earl. 1990. *Survey Research Methods*. 2nd ed. Belmont, CA: Wadsworth.

Bardes, Barbara A. 1995. "From the Cold War to the Clinton Years: the American Public Views a Changing World," presented at the annual meeting of American Political Science Association, Chicago.

———. 1997. "Public Opinion and Foreign Policy: How Does the Public Think About America's Role in the World." *Understanding Public Opinion*. Ed. Barbara Norrander and Clyde Wilcox. Washington, D.C.: Congressional Quarterly Press.

Bardes, Barbara A., and Robert W. Oldendick. 1978. "Beyond Internationalism: The Case for Multiple Dimensions in the Structure of Foreign Policy Attitudes." *Social Science Quarterly* 59 (December): 496–508.

Barone, Michael. 1997. "Polls Are Part of the Air Politicians Breathe." *Public Perspective* 9 (April/May): 1–2.

Beck, Paul Allen. 1977. "The Role of Agents in Political Socialization." *Handbook of Political Socialization*. Ed. Stanley A. Renshon. New York: Free Press.

Bennet, James. 1996. "The Delegates: Where Image Meets Reality." *New York Times*, 12 August: A1.

Bennett, W. Lance. 1996. *News: The Politics of Illusion*. 3rd ed. New York: Longman.

Bennett, Linda L. M., and Stephen Earl Bennett. 1990. *Living with Leviathan: Americans Coming to Terms with Big Government*. Lawrence, KN: University of Kansas Press.

Bennett, Stephen Earl. 1995. "Americans' Knowledge of Ideology, 1980–1992." *American Politics Quarterly* 23 (July): 259–278.

Bennett, Stephen E., and Robert W. Oldendick. 1977. "The Power of the Federal Government," presented at the annual meeting of the Midwest Political Science Association, Chicago.

Bennett, Stephen E., and David Resnick. 1990. "The Implications of Nonvoting for Democracy in the United States." *American Journal of Political Science* 34 (August): 771–802.

Bishop, George F., Robert W. Oldendick, and Alfred J. Tuchfarber. 1983. "Effects of Filter Questions in Public Opinion Surveys." *Public Opinion Quarterly* 47 (Winter): 528–546.

———. 1984. "What Must My Interest in Politics Be If I Just Told You 'I Don't Know'?" *Public Opinion Quarterly* 48 (Winter): 510–519.

Bishop, George F., Robert W. Oldendick, Alfred J. Tuchfarber, and Stephen E. Bennett. 1978. "The Changing Structure of Mass Belief Systems: Fact or Artifact?" *Journal of Politics* 40 (August): 781–787.

———. 1980. "'Pseudo-Opinions' on Public Affairs." *Public Opinion Quarterly* 44 (Summer): 198–209.

Bishop, George F., Alfred J. Tuchfarber, and Robert W. Oldendick. 1978. "Change in the Structure of American Political Attitudes: The Nagging Question of Question Wording." *American Journal of Political Science* 22 (May): 250–269.

Blendon, Robert J., Drew E. Altman, John M. Benson, Humphrey Taylor, Matt James, and Mark Smith. 1992. "The Implications of the 1992 Presidential Election for Health Care Reform." *Journal of the American Medical Association* 268 (December): 3371–3375.

Blendon, Robert J., John M. Benson, Mollyann Brodie, Drew E. Altman, and Mario Brossard. 1998. "The Public and the President's Commission on Race." *The Public Perspective* 9 (February/March): 66–69.

Blendon, Robert J., and Karen Donelan. 1991. "The Public and the Future of U.S. Health Care System Reform." *System in Crisis: The Case for Health Care Reform*. Ed. Robert J. Blendon and Jennifer N. Edwards. New York: Faulkner and Gray.

Blendon, Robert J., and Jennifer N. Edwards, eds. 1991. *System in Crisis: The Case for Health Care Reform*. New York: Faulkner and Gray.

Blendon, Robert J., Ulrike S. Szalay, Drew E. Altman, and Gerald Chervinsky. 1992. "New Hampshire, Health Care, and the 1992 Election." *Journal of American Health Policy* 2 (May/June): 16–22.

Blumer, Herbert. 1948. "Public Opinion and Public Opinion Polling." *American Sociological Review*, 13 (October): 542–554.

Bradburn, Norman M., and Seymour Sudman. 1988. *Polls and Surveys: Understanding What They Tell Us*. San Francisco: Jossey-Bass.

Brehm, John. 1993. *The Phantom Respondents: Opinion Surveys and Political Representation*. Ann Arbor: University of Michigan Press.

———. 1994. "Stubbing Our Toes for a Foot in the Door? Prior Contact, Incentives, and Survey Response." *International Journal of Public Opinion Research* 6 (Spring): 45–63.

Brown v. Board of Education of Topeka, 347 U.S. 483 (1954).

Caddell, Patrick H. 1979. "Crisis of Confidence—I: Trapped in a Downward Spiral." *Public Opinion* 2 (October/November): 2–8.

Campbell, Angus, Philip E. Converse, Warren E. Miller, and Donald E. Stokes. 1960. *The American Voter*. New York: John Wiley and Sons.

Campbell, Angus, Gerald Gurin, and Warren E. Miller. 1954. *The Voter Decides*. New York: Harper and Row.

Cantrell, Paul. 1992. "Opinion Polling and American Democratic Culture," *International Journal of Politics, Culture, and Society* 5: 405–432.

Cantril, Albert, ed. 1980. *Polling on the Issues*. Cabin John, MD: Seven Locks Press.

Cantril, Hadley. 1967. *The Human Dimension: Experiences in Policy Research*. New Brunswick, NJ: Rutgers University Press.

Carmines, Edward G., and James A. Stimson. 1980. "The Two Faces of Issue Voting." *American Political Science Review* 74 (March): 78–91.

———. 1989. *Issue Evolution: Race and the Transformation of American Politics*. Princeton: Princeton University Press.

Citrin, Jack. 1996. "Affirmative Action in the People's Court." *The Public Interest* 122 (Winter): 39–48.

Clark, Nina. 1997. *The Politics of Physician Assisted Suicide*. New York: Garland Publishing.

Cohen, Steven M., and Charles S. Liebman. 1997. "American Jewish Liberalism: Unraveling the Strands." *Public Opinion Quarterly* 61 (Fall): 405–430.

Conover, Pamela Johnston. 1984. "The Influence of Group Identifications on Political Perceptions and Evaluation." *Journal of Politics* 46 (August): 760–784.

Converse, Jean M. 1987. *Survey Research in the United States: Roots and Emergence 1890–1960*. Berkeley, CA: University of California Press.

Converse, Jean M., and Stanley Presser. 1986. *Survey Questions: Handcrafting the Standardized Questionnaire*. Newbury Park, CA: Sage.

Converse, Philip E. 1964. "The Nature of Belief Systems in Mass Publics." *Ideology and Discontent*. Ed. David E. Apter. New York: Free Press.

———. 1970. "Attitudes and Non-Attitudes: Continuation of a Dialogue." *The Quantitative Analysis of Social Problems*. Ed. Edward R. Tufte. Reading, MA: Addison-Wesley Publishing.

————. 1972. "Change in the American Electorate." *The Human Meaning of Social Change.* Ed. Angus Campbell and Philip E. Converse. New York: Russell Sage Foundation.

————. 1976. *The Dynamics of Party Support: Cohort-Analyzing Party Identification.* Beverly Hills, CA: Sage Publications.

————. 1980. *American Social Attitudes Data Sourcebook, 1947–1978.* Cambridge, MA: Harvard University Press.

————. 1987. "Changing Conceptions of Public Opinion in the Political Process." *Public Opinion Quarterly* 51 (Winter): S12–S24.

Converse, Philip E., and Gregory B. Markus. 1979. "Plus ca change . . . The New CPS Election Study Panel." *American Political Science Review* 85 (March): 32–49.

Converse, Philip E., Warren E. Miller, Jerrold G. Rusk, and Arthur C. Wolfe. 1969. "Continuity and Change in American Politics: Parties and Issues in the 1968 Election." *American Political Science Review* 63 (December): 1083–1105.

Cook, Charles E., Jr. 1998. "Election '98: The Calm Before the Storm." *Public Perspective* (April/May): 2–5.

Cook, Elizabeth Adell, Ted G. Jelen, and Clyde Wilcox. 1992. *Between Two Absolutes: Public Opinion and the Politics of Abortion.* Boulder, CO: Westview Press.

Cooper, Sanford L. 1964. "Random Sampling by Telephone—An Improved Method." *Journal of Marketing Research* 1 (November): 45–48.

Council for Marketing and Opinion Research. 1995. *CMOR Refusal Rates and Industry Image Survey.* New York: Council for Marketing and Opinion Research.

Craig, Barbara Hinkson, and David M. O'Brien. 1993. *Abortion and American Politics.* Chatham, NJ: Chatham House Publishers.

Crigler, Ann N., ed. 1996. *The Psychology of Political Communication.* Ann Arbor, MI: University of Michigan Press.

"Crime in America," 1997. *Public Perspective* 8 (June/July): 9–33.

Crossen, Cynthia. 1991. "Studies Galore Support Products and Positions, But Are They Reliable?" *Wall Street Journal.* 14 November: A-1.

Cummings, Milton C., Jr., and David Wise. 1974. *Democracy Under Pressure.* 2nd ed. New York: Harcourt, Brace, Jovanovich.

Dahl, Robert A. 1950. *Congress and Foreign Policy.* New York: Harcourt, Brace.

Davis, Darren W. 1997. "Nonrandom Measurement Error and Race of Interviewer Effects Among African Americans." *Public Opinion Quarterly* 61 (Spring): 183–207.

Davis, Richard. 1996. *The Press and American Politics: The New Mediator.* 2nd ed. New York: Prentice-Hall.

Dawson, Richard E., Kenneth Prewitt, and Karen S. Dawson. 1977. *Political Socialization.* 2nd ed. Boston: Little, Brown and Co.

Della Carpini, Michael X., and Scott Keeter. 1992. "The Public's Knowledge of Politics." *Public Opinion, the Press, and Public Policy.* Ed. J. David Kannamer. Westport, CT: Praeger.

————. 1996. *What Americans Know About Politics and Why It Matters.* New Haven, CT: Yale University Press.

DeMaio, Theresa J., Catherine Marsh, and Charles F. Turner. 1984. "The Development and Contemporary Use of Subjective Surveys." *Surveying Subjective Phenomena.* Ed. Charles F. Turner and Elizabeth Martin. New York: Russell Sage Foundation.

Dennis, Jack. 1969. *Political Learning in Childhood and Adolescence.* Madison, WI: University of Wisconsin.

Dennis, Jack, and Carol Webster. 1975. "Children's Images of the President and of Government in 1962 and 1974." *American Politics Quarterly* 3 (October): 386–405.

Dillman, Don A. 1978. *Mail and Telephone Surveys: The Total Design Method.* New York: John Wiley and Sons.

Dran, Ellen M., and Anne Hildreth. 1995. "What the Public Thinks about How We Know What It Is Thinking." *International Journal of Public Opinion Research* 7 (Summer): 129–144.

———. 1997. "Studying Public Opinion about Public Opinion: To Poll or Not to Poll," presented at the annual meeting of the American Association for Public Opinion Research, Norfolk, VA.

Dred Scott v. Sanford, 19 Howard 393 (1857).

Easton, David, and Jack Dennis. 1969. *Children in the Political System: Origins of Political Legitimacy.* New York: McGraw-Hill.

Electronic Industries Association. 1991. *Consumer Electronics U.S. Sales.* Washington D.C.: Electronic Industries Association.

Erbring, Lutz, Edie N. Goldenberg, and Arthur H. Miller. 1980. "Front Page News and Real-World Cues: A New Look at Agenda-Setting by the Media." *American Journal of Political Science* 24 (February): 16–49.

Erikson, Robert S. 1979. "The SRC Panel Data and Mass Attitudes." *British Journal of Political Science* 9 (January): 89–114.

Erikson, Robert S., Norman R. Luttbeg, and Kent L. Tedin. 1980. *American Public Opinion: Its Origins, Content, and Impact.* 2nd ed. New York: John Wiley and Sons.

Erikson, Robert S., and Kent L. Tedin. 1995. *American Public Opinion: Its Origins, Content, and Impact.* 5th ed. Boston: Allyn and Bacon.

Evans, Marilyn. 1996. "The Next Generation and American Democracy: Encouraging Political Participation in the Next Generation: Kids Voting USA." *The Public Perspective* 7 (June/July): 47.

Exoo, Calvin F. 1994. *The Politics of the Mass Media.* Minneapolis: West Publishing Company.

The Federalist. No. 10, No. 63. New York: Mentor Books, 1961.

Field, John O., and Ronald Anderson. 1969. "Ideology in the Public's Conceptualization of the 1964 Election." *Public Opinion Quarterly* 33 (Fall): 380–398.

Finkel, Steven E., Thomas M. Guterbock, and Marian J. Borg. 1991. "Race-of-Interviewer Effects in a Presidential Poll: Virginia 1989." *Public Opinion Quarterly* 55 (Fall): 313–330.

Flanagan, Timothy J. 1996. "Public Opinion on Crime and Justice: History, Development, and Trends." *Americans View Crime and Justice: A National Public Opinion Survey.* Ed. Timothy J. Flanagan and Dennis R. Longmire. Thousand Oaks, CA: Sage.

Flanagan, Timothy J., and Dennis R. Longmire, eds. 1996. *Americans View Crime and Justice: A National Public Opinion Survey.* Thousand Oaks, CA: Sage.

Frankovic, Kathleen. 1982. "Sex and Politics—New Alignments, Old Issues." *PS* 15 (Summer): 439–448.

———. 1992. Interview. "The CBS News Call-In: Slipups in the Broadcast." *The Public Perspective* 3 (March/April): 19–21.

Free, Lloyd A., and Hadley Cantril. 1968. *The Political Beliefs of Americans: A Study of Public Opinion.* New York: Simon and Schuster.

Frey, James H. 1989. *Survey Research by Telephone.* 2nd ed. Newbury Park, CA: Sage.

Funk, Tim, and Jim Wrinn. 1992. "President Tells Large N.C. Crowds He Can Still Win," *The Charlotte Observer.* 22 October: 1A.

Furman v. Georgia, 408 U.S. 238 (1972).

Gallup, Alec, and David W. Moore. 1996. "Younger People Today Are More Positive About Polls Than Their Elders." *The Public Perspective* 7 (August/September): 50–53.

Gallup, George. 1947. "The Quintamensional Plan of Question Design." *Public Opinion Quarterly* 11 (Fall): 385–393.

Gallup, George, and Saul Forbes Rae. 1940. *The Pulse of Democracy*. New York: Simon and Schuster.

Gawiser, Sheldon. 1995. "Push Polls: Next Wave of Dangerous Pseudo Polls." *AAPOR News* 23 (Fall): 1.

Geer, John. 1996. *From Tea Leaves to Opinion Polls: A Theory of Democratic Leadership.* New York: Columbia University Press.

Gibbons v. Ogden, 9 Wheaton 1 (1824).

Gilroy, John M., and Robert Y. Shapiro. 1986. "The Polls: Environmental Protection." *Public Opinion Quarterly* 50 (Summer): 270–279.

Golay, Michael. 1997. *Where American Stands 1997.* New York: Wiley.

Goldwater, Barry. 1960. *The Conscience of a Conservative.* Shephardsville, KY: Victor Publishing Company.

Goyder, John. 1986. "Surveys on Surveys: Limitations and Potentialities." *Public Opinion Quarterly* 50 (Spring): 27–41.

Graber, Doris A. 1976. "Press and TV as Opinion Resources in Presidential Campaigns." *Public Opinion Quarterly* 40 (Fall): 285–303.

———. 1984. *Processing the News: How People Tame the Information Tide.* New York: Longman.

———. 1997. *Mass Media and American Politics.* 5th ed. Washington, D.C.: Congressional Quarterly Press.

Greenberg, Edward. 1970. "Black Children and the Political System." *Public Opinion Quarterly* 34 (Fall): 335–348.

Greenstein, Fred I. 1965. *Children and Politics.* New Haven, CT: Yale University Press.

———. 1969. *Personality and Politics.* Chicago: Markham Publishing Company.

———. 1973. "Sex-Related Political Differences in Childhood." *Socialization to Politics: A Reader.* Ed. Jack Dennis. New York: John Wiley and Sons.

———. 1975. "The Benevolent Leader Revisited: Children's Images of Political Leaders in Three Democracies." *American Political Science Review* 69 (December): 1371–1398.

Gregg v. Georgia, 428 U.S. 153 (1976).

Griswold v. Connecticut, 381 U.S. 479 (1965).

Groves, Robert M., and Mick P. Couper. 1998. *Nonresponse in Household Interview Surveys.* New York: John Wiley and Sons.

Groves, Robert M., and Robert M. Kahn. 1979. *Surveys by Telephone: A National Comparison with Personal Interviews.* New York: Academic Press.

Hatchett, Shirley, and Howard Schuman. 1975. "White Respondents and Race-of-Interviewer Effects." *Public Opinion Quarterly* 39 (Winter): 523–528.

Hennessy, Bernard H. 1981. *Public Opinion.* 4th ed. Monterey, CA: Brooks/Cole Publishing.

Hess, Robert D., and Judith V. Torney. 1967. *The Development of Political Attitudes in Children.* Chicago: Aldine Publishing Company.

Hetherington, Marc J. 1998. "The Political Relevance of Political Trust." *American Political Science Review* 92 (December): 791–808.

Hinckley, Ronald H. 1988. "Public Attitudes toward Key Foreign Policy Events." *Journal of Conflict Resolution* 32 (June): 95–318.

Holsti, Ole, and James N. Rosenau. 1984. *American Leadership in World Affairs and the Breakdown of Consensus.* Boston: Allen and Unwin.

Holsti, Ole R. 1996. *Public Opinion and American Foreign Policy.* Ann Arbor, MI: University of Michigan Press.

Honomichl, Jack J. 1986. *Honomichl on Marketing Research*. Lincolnwood, IL: NTC Business Books.

———. 1997. "Real Growth Driven by Overseas Research." *Marketing News* 31 (June): H1–H43.

Hubert, David A. 1992. "Publics, Polls, and Public Opinion." *The Public Perspective* 3 (January/February): 30–31.

Hunter, James Davison, and Daniel C. Johnson. 1997. "A State of Disunion?" *Public Perspective* (February/March): 35–38.

Hurwitz, Jon, and Mark Peffley. 1987. "How Are Foreign Policy Attitudes Structured: A Hierarchical Model." *American Political Science Review* 81 (December): 1099–1120.

Hyman, Herbert H. 1959. *Political Socialization: A Study in the Psychology of Political Behavior*. Glencoe, IL: The Fress Press.

Iyengar, Shanto, and Donald Kinder. 1987. *News That Matters*. Chicago: University of Chicago Press.

Jacobs, Lawrence R., and Robert Y. Shapiro. 1995. "The Rise of Presidential Polling: The Nixon White House in Historical Perspective." *Public Opinion Quarterly* 59 (Summer): 163–195.

———. 1997. "Debunking the Pandering Politician Myth." *Public Perspective* 8 (April/May): 3–5.

Jacoby, William G. 1988. "The Impact of Party Identification on Issue Attitudes." *American Journal of Political Science* 32 (August): 643–661.

———. 1991. "Ideological Identification and Issue Attitudes." *American Journal of Political Science* 35 (February): 178–205.

Jajich-Toth, Cindy, and Burns W. Roper. 1990. "Americans' Views on Health Care: A Study in Contradictions." *Health Affairs* 9 (Winter): 149–157.

Jaros, Dean, and Lawrence V. Grant. 1974. *Political Behavior: Choices and Perspectives*. New York: St. Martin's Press.

Jaros, Dean, Herbert Hirsch, and Frederic J. Fleron, Jr. 1968. "The Malevolent Leader: Political Socialization in an American Sub-Culture." *American Political Science Review* 62 (June): 564–575.

Jaros, Dean. 1973. *Socialization to Politics*. New York: Praeger.

Jelen, Ted G. 1989. "Biblical Literalism and Inerrancy: Does the Difference Make a Difference?" *Sociological Analysis* 49 (Winter): 421–429.

———. 1992. "Political Christianity: A Contextual Analysis." *American Journal of Political Science* 36 (August): 662–692.

Jennings, M. Kent, Lee H. Ehrman, and Richard G. Niemi. 1974. "Social Studies Teachers and their Students." *The Political Character of Adolescence*. Ed. M. Kent Jennings and Richard G. Niemi. Princeton NJ: Princeton University Press.

Jennings, M. Kent, and Gregory B. Markus. 1984. "Partisan Orientations over the Long Haul: Results from the Three-Wave Political Socialization Panel Study." *American Political Science Review* 78 (December): 1000–1018.

Jennings, M. Kent, and Richard Niemi. 1968. "The Transmission of Political Values from Parent to Child." *American Political Science Review* 62 (March): 169–184.

———. 1974. *The Political Character of Adolescence: The Influence of Families and Schools*. Princeton, NJ: Princeton University Press.

———. 1975. "Continuity and Change in Political Orientations: A Longitudinal Study of Two Generations." *American Political Science Review* 69 (December): 1316–1335.

Jensen, Richard. 1980. "Democracy by the Numbers." *Public Opinion* 3 (February/March): 53–59.

Jentleson, Bruce. 1992. "The Pretty Prudent Public: Post Post-Vietnam American Opinion on the Use of Military Force." *International Studies Quarterly* 36 (March): 49–74.

Kalton, Graham. 1983. *Introduction to Survey Sampling.* Beverly Hills, CA: **Sage** Publications.

Katz, Daniel. 1960. "The Functional Approach to the Study of Attitudes." *Public Opinion Quarterly* 24 (Summer): 163–177.

Kegeles, S. Stephen, Clinton F. Fink, and John P. Kirscht. 1969. "Interviewing a National Sample by Long-Distance Telephone." *Public Opinion Quarterly* 33 (Fall): 412–419.

Kerber, Linda K. 1980. *Women of the Republic: Intellect and Ideology in Revolutionary America.* Chapel Hill: University of North Carolina Press.

Key, V. O., Jr. 1967. *Public Opinion and American Democracy.* New York: Knopf.

Kinder, Donald R., and D. Roderick Kiewiet. 1979. "Economic Grievance and Political Behavior: The Role of Personal Discontents and Collective Judgments in Congressional Voting." *American Journal of Political Science* 23 (August): 495–527.

Kirkpatrick, Samuel A., and Melvin E. Jones. 1974. "Issue Publics and the Electoral System: The Role of Issues in Electoral Change." *Public Opinion and Political Attitudes.* Ed. Allen R. Wilcox. New York: John Wiley and Sons.

Kohl, Rhiana, Diana Brensilber, and William Holmes. 1995. *Elderly Protection Project, Final Report.* Washington: United States Department of Justice, National Institute of Justice.

Kohut, Andrew. 1986. "Rating the Polls: The Views of Media Elites and the General Public." *Public Opinion Quarterly* 50 (Spring): 1–9.

Krysan, Maria, Howard Schuman, Lesli Jo Scott, and Paul Beatty. 1994. "Response Rates and Response Content in Mail Versus Face-to-Face Surveys." *Public Opinion Quarterly* 58 (Fall): 381–399.

Ladd, Everett Carll. 1990. "What Do Americans Really Think About the Environment?" *The Public Perspective* 1 (May/June): 11–13.

———. 1992. "The Trials of Election Polling: Election Polls—1948 and Today." *The Public Perspective* 3 (May/June): 24–28.

———. 1995. "Americans on Public Education." *The Public Perspective* 6 (October/November): 22–37.

———. 1996a. "The Election Polls: an American Waterloo." *Chronicle of Higher Education* 43 (November): A52.

———. 1996b. "Election 1996: A Roper Center Data Review." *The Public Perspective* 7 (October/November): 15–54.

———. 1998a. "The American Ethnic Experience As It Stands in the Nineties." *The Public Perspective* 9 (February/March): 50–65.

———. 1998b. "What's the Biggest Hurdle for the Polls?" *The Public Perspective* 9 (February/March): 86.

Ladd, Everett C., and Karlyn H. Bowman. 1997. *Public Opinion About Abortion: Twenty-Five Years after Roe v. Wade.* Washington, D.C.: American Enterprise Institute.

Ladd, Everett C., and G. Donald Ferree. 1981. "Were the Pollsters Really Wrong?" *Public Opinion* 3 (December/January): 13–20.

Lamare, James W. 1974. "Language Environment and Political Socialization of Mexican-American Children." *The Politics of Future Citizens.* Ed. Richard G. Niemi and Associates. San Francisco: Jossey-Bass Publishers.

Langton, Kenneth P. 1969. *Political Socialization.* New York: Oxford University Press.

Langton, Kenneth, and M. Kent Jennings. 1968. "Political Socialization and the High School Civics Curriculum in the United States." *American Political Science Review* 62 (September): 852–867.

Langton, Kenneth, and D. Karns. 1969. "A Cross National Study of the Relative Influence of School Education: A Causal Analysis." ERIC, ED 034 320.

Lau, Richard R., and Ralph Erber. 1987. "Political Sophistication: An Information-Processing Perspective," *Mass Media and Political Thought: An Information Processing Approach.* Ed. Sidney Kraus and Richard M. Perloff. New York: **Sage** Publications.

Lazarsfeld, Paul, Bernard Berelson, and Hazel Gaudet. 1944. *The People's Choice.* New York: Columbia University Press.

Leege, David C., and Michael R. Welch. 1989. "Religious Roots of Political Orientations: Variations Among American Catholic Parishioners." *Journal of Politics* 51 (February): 137–162.

Levy, Mark R. 1983. "The Methodology and Performance of Election Day Polls." *Public Opinion Quarterly* 47 (Spring): 54–67.

Link, Michael W. 1997a. *South Carolina State Survey: Summary Findings for the South Carolina State Park Service.* Columbia, SC: Institute of Public Affairs.

———. 1997b. *Survey of South Carolina Registered Voters Regarding Youth Sexuality.* Columbia, SC: Institute of Public Affairs.

———. 1997c. *Public Perceptions of the South Carolina Department of Revenue.* Columbia, SC: Institute of Public Affairs.

Link, Michael W., and Robert W. Oldendick. 1996. "Social Construction and White Attitudes Toward Equal Opportunity and Multiculturalism." *Journal of Politics* 58 (February): 149–168.

———. 1998. "Caller-ID: Does It Help or Hinder Survey Research?" presented at the annual meeting of the American Association for Public Opinion Research, St. Louis.

Lippmann, Walter. 1922. *Public Opinion.* New York: Harcourt, Brace.

———. 1956. *The Public Philosophy.* New York: Mentor.

Lipset, Seymour Martin, and William Schneider. 1978. "The Bakke Case: How Would It Be Decided at the Bar of Public Opinion?" *Public Opinion* 1 (March/April): 38–44.

———. 1983. *The Confidence Gap: Business, Labor, and Government in the Public Mind.* New York: The Free Press.

———. 1987. "The Confidence Gap During the Reagan Years, 1981–1987." *Political Science Quarterly* 102 (Spring): 1–23.

Litt, Edgar. 1963. "Civic Education, Community Norms, and Political Indoctrination." *American Sociological Review* 28 (February): 69–75.

Luevano, Patricia. 1994. "Response Rates in the National Election Studies, 1948–1992." NES Technical Report #44. Ann Arbor: Center for Political Studies.

MacKuen, Michael Bruce. 1981. "Social Communication and the Mass Policy Agenda." *More Than News: Media Power in Public Affairs.* Ed. Michael Bruce MacKuen and Steven Coombs. Beverly Hills, CA: Sage.

MacKuen, Michael B., Robert S. Erikson, and James A. Stimson. 1992. "Peasants or Bankers? The American Electorate and the U.S. Economy." *American Political Science Review* 86 (September): 1125–1142.

Martin, Elizabeth. 1984. "The Role of the Respondent." *Surveying Subjective Phenomena.* Ed. Charles F. Turner and Elizabeth Martin. New York: Russell Sage Foundation.

Massey, James T. 1988. "An Overview of Telephone Coverage." *Telephone Survey Methodology.* Ed. Robert M. Groves, Paul P. Biemer, Lars E. Lyberg, James T. Massey, William L. Nicholls, II, and Joseph Waksberg. New York: John Wiley and Sons.

Mayer, William G. 1992. *The Changing American Mind: How and Why American Public Opinion Changed between 1960 and 1988.* Ann Arbor, MI: The University of Michigan Press.

McCloskey, Herbert, Paul Hoffman, and Rosemary O'Hara. 1960. "Issue Conflict and Consensus Among Party Leaders and Followers." *American Political Science Review* 54 (June): 406–427.

McClure, Robert D., and Thomas E. Patterson. 1976. *The Unseeing Eye: The Myth of Television Power in National Elections.* New York: Putnam.

McCormick, James M. 1998. *American Foreign Policy and Process,* 3rd. ed. Itasca, IL: F. E. Peacock.

McSweeney, Dean, and John Zvesper. 1991. *American Political Parties: The Formation, Decline, and Reform of the American Party System.* New York: Routledge.

Merelman, Richard M. 1971. *Political Socialization and Educational Climates: A Study of Two School Districts.* New York: Holt, Rinehart and Winston.

Milbrath, Lester W. 1965. *Political Participation.* Chicago: Rand McNally.

Miller, Arthur H. 1974. "Political Issues and Trust in Government, 1964–1970." *American Political Science Review* 68 (September): 951–972.

Miller, Warren E. 1979. "Crisis of Confidence—II: Misreading the Public Pulse." *Public Opinion* 2 (October/November): 9–17.

———. 1991. "Party Identification, Realignment, and Party Voting: Back to Basics." *American Political Science Review* 85 (June): 557–568.

Miller, Warren E., and Donald E. Stokes. 1963. "Constituency Influence in Congress." *American Political Science Review* 57 (March): 45–56.

Miller, Warren E., and Santa Traugott. 1989. *American National Election Studies Data Sourcebook, 1952–1986.* Cambridge, MA: Harvard University Press.

Minow, Newton N., John Bartlow Martin, and Lee M. Mitchell. 1973. *Presidential Television.* New York: Basic Books.

Mitofsky, Warren J., 1989. Rev. of *Polling and the Public,* by Herbert Asher. *Public Opinion Quarterly* 53 (Winter): 617–619.

Monroe, Alan D. 1979. "Consistency Between Public Preferences and National Policy Decisions." *American Politics Quarterly* 7 (January): 3–20.

Monroe, Alan D. 1998. "Public Opinion and Public Policy, 1980–1993." *Public Opinion Quarterly* 62 (Spring): 6–28.

Monroe, Alan D. 1975. *Public Opinion in America.* New York: Dodd, Mead.

Morgenthau, Hans J. 1978. *Politics Among Nations.* 5th ed. New York: Alfred A. Knopf.

Moore, David W. 1992. *The Superpollsters: How They Measure and Manipulate Public Opinion in America.* New York: Four Walls Eight Windows.

———. 1996a. "The Party Really Isn't Over." *The Public Perspective* 7 (October/November): 1–3.

———. 1996b. "Perils of Polling '96: Myth and Fallacy." *The Polling Report* 12 (December): 1–8.

Mosteller, Frederick, Herbert Hyman, Philip J. McCarthy, Eli S. Marks, and David B. Truman. 1949. *The Pre-election Polls of 1948: Report to the Committee on Analysis of Pre-election Polls and Forecasts.* New York: Social Science Research Council.

Mueller, John. 1971. "Trends in Popular Support for the Wars in Korea and Vietnam." *American Political Science Review* 65 (June): 358–375.

———. 1973. *Wars, Presidents, and Public Opinion.* New York: John Wiley.

———. 1994. *Policy and Opinion in the Gulf War.* Chicago: University of Chicago Press.

Natchez, Peter B., and Irvin C. Bupp. 1968. "Candidates, Issues, and Voters." *Public Policy* 17 (Summer): 409–437.

New York Times. 1936. "Dr. Gallup Chided by *Digest* Editor." *New York Times,* 19 July: 21.

Neuman, W. Russell. 1986. *The Paradox of American Politics: Knowledge and Opinion in the American Electorate.* Cambridge, MA: Harvard University Press.

Newcomb, Theodore M., et al. 1958. "Attitude Development as a Function of Reference Groups: The Bennington Study." *Readings in Social Psychology*. Ed. Eleanor E. Maccoby, et al. New York: Holt, Rinehart and Winston.

Newmark, Lisa, Adele Harrell, and Bill Adams. 1995. *Evaluation of Police Training Conducted Under the Family Violence Prevention and Services Act, Final Report.* Washington: United States Department of Justice, National Institute of Justice.

Newport, Frank. 1998. "Reporting Poll Results Better." *The Public Perspective* 9 (February/March): 87.

Nicholls II, William L., 1988. "Computer-Assisted Telephone Interviewing: A General Introduction." *Telephone Survey Methodology*. Ed. Robert M. Groves, Paul P. Biemer, Lars E. Lyberg, James T. Massey, William L. Nicholls, II, and Joseph Waksberg. New York: John Wiley and Sons.

Nie, Norman H., with Kristi Anderson. 1974. "Mass Belief Systems Revisited: Political Change and Attitude Structure." *Journal of Politics* 36 (August): 541–591.

Nie, Norman H., Sidney Verba, and John R. Petrocik. 1976. *The Changing American Voter.* Cambridge, MA: Harvard University Press.

Niemi, Richard, and M. Kent Jennings. 1974. *The Political Character of Adolescence.* Princeton NJ: Princeton University Press.

Noelle-Neumann, Elisabeth. 1984. *The Spiral of Silence.* Chicago: University of Chicago Press.

Oldendick, Robert, and Barbara Bardes. 1981. "The Continuing Case for Multiple Dimensions in the Structure of Foreign Policy Attitudes." *Social Science Quarterly* 62 (March): 124–126.

Oldendick, Robert W. 1992a. *What Does the Public Want? Health Care Issues in South Carolina.* Columbia, SC: Institute of Public Affairs.

———. 1992b. *Opinion on an Income Tax Check-Off for an Eldercare Trust Fund: A South Carolina State Survey Report.* Columbia, SC: Institute of Public Affairs.

———. 1994. *Recreation Participation and Preference Study, 1994.* Columbia, SC: Institute of Public Affairs.

———. 1996. *Georgetown County (S.C.) Recreation Needs Assessment.* Columbia, SC: Institute of Public Affairs.

Oldendick, Robert W., and Michael W. Link. 1994. "The Answering Machine Generation: Who Are They and What Problem Do They Pose for Survey Research?" *Public Opinion Quarterly* 58 (Summer): 264–273.

———. 1998. "Race-of-Interviewer and the Study of Public Opinion," presented at the annual meeting of the American Association for Public Opinion Research, St. Louis.

Oldendick, Robert W., and Alfred J. Tuchfarber. 1984. *Evaluation of Queen City Metro's Weekend Fare Experiment.* Cincinnati, OH: Institute for Policy Research.

O'Neill, Harry W. 1996. "Our Greatest and Most Frustrating Challenge Is How to Increase the Rate of Public Participation in Polls." *The Public Perspective* 7 (August/September): 54–56.

Opinion Research Service. 1998. *American Public Opinion Index—1997.* Bethesda, MD: ORS Publishing.

O'Reilly, James M., Michael L. Hubbard, Judith T. Lessler, Paul P. Biemer, and Charles F. Turner. 1994. "Audio and Video Computer Assisted Self-Interviewing: Preliminary Tests of New Technologies for Data Collection." *Journal of Official Statistics* 10 (2): 197–214.

O'Rourke, Diane, Seymour Sudman, and Marya Ryan. 1996. "The Growth of Academic and Not-for-Profit Survey Research Organizations." *Survey Research* 27 (Winter-Spring): 2–5.

Page, Benjamin I., and Robert Y. Shapiro. 1982. "Changes in Americans' Policy Preferences, 1935–1979." *Public Opinion Quarterly* 46 (Spring): 24–42.

———. 1983. "Effects of Public Opinion on Policy." *American Political Science Review* 77 (March): 175–190.

————. 1992. *The Rational Public: Fifty Years of Trends in Americans' Policy Preferences*. Chicago: University of Chicago Press.

Palmer, Paul A. 1936. "The Concept of Public Opinion in Political Theory." *Essays in History and Political Theory*. Ed. Carl Wittke. Cambridge, MA: Harvard University Press.

Parker, Suzanne. 1995. "Toward an Understanding of 'Rally' Effects: Public Opinion in the Persian Gulf War." *Public Opinion Quarterly* 59 (Winter): 526–546.

Patterson, Kelly D., and David B. Magelby. 1992. "The Polls—Poll Trends: Public Support for Congress." *Public Opinion Quarterly* 56 (Winter): 539–551.

Patterson, Thomas E. 1980. *The Mass Media Election*. New York: Praeger.

Payne, Stanley L. 1951. *The Art of Asking Questions*. Princeton, NJ: Princeton University Press.

Penner, Rudolph. 1982. "Spooking the Public: The Social Security Specter." *Public Opinion* 5 (October/November): 16–18.

Perry, James M. 1994. "Clinton Relies Heavily on White House Pollster To Take Words Right Out of Public's Mouth." *Wall Street Journal*. 23 March: A16.

Pierce, John C., and Paul R. Hagner. 1980. "Changes in the Public's Political Thinking: The Watershed Years, 1956–1968." *The Electorate Reconsidered*. Ed. John C. Pierce and John L. Sullivan. Beverly Hills: CA: Sage.

Plessy v. Ferguson 163 U.S. 537 (1896).

Polling Report. 1986. "Campaign '00 Update." *Polling Report* 12 (November): 4.

Prothro, James W., and Charles M. Grigg. 1960. "Fundamental Principles of Democracy: Bases of Agreement and Disagreement." *Journal of Politics* 22 (May): 276–294.

Public Perspective. 1994. "The Public Decides on Health Care Reform: A Polling Review of a Great Debate." *The Public Perspective* 5 (September/October): 23–28.

————. 1998a. "Thinking About Government: Health Care Reform, 1993–94." *The Public Perspective* 9 (February/March): 36–39.

————. 1998b. "Thinking About Polls and Polling." *The Public Perspective* 9 (February/March): 86–94.

Ragsdale, Lyn. 1997. "Disconnected Publics: Public Opinion and Presidents." *Understanding Public Opinion*. Ed. Barbara Norrander and Clyde Wilcox. Washington: Congressional Quarterly Press.

Reilly, John E. 1995a. "The Public Mood at Mid-Decade." *Foreign Policy* 98 (Spring): 76–93.

Reilly, John E., ed. 1995b., *American Public Opinion and Foreign Policy*. Chicago, Illinois: The Chicago Council on Foreign Relations.

Regents of the University of California v. Bakke, 438 U.S. 265 (1978).

Research Industry Coalition. 1996. *Integrity and Good Practice in Marketing and Opinion Research*. Port Jefferson, NY: Research Industry Coalition.

Rice, Tom W., and Tracey A. Hilton. 1996. "Partisanship Over Time: A Comparison of United States Panel Data." *Political Research Quarterly* 49 (March): 191–201.

Richman, Alvin. 1996. "Trends: American Support for International Involvement, General and Specific Components of Post-Cold War Changes." *Public Opinion Quarterly* 60 (Summer): 305–321.

Roberts, Julian V., and Loretta J. Stalans. 1997. *Public Opinion, Crime and Criminal Justice*. Boulder, CO: Westview Press.

Robinson, Claude E. 1932. *Straw Votes: A Study of Political Prediction*. New York: Columbia University Press.

Rodgers, Harrell R., and George Taylor. 1971. "The Policeman as an Agent of Regime Legitimation." *Midwest Journal of Political Science* 15 (February): 72–86.

Roe v. Wade, 410 U.S. 113 (1973).

Roll, Charles W., and Albert H. Cantril. 1980. *Polls: Their Use and Misuse in Surveys*. Cabin John, MD: Seven Locks Press.

Roper, Burns W. 1986. "Evaluating the Polls with Poll Data." *Public Opinion Quarterly* 50 (Spring): 10–16.

Rosenberg, Milton J., Sidney Verba, and Philip E. Converse. 1970. *Vietnam and the Silent Majority: The Dove's Guide*. New York: Harper and Row.

Royko, Mike. 1992. "Annoy Pollster—Resort to Lying." *Chicago Tribune,* 28 October: 3.

Saad, Lydia K. 1998. "After 25 Years, Abortion Attitudes Register a Slight Conservative Shift." *The Public Perspective* 9 (February/March): 7–8.

Scammon, Richard M., and Ben J. Wattenberg. 1970. *The Real Majority: An Extraordinary Examination of the American Electorate*. New York: Coward, McCann and Geoghegan.

Schmidt, Steffen W., Mack C. Shelley, II, and Barbara A. Bardes. 1997. *American Government and Politics Today, 1997–1998 Edition*. Belmont, CA: **Wadsworth** Publishing Company.

Schneider, William. 1997. "The Pollster General: A Brief History of Polling for the President." *The Polling Report* 13 (May): 7.

Schuman, Howard, and Stanley Presser. 1981. *Questions and Answers in Attitude Surveys*. New York: Academic Press.

Schuman, Howard, Charlotte Steeh, and Lawrence Bobo. 1985. *Racial Attitudes in America: Trends and Interpretations*. Cambridge, MA: Harvard University Press.

Schuman, Howard, Charlotte Steeh, Lawrence Bobo, and Maria Krysan. 1997. *Racial Attitudes in America: Trends and Interpretations*. Revised. Cambridge, MA: Harvard University Press.

Sears, David O. 1990. "Whither Political Socialization Research? The Question of Persistence." *Political Socialization, Citizenship Education. and Democracy*. Ed. Orit Ichilov. New York: Columbia University Press.

Sears, David O., Carl P. Hensler, and Leslie K. Speer. 1979. "Whites' Opposition to 'Busing': Self-Interest or Symbolic Politics?" *American Political Science Review* 73 (June): 369–384.

Sears, David O., Collette van Laar, Mary Carillo, and Rick Kosterman. 1997. "Is it Really Racism? The Origins of White Americans' Opposition to Race-Targeted Policies." *Public Opinion Quarterly* 61 (Spring): 16–53.

Selltiz, Claire, Marie Jahoda, Morton Deutsch, and Stuart W. Cook. 1959. *Research Methods in Social Relations*. New York: Holt, Rinehart and Winston.

"Sensible Internationalism." 1993. *Public Perspective* 4 (March/April): 95–104.

Shapiro, Robert Y., Kelly D. Patterson, Judith Russell, and John T. Young. 1987a. "The Polls: Public Assistance." *Public Opinion Quarterly* 51 (Spring): 120–130.

———. 1987b. "The Polls: Employment and Social Welfare." *Public Opinion Quarterly* 51 (Summer): 268–281.

Shapiro, Robert, and Harpreet Mahajan. 1986. "Gender Differences in Policy Preferences: A Summary of Trends from the 1960s to the 1980s." *Public Opinion Quarterly* 50 (Spring): 42–61.

Shapiro, Robert, and Benjamin I. Page. 1988. "Foreign Policy and the Rational Public." *Journal of Conflict Resolution* 32 (June): 211–247.

Shapiro, Robert Y., and Tom W. Smith. 1985. "The Polls: Social Security." *Public Opinion Quarterly* 49 (Winter): 561–572.

Sharp, Laure M. 1984. "Researchers and Respondents in the 1980s." *Public Opinion Quarterly* 48 (Fall): 680–685.

Sheatsley, Paul B. 1966. "White Attitudes Toward the Negro." *Daedalus* 95 (Winter): 217–238.

Sigel, Roberta S. , ed. 1970. *Learning About Politics: A Reader in Political Socialization*. New York: Random House.

Sigelman, Lee, and Susan Welch. 1991. *Black Americans View of Racial Inequality—the Dream Deferred*. Cambridge, England: Cambridge University Press.

Simon, Rita James. 1974. *Public Opinion in America: 1936–1970*. Chicago: Rand McNally.

Singhania, Lisa. 1996. "Push Polling." *Associated Press Wire* 9 February.

Smith, Andrew E., Alfred J. Tuchfarber, Eric W. Rademacher, and Stephen E. Bennett. 1995. "Partisan Leaners are NOT Independents." *The Public Perspective* 6 (October/November): 9–12.

Smith, Eric R. A. N. 1989. *The Unchanging American Voter*. Berkeley, CA: University of California Press.

Smith, Tom W. 1987. "That Which We Call Welfare by Any Other Name Would Smell Sweeter: An Analysis of the Impact of Question Wording on Response Patterns." *Public Opinion Quarterly* 51 (Spring): 75–83.

———. 1990. "The First Straw: A Study of the Origins of Election Polls." *Public Opinion Quarterly* 54 (Spring): 21–36.

———. 1995. "Trends in Non-Response Rates." *International Journal of Public Opinion Research* 7 (Summer): 157–171.

———. 1997. "Tall Oaks from Little Acorns Grow: The General Social Surveys, 1971–1996." *The Public Perspective* 8 (February/March): 28–30.

Smith, Tom W., and Frederick D. Weil. 1990. "The Polls—A Report. Finding Public Opinion Data: A Guide to Sources." *Public Opinion Quarterly* 54 (Winter): 609–626.

Sniderman, Paul M., Thomas Piazza, Philip E. Tetlock, and Ann Kendrick. 1991. "The New Racism." *American Journal of Political Science* 35 (May): 423–447.

Sorenson, Theodore C. 1965. *Kennedy*. New York: Harper and Row.

Southwick, Jessie C., ed. 1975. *Survey Data for Trend Analysis: An Index of Repeated Questions in U.S. National Surveys Held by the Roper Public Research Center*. Williamstown, MA: Roper Public Opinion Research Center.

Squire, Peverill. 1988. "Why the 1936 *Literary Digest* Poll Failed." *Public Opinion Quarterly* 52 (Spring): 125–133.

Stanley, Harold W., and Richard G. Niemi. 1988. *Vital Statistics on American Politics*. Washington, D.C.: Congressional Quarterly Press.

———. 1995. *Vital Statistics on American Politics*. 5th ed. Washington, D.C.: Congressional Quarterly Press.

Stein, Lana. 1996. "American Jews and Their Liberal Political Behavior." *The Politics of Minority Coalitions: Race, Ethnicity and Shared Uncertainties*. Ed. Wilbur C. Rich. Westport, CT: Praeger.

Stimson, James A. 1991. *Public Opinion in America: Moods, Cycles and Swings*. Boulder, CO: Westview Press.

Stokes, Donald E. 1966. "Some Dynamic Elements of Contests for the Presidency." *American Political Science Review* 60 (March): 19–28.

Sudman, Seymour, and Norman H. Bradburn. 1987. "The Organizational Growth of Public Opinion Research in the United States." *Public Opinion Quarterly* 51 (Winter): S67–S78.

Sullivan, John L., James E. Piereson, and George E. Marcus. 1978. "Ideological Constraint in the Mass Public." *American Journal of Political Science* 22 (May): 233–249.

Swann v. Charlotte-Mecklenburg Board of Education, 402 U.S. 1 (1971).

Trop v. Dulles, 356 U.S. 86 (1958).

Tuchfarber, Alfred J., and William R. Klecka. 1976. *Random Digit Dialing: Lowering the Cost of Victimization Surveys*. Washington: The Police Foundation.

Tuchfarber, Alfred J., and Robert W. Oldendick. 1986. *Queen City Metro: Marketing Baseline Study*. Cincinnati, OH: Institute for Policy Research.

Tuchfarber, Alfred J., Robert W. Oldendick, and George F. Bishop. 1984. "Citizen Attitudes Toward Taxation and Spending: Inconsistent Answers or the Wrong Questions?" presented at the annual meeting of the American Political Science Association, Washington.

Tuchfarber, Alfred J., and Andrew E. Smith. 1995. *City of Cincinnati Citizen Attitude Survey.* Cincinnati, OH: Institute for Policy Research.

Tuchfarber, Alfred J., and R. Eric Weise. 1982. *Queen City Metro Public Financing Study Report.* Cincinnati, OH: Institute for Policy Research.

Tuckel, Peter, and Barry M. Feinberg. 1991. "The Answering Machine Poses Many Questions for Telephone Survey Researchers." *Public Opinion Quarterly* 55 (Summer): 200–217.

Tuckel, Peter, and Harry W. O'Neill. 1996. "Screened Out." *Marketing Research* 8 (Fall): 34–43.

U.S. Department of Commerce, Bureau of the Census. 1996. *Statistical Abstract of the United States 1996.* Washington: Government Printing Office.

Verba, Sidney, and Richard A. Brody, Edwin B. Parker, Norman H. Nie, Nelson W. Polsby, Paul Ekman, and Gordon S. Black. 1967. "Public Opinion and the War in Vietnam." *American Political Science Review* 61 (June): 317–333.

Verba, Sidney, Nancy Burns, and Kay Lehman Schlozman. 1997. "Knowing and Caring about Politics: Gender and Political Engagement." *Journal of Politics* 59 (November): 1051–1072.

Waksberg, Joseph. 1978. "Sampling Methods for Random Digit Dialing." *Journal of the American Statistical Association* 73 (March): 40–46.

Waller, Robert. 1992. *Caveat Populi Quaestor.* The 1992 British General Election Polling Debacle." *The Public Perspective* 3 (May/June): 25–26.

Weaver, Carolyn L., and Derrick A. Max. 1995. "The Economics of an Aging Social Security Program." *The Public Perspective* 6 (February/March): 16–18.

Weeks, Michael F. 1992. "Computer-Assisted Survey Information Collection: A Review of CASIC Methods and Their Implications for Survey Operations." *Journal of Official Statistics* 8 (4): 445–465.

Weisberg, Herbert E. 1980. "A Multidimensional Conceptualization of Party Identification." *Political Behavior* 2 (1): 33–60.

Weissberg, Robert. 1974. *Political Learning, Political Choice, and Democratic Citizenship.* Englewood Cliffs, NJ: Prentice-Hall.

———. 1976. *Public Opinion and Popular Government.* Englewood Cliffs, N.J.: Prentice-Hall.

Wheeler, Michael. 1980. "Reining in Horserace Journalism." *Public Opinion* 3 (February/March): 41–45.

Wilcox, Clyde, J. Ferrara, and Dee Alsop. 1991. "Before the Rally: The Dynamics of Attitudes toward the Gulf Crisis before the War," presented at the annual meeting of the American Political Science Association, Washington, D.C.

Wittkopf, Eugene R. 1990. *Public Faces of Internationalism Opinion and American Foreign Policy.* Durham, NC: Duke University Press.

Wittkopf, Eugene R., and Michael Maggiotto. 1983. "The Two Faces of Internationalism: Public Attitudes toward American Foreign Policy and Beyond? *Social Science Quarterly* 64 (June): 288–304.

Yankelovich, Daniel. 1991. *Coming to Public Judgment.* Syracuse. N.Y.: Syracuse University Press.

Zaller, John. 1992. *The Nature and Origins of Mass Opinions.* Cambridge, England: Cambridge University Press.

Zogby, John. 1998. "Harnessing the Internet." *The Public Perspective* 9 (February/March): 94.

Index

ABC News, 38, 39, 174, 206, 239, 240
Abortion issue
  political system and, 170
  protests and, 169
  public opinion on, 179–184, 230
  situationalists and, 181–182
  question context effect and, 62
Abortions, traumatic versus elective, 180–181
Abramowitz, Alan I., 98
Abramson, Paul R., 220
Academic research
  American National Election Studies (NES), 42–43
  General Social Survey (GSS), 43–44
  web sites for, 240
  See also Universities
Achen, Christopher H., 4, 99
Acquiescence response set, 58
Adams, Bill, 35
Adams, Kenneth, 186, 187
Adams, William C., 9
Adarand Constructors, Inc. v. Pena, 155

Adolescents, political learning of, 73–76
Adults
  definition of public opinion and, 6
  peer influence and, 89–90
Affirmative action, 154–157, 229
African Americans, opinions of
  on affirmative action, 155–157, 229
  on aid to minorities, 159
  on capital punishment, 177–178
  on civil rights movement, 162–163
  on crime, 173, 175–176
  on domestic policy, 83
  education and, 78, 80–81
  ethnic identity and, 82
  on fair employment, 153–154
  on government, 113–114, 117–118
  interview situation and, 220
  on military force, 202, 231
  on minority candidates, 164–165
  party identification and, 83, 91, 105–106, 225

  on racial issues spending, 161
  on racism, 83–84
  on residential integration, 151–152
  on school busing, 148, 150
  on school desegregation, 147–150, 229
  on slavery, 163–165
  on social welfare, 139–141
  on Vietnam conflict, 200
  ideology and, 102–103
Age
  and abortion issue opinions, 182
  and crime/punishment opinions, 175–176
  and fear of crime, 172–173
  and foreign policy opinions, 208
  and government opinions, 113–114, 117–118
  and ideology, 102–103
  and opinions (generational effects), 76, 90–91
  and party identification, 106, 108, 225
  and social welfare opinions, 139–140